THE STORYMAKERS:
ILLUSTRATING CHILDREN'S BOOKS

THE STORYMAKERS:
ILLUSTRATING CHILDREN'S BOOKS

72 Artists and Illustrators
Talk About Their Work

Compiled by The Canadian Children's Book Centre

HEATHER COLLINS

Pembroke Publishers Limited

© 1999 The Canadian Children's Book Centre

Pembroke Publishers
538 Hood Road
Markham, Ontario, Canada L3R 3K9
www.pembrokepublishers.com

Distributed in the U.S. by Stenhouse Publishers
P.O. Box 360
York, Maine 03909
www.stenhouse.com

This project was made possible through
the generous support of The Canada Council for the Arts
Writing and Publications Section.

Compiler: Ian Krykorka
Editor: Gillian O'Reilly
Cover and design: Loris Lesynski
Proofreader: Lori Eckler

The Storymakers: Illustrating Children's Books is the first volume of the updated and revised
edition of the Centre's groundbreaking *Writing Stories, Making Pictures* (1994). A companion
volume, *The Storymakers: Writing Children's Books*, looks at children's book authors.

Canadian Cataloguing in Publication Data
Main entry under title:
The storymakers: illustrating children's books; 72 artists and illustrators talk about their work

Includes bibliographical references and index.
ISBN 1-55138-107-9

1. Illustrators – Canada – Biography – Juvenile literature. 2. Illustration of books – 20th century --
Canada – Juvenile literature. I. Canadian Children's Book Centre.

NC975.6.S76 1999   j741.6'42'092271   C98-932987-9

Printed and bound in Canada
9 8 7 6 5 4 3 2 1

Introduction

Welcome to *The Storymakers: Illustrating Children's Books*—the resource that brings you colourful biographies of 72 Canadian illustrators and artists whose works are considered among the best in the world. Told in the artists' own words, these biographies offer a fascinating and delightful insight into the worlds of these talented creators. Every biography also shows an illustration from one of the artist's books, giving you a sample of the style.

The Storymakers: Illustrating Children's Books has grown out of previous work by The Canadian Children's Book Centre that made available biographical and bibliographical information on talented illustrators and authors who create the wonderful books being published today. Such information allows readers of all ages to more fully understand and enjoy the books—both illustration and text.

In compiling the list of illustrators to be included, the Centre consulted experts in the children's literature field—librarians, booksellers and academics—and also looked at award-winning books. The resulting list includes artists at the height of their careers as well as rising stars in the field of children's book illustration.

Particular thanks for their assistance in developing the list go to: Ken Setterington, Trudy Carey, Dr. David Jenkinson, Karin Paul, Judy Sarick, André Gagnon, Nora Lester, Arlene Perly Rae, Muriel Morton, Virginia Davis, and Phyllis Simon. Thanks are also due to researcher Ian Krykorka and to Anne Dumont who assisted him in the task.

Thank you to The Canada Council for the Arts Writing and Publishing Section, whose support made the publication of this book possible.

Of the 72 illustrators featured here, those who write the text for many or all of their books are listed as author/illustrators. The bibliographies list the books alphabetically by the author of the work. The fleur de lis symbol (✻) indicates titles also available in French.

In these pages, you will meet many talented, award-winning and wonderfully creative children's illustrators. Discover their passions, their techniques and their histories. Find out how they create works that fire the imagination and stoke the enthusiasm of young readers today. Here are their stories... Read and enjoy!

CONTENTS

LINDA HENDRY

Warabé Aska
AUTHOR/ILLUSTRATOR

Born
February 3, 1944, Kagawa, Japan

School
Polytechnic School, Kagawa, Japan

Where I live now
Mississauga, Ontario

My favourite book when I was young
Hans Christian Andersen

My favourite books now
Biographies

Career
"I started as a graphic designer and illustrator of books for both adults and children. I now work as a full-time artist."

Family
"I live with my wife, two sons and a daughter."

The room where I create
"I have converted a part of my house into a studio."

Spare time
"I like driving and camping with my family. I also would like to travel to a part of the world unknown to me."

When I was growing up
"I used to play outside by myself. I caught fish from the river, climbed trees, chased butter-flies, swam in the sea. Everyday I absorbed the nature around me.

"In junior high school I had my leg operated on and was in the hospital for eight months. I used to lie in bed looking out the window and imagine all of nature in the sky and clouds. When later I started to paint, these images welled out from my imagination onto the canvas."

My first book (and how it happened)
"When I had my first one-man exhibition in Tokyo after travel-ling around Japan for three months, a chief editor came into my gallery and asked me, 'Why don't you write and illustrate your trip for children?' A year later, my first book, *Discovering Japan in 80 Days*, was published. It was a turning point in my career because I then began to focus on illustrating children's books."

Where my ideas come from
"I always find that sitting out in the open air inspires me. Natural objects such as trees, flowers, birds, animals, the sun and moon, clouds and water, trigger my imagination. Many of my paintings have their origin in reality. For *Aska's Animals*, I went on a safari in Kenya. There I saw and was able to paint the real life of African animals in their own habitat. Such observations were important to get a real 'feel' in my book."

Once Warabé gets an idea, he either writes it down in Japanese, to be translated into English later, or draws it in his notebook for future development.

Who and what influenced me
"My art work has been influenced by the natural environment such as fresh air, clear water, and green trees."

How I work
"I spend a lot of time observing how people and animals com-mune or communicate in nature. Then I draw my rough sketches in pencil, ink or watercolour on paper before starting to paint in oil on canvas."

Even with a schedule of eight to ten hours a day, it can take one or two years to complete a book. Much of his time is spent researching the topic. The research can lead him to a library, museum, or even to the actual location of the book, where he makes as many sketches as possible. It takes him approxi-mately a year to pull his ideas for the paintings into shape. Generally, Aska paints from sunup to sundown because day-light is so important when trying to express colour and light. In addition to the paintings, Aska usually designs the book cover and does the layout of the book himself.

Something nobody knew about me (until now)

"I am a self-taught artist. I have never taken any art class and have never had a teacher of fine art."

My favourite book that I've created

"*Aska's Sea Creatures.* As the sun sinks to meet the creatures of the sea, and rises again to its home in the sky, it symbolizes the cycle of nature and of life."

Tips for young creators

"Originality and personality are most important to create something. Don't copy anyone else; draw what you see, and develop your own style."

Warabé Aska

BIBLIOGRAPHY

Aska, Warabé. *Who Goes to the Park?* Montreal: Tundra Books, 1986 Paper 0-88776-187-9. Illustrations by the author. Out of print.

—. *Who Hides in the Park.* (Multilingual) Translated by Michele Boileau and Teresa Yu. Montreal: Tundra Books, 1990 Paper 0-88776-244-1. Illustrations by the author.

Manguel, Alberto, ed. *Seasons.* Toronto: Doubleday Canada, 1990. Illustrations by Warabé Aska. Out of print.

Day, David. *Aska's Animals.* Toronto: Doubleday Canada, 1991. Illustrations by Warabé Aska. Out of print.

—. *Aska's Birds.* Toronto: Doubleday Canada, 1992. Illustrations by Warabé Aska. Out of print.

—. *Aska's Sea Creatures.* Toronto: Doubleday Canada, 1994 Cloth 0-385-32107-4. Illustrations by Warabé Aska.

Princess Hisako of Takamado, Her Imperial Highness. *Lulie the Iceberg.* New York: Kodansha America, 1998 Cloth 1-56836-272-2. Illustrations by Warabé Aska.

Warabé Aska has also written, illustrated and designed a number of books in his native Japan.

Awards

1985 City of Toronto Book Award for *Who Goes to the Park?*

1990 Studio Magazine Awards Gold Medal for *Seasons*

1993 Tehran International Biennale of Illustration 1st Prize for *Aska's Birds*

From *Aska's Sea Creatures*

Eric Beddows (a.k.a Ken Nutt)
ILLUSTRATOR

Born
November 29, 1951, Woodstock, Ontario

School
York University, Toronto, Ontario

Where I live now
Stratford, Ontario

My favourite book when I was young
"*The Time Machine* by H.G. Wells (for the illustrations by W.A. Dwiggins)."

My favourite book now
"William Steig is my favourite children's writer."

Career
A painter and an illustrator for fifteen years.

Family
"I have three cats: Buddy, Nemo and Emily."

The room where I create
"I paint in a big messy studio. I draft in my small neat studio."

Spare time
"I like to collect fossils and read about cosmology, geology and evolution."

When I was growing up
"I was a loner. I liked to look, to draw and to daydream. I still do. I have been drawing for as long as I can remember. Everyone, my parents, teachers and friends encouraged me. I was always the kid who drew. My early jobs were mostly boring, which was probably a good thing. I was a carpenter for a while, but I worried about losing my fingers, so I quit."

My first book (and how it happened)
"My friend Tim Wynne-Jones had written a story about his cat, Montezuma, who was in love with water. He asked me to make the pictures for it. That book, *Zoom at Sea*, was the first I illustrated."

Where my ideas come from
"I read lots, especially about art and the way people lived in the past. I love collecting old books with offbeat pictures in them like old science texts or outdated encyclopedias of the 'modern' world. I like books with a sense of wonder in them which is what I try to create in my own drawings."

Who and what influenced me
"Nature first. Then books influenced me; science books and illustrated books. I had (and still have) lots of heroes in science and art like Charles Darwin and the surrealist painter Max Ernst.

"From reading Charles Darwin, I learned to look for order in diversity. From looking at Max Ernst's paintings, I learned to see fantasy in the ordinary. Some illustrators who influenced me were Walter Crane, Gustave Doré and Rockwell Kent."

How I work
"I start work on a book or painting by scribbling. I try to let the images come unconsciously at first, and they can be quite fantastic.

"Once I can see pictures in the scribbles, I start work on making the pictures 'look real.' I work out floor plans for the action in a book, I build models to get lighting and perspective and I research details. When all my preliminary drawings are done, I trace them onto good paper and begin the final artwork."

My favourite book that I've created
"*Shadow Play*. It is a bit overlooked, but I like the little fellow who is the surprise hero as well as imagining that I am visiting a turn-of-the-century travelling fair."

Tips for young creators

"Keep drawing things that you like. Your drawings will change and grow. Read a lot. Look a lot, with your brain as well as your eyes. Anything that is known, you can find out about. You may even discover something no one else knows."

Eric Beddows (Ken Nutt)

BIBLIOGRAPHY

Beddows, Eric. *Zoom: How Preposterous Became Pharaoh* (A puzzle/poster). Toronto: Groundwood Books, 1993 0-88899-186-X.

Conrad, Pam. *The Rooster's Gift.* New York: HarperCollins; Toronto: Douglas and McIntyre, 1996 Cloth 0-88899-273-4. Illustrations by Eric Beddows.

Day, David. *The Emperor's Panda.* Toronto: McClelland & Stewart, 1986 Cloth 0-7710-2573-4. Illustrations by Eric Beddows.

Esbensen, Barbara. *Who Shrank My Grandmother's House?* Vancouver: Douglas & McIntyre, 1992 Cloth 1-55054-211-7. Illustrations by Eric Beddows.

Fleischman, Paul. *I Am Phoenix: Poems for Two Voices.* New York: HarperCollins, 1985 Cloth 0-06-021882-7. 1989 Paper 0-06-446092-4. Illustrations by Ken Nutt.

—. *Joyful Noise: Poems for Two Voices.* New York: HarperCollins, 1988 Cloth 0-06-021853-3. 1992 Paper 0-06-446093-2. Illustrations by Eric Beddows.

—. *Shadow Play.* New York: HarperCollins, 1990 Cloth 0-06-021865-7. Illustrations by Eric Beddows.

Hasely, Dennis. *The Cave of Snores.* New York: Harper & Row, 1987. Illustrations by Eric Beddows. Out of print.

Jam, Teddy. *Night Cars.* Toronto: Groundwood Books, 1988 Paper 0-88899-134-7. Illustrations by Eric Beddows.

Wynne-Jones, Tim. *Zoom at Sea.* Toronto: Groundwood Books, 1983. Rev. ed. 1993 Cloth 0-88899-172-X. 1997 Paper 88899-106-1. Illustrations by Eric Beddows.

—. *Zoom Away.* Toronto: Groundwood Books, 1985. Rev. ed. 1993 Cloth 0-88899-173-8. 1997 Paper 0-88899-151-7. Illustrations by Eric Beddows.

—. *Zoom Upstream.* Toronto: Groundwood Books, 1992 Cloth 0-88899-109-6. 1993 (Meadow Mouse Paperback) 0-88899-188-6. Illustrations by Eric Beddows.

Awards

1984 Amelia Frances Howard-Gibbon Illustrator's Award for *Zoom at Sea*

1984 Ruth Schwartz Children's Book Award for *Zoom at Sea*

1986 Amelia Frances Howard-Gibbon Illustrator's Award for *Zoom Away*

1988 IODE Book Award - Toronto Chapter for *Night Cars*

1988 IBBY Youth Honour List for *Emperor's Panda*

1989 Elizabeth Mrazik-Cleaver Picture Book Award for *Night Cars*

1992 School Library Journal's Best Book Award for *Who Shrank My Grandmother's House?*

1993 American Library Association Notable Children's Books List for *Who Shrank My Grandmother's House?*

1996 Governor General's Literary Award for Children's Book Illustration for *The Rooster's Gift*

Selected articles about Eric Beddows

Granfield, Linda. "Beyond the Shadows: The Illustrations of Eric Beddows." *Teaching Librarian* Autumn 1995: 10-12.

Jenkinson, David. "Portraits: Eric Beddows, Award Winning Children's Illustrator." *Emergency Librarian* May-June 1993: 68-71.

Oppel, Kenneth. "Ken Nutt (a.k.a. Eric Beddows): Zooming to the Top." *Quill and Quire* Aug. 1989.

From *The Rooster's Gift*

Ron Berg
ILLUSTRATOR

Born
April 10, 1952, Niagara-on-the-Lake, Ontario

School
Sheridan College, Oakville, Ontario; Ontario College of Art, Toronto, Ontario

Where I live now
Toronto, Ontario

My favourite book now
The Hobbit and *Lord of the Rings* by J.R.R. Tolkien

Career
Illustrator

Family
Wife, Josie; daughter, Jennifer; son, Christopher; dog, Corky; cat, Muffy

The room where I create
"Third-floor studio in our house."

When I was growing up
"When I was a kid living in Niagara-on-the-Lake, I remember the half-acre of property we had, with its small creek winding its way through bulrushes, and the large willow trees whose leaves made wonderful rustling sounds in the breeze. I remember being lost in a world of make-believe where I was the conqueror, the hero, making long journeys across the overgrown terrain of our yard until it was time for lunch. I remember in winter the snow being piled so high that the banks seemed like mountains. My friends and I would dig a network of tunnels and rooms and ambush each other with snowballs."

My first book (and how it happened)
"My first book was *The King's Loon* written by Mary Alice Downie and it was published by Kids Can Press in 1979. I did six or seven pen and ink (black and white) illustrations and a colour cover. The story was fictional but elements were based on historical fact. The story takes place in New France (Quebec) and is about a little boy and his destiny with Count Frontenac. This book was the beginning of a series of historically-based fiction books that I illustrated for Kids Can Press."

Where my ideas come from
"I have yet to write a children's book so I'm in the situation where I receive a manuscript and am asked to give a visual interpretation of the story. Sometimes it is enough to just interpret, but then there are times when I long to create the story as well as the pictures. My mind easily drifts off into visual scripts but making sense of the visions and translating them into words seems an impossible task for me."

Who and what influenced me
"I've been influenced by the Old Masters like Dürer, (etching style), Chagall (fantasy), the Symbolists of the late 1800's, and the Dutch and Italian Renaissance painters. During my school and professional life, I have been influenced by students, teachers and other illustrators. But maybe the biggest influence has been the half-acre of property in Niagara-on-the-Lake."

How I work
"I like to work in quiet seclusion (I don't always achieve this, it gets quite active in the summer when the kids are home). My studio provides a very comfortable and well-lit place to work and think. If you're wondering what materials I use, I rough in colour on my illustrations with an airbrush (tinting the paper) and then work over top of it with chalk pastel pencils.

"I really enjoy working at home because it allows me to sit in the back yard or take a walk in the park nearby when I need a break." In fact, a lot of Ron's work time is spent sitting and working out problems in his head before he starts to draw. "People who create need to think of the impossible. A lot of my time is spent on gathering things in and then there's a spurt of output."

Ron Berg

BIBLIOGRAPHY

Bilson, Geoffrey. *Goodbye Sarah*. Toronto: Kids Can Press, 1982. Illustrations by Ron Berg. Out of print.

Downie, Mary Alice. *The King's Loon*. Toronto: Kids Can Press, 1979. Illustrations by Ron Berg. Out of print.

Downie, Mary Alice and George Rawlyk. *A Proper Acadian*. Toronto: Kids Can Press, 1980 Paper 0-919964-29-X. Illustrations by Ron Berg.

Field, Eugene. *Wynken, Blynken, and Nod*. Richmond Hill: Scholastic Canada, 1985 Cloth 0-590-71597-6; Big Book 0-590-71588-7. 1987 Paper 0-590-71589-5. Illustrations by Ron Berg.

Hamilton, Mary. *The Tin-Lined Trunk*. Toronto: Kids Can Press, 1980 Paper 0-919964-28-1. Illustrations by Ron Berg.

Lear, Edward. *The Owl and the Pussycat*. Richmond Hill: Scholastic Canada, 1984 Paper 0-590-71407-4; Cloth 0-590-71457-0; Big Book 0-590-71406-6. Illustrations by Ron Berg.

Quinlan, Patricia. *Night Fun*. Toronto: Annick Press, 1997 Cloth 1-55037-487-7. Illustrations by Ron Berg.

Tanaka, Shelley. *Michi's New Year* (Northern Lights Series). Concord: Irwin, 1980. Illustrations by Ron Berg.

From *Night Fun*

John Bianchi
AUTHOR/ILLUSTRATOR

Born
August 23, 1947, Rochester, New York, U.S.A.

Where I live now
Tucson, Arizona, U.S.A.

My favourite book when I was young
"*The Travels of Babar* by Jean de Brunhoff, for the writing and the simple watercolour illustrations."

Career
Publisher, illustrator and writer

Family
Wife, Margaret Cameron; two daughters, Jessica and Sascha

The room where I create
"I work at a large oak desk and generally have the family dog, a small, dusty-coloured mutt named Kasey, lying at my feet."

When I was growing up
"My first interest was sports — baseball, soccer, basketball and track were my favourites. I always loved to draw — especially cartoons. I could impress my friends with a quick drawing of Mickey Mouse or Pluto. My parents encouraged my creativity, but it wasn't until I turned 20 that I decided to make my living as an artist."

Becoming an artist
"When I first came to Canada, I worked at whatever jobs I could find. But no matter what I did by day, by night I was an artist. How did I know how to paint? I read books!

"After a few years, I went to work for Crawley Films, painting backgrounds for their animated films, then designing characters and doing storyboards."

My first book (and how it happened)
"By 1974, we moved from the city to a big old house in the country. Life was different; lots of funny things happened to us (like the time when I thought it might be fun to keep bees). I couldn't resist doing cartoons about all these funny experiences. I even started writing short stories for *Harrowsmith Magazine*.

"In 1985, I was asked to illustrate my first picture book, *The Dingles* by Helen Levchuk, and my career took on a whole new meaning. For me, the medium was the perfect marriage between words and pictures. Soon I was ready to try my own stories.

"I showed my work to Frank Edwards, a friend from *Harrowsmith Magazine*, and he liked it. We formed our own publishing company and called it Bungalo Books."

From *The Lab Rats of Doctor Éclair*

Where my ideas come from

"Ideas for books come to me all the time — driving with the family, jogging, biking, visiting schools, playing with my children. Whenever I have an idea for a book, I write it down — on a notepad, the back of a parking ticket — anywhere. I put all of these scraps of paper into the Bungalo Book folder. When it comes time to write another book, it's just a matter of consulting the ideas folder."

How I work

"I work with a large papier maché model of Johnny Bob Bungalo next to my desk. He's in a perfect position to hold my drawing tools for me. I work six to eight hours a day writing or illustrating. Sometimes I use a Macintosh computer for writing. Sometimes I'll use plain old pencil and paper. For illustrating I use my computer to colour all my pictures. I scan in a line drawing and then use a program called Adobe Photoshop to complete the work.

"I like reading my unfinished stories to my daughters. They always offer intelligent criticisms. Sometimes I'll bring along a work in progress on one of my school visits and read it to the students. Their reactions always help me make the story better."

John Bianchi

BIBLIOGRAPHY

All books illustrated by John Bianchi

Atwood, Margaret. *For the Birds.* Toronto: Groundwood Books, 1990 Paper 0-88894-825-5.

Bianchi, John. *The Bungalo Boys I: Last Of The Tree Ranchers.* Newburgh: Bungalo Books, 1986 Paper 0-921285-00-0; Cloth 1-921285-02-7.

—. *The Bungalo Boys II: Bushmen Brouhaha.* Newburgh: Bungalo Books, 1987 Paper 0-921285-08-6; Cloth 0-921285-10-8.

—. *Princess Frownsalot.* Newburgh: Bungalo Books, 1987 Paper 0-921285-04-3; Cloth 0-921285-06-X.

—. *The Swine Snafu.* Newburgh: Bungalo Books, 1988 Paper 0-921285-12-4; Cloth 0-921285-14-0.

—. *The Bungalo Boys III: Champions Of Hockey.* Newburgh: Bungalo Books, 1989 Paper 0-921285-16-7; Cloth 0-921285-18-3. I

—. *Snowed In at Pokeweed School.* Newburgh: Bungalo Books, 1991 Paper 0-921285-05-1; Cloth 0-921285-07-8.

—. *Penelope Penguin, The Incredibly Good Baby.* Newburgh: Bungalo Books, 1992 Paper 0-921285-11-6; Cloth 0-921285-13-2.

—. *The Artist.* Newburgh: Bungalo Books, 1993 Paper 0-921285-28-0; Cloth 0-921285-29-9.

—. *Spring Break at Pokeweed Public School.* Newburgh: Bungalo Books, 1994 Paper 0-921285-32-9; Cloth 0-921285-33-7.

—. *The Toad Sleeps Over.* Kingston: Bungalo Books, 1995 Paper 0-921285-40-X; Cloth 0-921285-41-8.

—. *Welcome Back to Pokeweed Public School.* Kingston: Bungalo Books, 1996 Paper 0-921285-44-2; Cloth 0-921285-45-0.

—. *Melody Mooner Takes Lessons.* Kingston: Bungalo Books, 1996 Paper 0-921285-46-9; Cloth 0-921285-47-7.

—. *The Lab Rats of Doctor Éclair.* Kingston: Bungalo Books, 1997 Paper 0-921285-48-5; Cloth 0-921285-49-3.

Dickinson, Terence. *Exploring the Night Sky.* Camden East: Camden House, 1987 Paper 0-920656-66-8; Cloth 0-920656-64-1.

—. *Exploring The Sky By Day.* Camden East: Camden House, 1988 Paper 0-920656-71-4; Cloth 0-920656-73-0.

Edwards, Frank B. *Mortimer Mooner Stopped Taking a Bath.* Newburgh: Bungalo Books, 1990 Paper 0-921285-20-5; Cloth 0-921285-21-3.

—. *Snow: Learning for the Fun of It.* Newburgh: Bungalo Books, 1992 Paper 0-921285-09-4; Cloth 0-921285-07-8.

—. *A Dog Called Dad.* Newburgh: Bungalo Books, 1994 Paper 0-921285-34-5; Cloth 0-921285-35-3.

—. *Melody Mooner Stayed Up All Night.* Newburgh: Bungalo Books, 1991 Paper 0-921285-01-9; Cloth 0-921285-03-5.

—. *Grandma Mooner Lost Her Voice!* Newburgh: Bungalo Books, 1992 Paper 0-921285-17-5; Cloth 0-921285-19-1.

—. *Mortimer Mooner Makes Lunch.* Newburgh: Bungalo Books, 1995 Paper 0-921285-36-1; Cloth 0-921285-37-X.

—. *Downtown Lost and Found* (New Reader Series). Kingston: Bungalo Books, 1997 Paper 0-921285-50-7; Cloth 0-921285-51-5.

—. *Peek-a-Boo at the Zoo* (New Reader Series). Kingston: Bungalo Books, 1997 Paper 0-921285-52-3; Cloth 0-921285-53-1.

—. *The Zookeepers Sleepers* (New Reader Series). Kingston: Bungalo Books, 1997 Paper 0-921285-54-X; Cloth 0-921285-67-1.

—. *Is the Spaghetti Ready?* (New Reader Series). Kingston: Bungalo Books, 1998 Paper 0-921285-66-3; Cloth 0-921285-67-1.

—. *New at the Zoo* (New Reader Series). Kingston: Bungalo Books, 1998 Paper 0-921285-69-8; Cloth 0-921285-70-1.

—. *Troubles with Bubbles* (New Reader Series). Kingston, Bungalo Books, 1998 Paper 0-921285-64-7; Cloth 0-921285-63-9.

Foon, Dennis. *The Short Tree and the Bird That Could Not Sing.* Toronto: Groundwood Books, 1986 Cloth 0-88899-046-4.

Levchuk, Helen. *The Dingles.* Toronto: Groundwood Books, 1985 Paper 0-88899-044-8.

Levchuk, Helen. *Doris Dingle's Crafty Cat Activity Book.* Toronto: Groundwood Books, 1990. Out of print.

Ann Blades
AUTHOR/ILLUSTRATOR

Born
November 16, 1947, Vancouver, British Columbia

School
"Seven schools, in West Vancouver, North Vancouver, Vancouver, New York and England."

Where I live now
Crescent Beach, British Columbia

My favourite book when I was young
"I was not a reader. I was generally outside climbing trees, riding my bike, building rafts, etc. When I was inside I painted in my spare time."

My favourite book now
"Dick King-Smith books, which I read to my sons."

Career
Elementary school teacher from 1967 to 1971; registered nurse from 1974 to 1980; writer and illustrator of children's books since 1968; artist, exhibited at Bau Xi Gallery since 1982.

Family
Two sons and a black lab named Digger

The room where I create
"A very messy room with a big window looking out into my garden."

Spare time
"Gardening, going to my cabin."

When I was growing up
"I was a tomboy, built rafts and forts and did not want childhood to end. When I was 11, I spent a year at school in England, where I was encouraged to draw and paint with watercolours. From that time I continued painting as a hobby, but never expected to have a career as an artist."

My first book (and how it happened)
"When I was 19 years old I went to the Peace River north country in B.C. I taught Grades 1 to 3 in a two-room school at Mile 18, a small, isolated farming community. Every week or two, a librarian on a bus brought books to the school, and I found that most of the books were published in New York and had very little relevance to the children I was teaching. Because of the isolation, I decided to write and illustrate a story of my own and I began work on what would become *Mary of Mile 18*, about Mary Bergen, who was in Grade 2 in my class."

Where my ideas come from
"I work mainly as an illustrator. The few books I have written and illustrated were all based on places and people I knew.

"*Mary of Mile 18* and *A Boy of Taché* were about children in communities where I had taught school, *The Cottage at Crescent Beach* was about my summers as a child, *By the Sea* had illustrations of Crescent Beach.

"*Back to the Cabin* is about going with my sons to our cabin in the Cariboo."

Who and what influenced me
"I was inspired by Harold Wiberg's beautiful illustrations in *The Tomten* and *The Fox*, which I read to the children I was teaching at Mile 18."

How I work
"I split the text into the number of pages needed, unless the publisher has done this already, and then do a storyboard (quick sketches to plan the illustration). If it's necessary, I do research and meet with the writer to discuss details.

"After all this, I do rough drawings (very quick, scribbled drawings) which are checked by the publisher. When they have been approved, I do detailed drawings (also checked by the publisher). Finally, I'm all set to do the final watercolour paintings."

Something nobody knew about me (until now)

"When I was in New York for three months during my Grade 11 year, trying to work on subjects by correspondence, I dreamed of making money by publishing a children's book, having a car, and taking my friends on a ski trip."

My favourite book that I've created

"I don't have a favourite. I am inclined to view them all very critically, and feel dissatisfied with some aspect of the illustrations. This criticism seems to fade as time passes."

Tips for young creators

"Paint for the fun of it, not to create a 'good' painting. Your painting is your impression of something, not an exact duplication."

Ann Blades

BIBLIOGRAPHY

All books illustrated by Ann Blades

Alderson, Sue Ann. *Ida and the Wool Smugglers.* Toronto: Groundwood Books, 1990 Paper 0-88899-119-3.

—. *A Ride for Martha.* Toronto: Groundwood Books, 1993 Cloth 0-88899-1-827.

—. *Pond Seasons.* Toronto: Groundwood, 1997 Cloth 0-88899-283-1.

Atwood, Margaret and Joyce Barkhouse. *Anna's Pet.* Toronto: James Lorimer & Co., 1980. 1986 Paper 0-88862-941-9; Cloth 0-88862-250-3.

Blades, Ann. *Mary of Mile 18.* Montreal: Tundra Books, 1971. 1988 Paper 0-88776-059-7; Cloth 0-88776-015-5.

—. *A Boy of Taché.* Montreal: Tundra Books, 1973. 1984 Cloth 0-88776-023-6. 1995 Paper 0-88776-350-2.

—. *The Cottage at Crescent Beach.* Toronto: Magook, 1977. Out of print.

—. *By the Sea: An Alphabet Book.* Toronto: Kids Can Press, 1985. Out of print.

—. *The Seasons Board Books.* Toronto: Groundwood Books, 1989.
   Spring 0-88899-090-1
   Summer 0-88899-091-X
   Fall 0-88899-092-8
   Winter 0-88899-093-6.

—. *Back to the Cabin.* Victoria: Orca Books, 1997 Paper 1-55143-051-7; Cloth 1-55143-049-5.

Laurence, Margaret. *Six Darn Cows* (The Kids of Canada Series). Toronto: James Lorimer & Co., 1986 Paper 0-88862-942-7; Cloth 0-88862-247-3.

Macklem, Michael. *Jacques the Woodcutter.* Ottawa: Oberon Press, 1977. Out of print.

Manson, Ainslie. *A Dog Came Too.* Toronto: Groundwood Books, 1992 Cloth 0-88899-140-1. 1993 Paper 0-88899-187-8.

Pearson, Kit. *The Singing Basket.* Toronto: Groundwood Books, 1990 Cloth 0-88899-104-5.

Speare, Jean. *A Candle for Christmas.* Toronto: Groundwood Books, 1986 Cloth 0-88899-050-2; Paper 0-88899-149-5.

Waterton, Betty. *A Salmon for Simon.* Toronto: Groundwood Books, 1986 0-590-71750-2. Rev. ed. 1996 Paper 0-88899-276-9; Cloth 0-88899-265-3.

—. *Pettranella.* Toronto: Groundwood Books, 1990 Paper 0-88899-108-8. ♣

Awards

1972 Canadian Library Association Book of the Year Award for Children for *Mary of Mile 18*

1978 Canada Council Children's Literature Prize for *A Salmon for Simon*

1979 The Amelia Frances Howard-Gibbon Illustrator's Award for *A Salmon for Simon*

1986 Elizabeth Mrazik-Cleaver Canadian Picture Book Award for *By the Sea: An Alphabet Book*

Selected articles about Ann Blades

Cory Davies. "A Conversation with Ann Blades." *Canadian Children's Literature* 39/40 (1985): 21.

Pearson, Kit. "Introducing Ann Blades." *CANSCAIP News* Summer 1993: 1-3.

From *Back to the Cabin*

Ron Broda
ILLUSTRATOR

Born
May 26, 1954, New Hamburg, Ontario

School
Conestoga College of Applied Arts Technique

Where I live now
Sarnia, Ontario

My favourite books when I was young
Dr. Seuss and Beatrix Potter

My favourite book now
Fox's Dream, by Telima; *The Party*, by Barbara Reid

Career
Drummer in a band, art director and designer for advertising agency. Currently illustrator in advertising and children's books, and director and curator for a children's museum.

Family
Wife, Joanne; children, Taylor, Dylan and Eden

The room where I create
"I'm just about to move into a new studio on the main floor of our new house. It's going to be jammed with all my stuff. I'll have a window by my drawing table, which is important to me, and I'll have my music by me which inspires me."

Spare time
"Enjoy my family. We like to do a lot of arts and crafts and tell stories before bedtime. We also like to go on nature walks together. Taylor and Eden love to catch frogs, snakes and insects."

When I was growing up
"I enjoyed the outdoors a lot in my childhood and I loved listening to all kinds of music."

My first book (and how it happened)
"My first book was *The Little Crooked Christmas Tree*. I had been doing a lot of illustrating in advertising, and one of my jobs was to do a short two-page poem about Icarus. The art director at Scholastic Canada saw that piece of work and called me to see if I would be interested in doing this book. I said yes!"

Where my ideas come from
"I get my ideas from all over; just everyday living can give me a lot of inspiration. When I need to know something specific I find the library is a good source."

Who and what influenced me
"A lot of artists have influenced me in the past and present. Norman Rockwell, Barbara Reid, Jonathan Milne, Reinard, Maxfield Parrish, Beatrix Potter, I can go on. What I like most about these people is their creativity and their drive for excellence. Each time I see something new from these people it makes me want to go to my studio."

How I work
"Lately I have been working at night on my books. I start by reading the story and doing rough thumbnails of ideas, then talking them over with my publisher and my wife. Once I have an idea that I want to work on, I do a couple of dummy books. Each one becomes a little bit more detailed in drawing. When my drawing is finished, it's time to figure out how I want to sculpt it. I do the hardest ones first, then finish the sculptures one by one. When every piece is done, I then take them to my photographer and we photograph each one with different lighting. The photo transparencies then go to the publisher to be reprinted."

Something nobody knew about me (until now)
Ron has A.D.D. (attention deficit disorder).

My favourite book that I've created
"*The Little Crooked Christmas Tree* is my favourite, because it was my first."

Tips for young creators

"For young artists, always keep a sketchbook with you and practise every day, even if it's only for 10 minutes."

Ron Broda

BIBLIOGRAPHY

Chase, Edith Newlin. *Waters.* Toronto: Scholastic, 1993 Cloth 0-590-74202-7. 1994 Paper 0-590-74201-9. Illustrations by Ron Broda.♣

Cole, Joanna. *Spider's Lunch.* New York: Putnam, 1995 Paper 0-448-40223-8. Illustrations by Ron Broda.

Cutting, Michael. *The Little Crooked Christmas Tree.* Toronto: Scholastic, 1991 Cloth 0-590-73652-3. 1993 Paper 0-590-73653-1. Illustrations by Ron Broda.

Eugene, Toni. *Caterpillar Magic.* Washington, DC: National Geographic, 1990. Illustrations by Ron Broda. Out of print.

Lawrence, Bonnie S. *Blue Jay Babies.* Washington, DC: National Geographic, 1991 Cloth 0-7922-1995-3. Illustrations by Ron Broda. Out of print.

Oppenheim, Joanne. *Have You Seen Bugs?* Toronto: Scholastic, 1996 Cloth 0-590-24322-5. Illustrations by Ron Broda.♣

Webb, Joanne. *3D Paper Crafts.* Toronto: Scholastic, 1997. Illustrations by Ron Broda.♣

Selected articles about Ron Broda

Muldoon, Kathy. "The Big Picture." *The Toronto Star* 2 Nov. 1996.

From *Have You Seen Bugs?*

William Roy Brownridge
AUTHOR/ILLUSTRATOR

Born
October 14, 1932, Rosetown, Saskatchewan

School
Institute of Technology and Art in Calgary

Where I live now
Calgary, Alberta

My favourite books when I was young
The *Books of Knowledge* and the *Big Little Books*

Career
"Partner at a graphic design studio. Associate creative director at F.W.J. Communications. Presently, I am a self-employed fine artist."

Family
Five children: Boyd, Beth, Nancy, Leanne and David

The room where I create
"Square room — north facing wall of windows — great view of downtown core — sunrise, moonrise."

Spare time
"Reading, photography, sports fan, wheelchair basketball."

When I was growing up
"Before electricity arrived in our village, Dad would light the candles on our 10-foot tree on Christmas Eve. All the family and friends would crowd into our living room for a wondrous moment.

"Brother Bob arriving home from playing hockey in New York with a surprise package for me: a complete cowboy outfit including vest and chaps. I was seven; the year was 1939. What a thrill!

"As a boy, my greatest love was the rink and playing hockey in all kinds of weather."

My first book (and how it happened)
"Having five children and being an artist, I often thought of trying to write and illustrate a children's book. An incident in my youth had always tugged at my memory. I knew it had a potential. As a handicapped teenager, I had been officially sanctioned to play in one final playoff game of hockey *without wearing skates.* (I couldn't wear skates. I had two crippled feet.) Years later, I did a painting of how I used to play goal in my moccasins. The title of the painting, 'The Moccasin Goalie,' sparked the book."

Where my ideas come from
"Most of my stories start with a few kernels of truth gleaned from my own feelings and experiences. Being born with a handicap, I've always been an outsider — different from the 'norm.' I've always identified with the underdog and this has shaped my view of the world and how I approach life."

Who and what influenced me
"My family has played a dominant role in shaping my personality, they were nurturing and supportive without being indulgent. My brother Bob was my role model. He was a great hockey player and a softspoken, strong and loving family man. He was a pilot during the war. He was everything I wanted to be as a growing boy.

"Team sports, and especially hockey, have influenced my outlook greatly. In a single team game you can learn the vital lessons of life. You learn to be tough mentally and physically. You learn fellowship and the true meaning of selflessness, a characteristic in very short supply today.

"Art instructors who influenced me: Illingworth Kerr, Stan Perrott, Ken Sturdy."

How I work

"I work on the storyline in my mind for some time, then do a rough draft — at the same time trying to explore the visual scenes within the story. Lastly, I do a final draft accompanied by line drawings.

"Once the draft and the line drawings are approved by the publisher, I photograph the line drawings on transparencies and enlarge them onto my panel or canvas. Then I start painting, using fast-drying alkyd oils.

"I like to work with a colour base (as opposed to a white canvas) and paint contrasting dots of colour over it. When I do school readings, I refer to pointillism as the historical term for this method, but my style isn't really pointillism; it's much cruder. I say it's broken colour.

"It gives a vibrancy to the painting. I like the surface to be activated as opposed to being flat. I love the interaction of contrasting colours and what the eye does to those colours when you step back to look at it.

"I prefer painting winter scenes. I like the starkness of the winter landscapes and the way the light looks on the snow."

Something nobody knew about me (until now)

"I'm 65 and still playing competitive wheelchair basketball."

My favourite book I've created

The Moccasin Goalie

Tips for young creators

"Look inside your own life and world for possible stories. It's there you will find ideas to feel passionate about."

William Roy Brownridge

BIBLIOGRAPHY

Brownridge, William Roy. *The Final Game*. Victoria: Orca Book Publishers, 1995 Cloth 1-55143-100-9. Illustrations by the author.

—. *The Moccasin Goalie*. Victoria: Orca Book Publishers, 1997 Paper 1-55143-054-1. Illustrations by the author.

Selected articles about William Roy Brownridge

Quill and Quire 23 Feb. 1996: 14.

McGoogan, Ken. *Calgary Herald* 18 Nov. 1995.

From *The Final Game*

Rhian Brynjolson
AUTHOR/ILLUSTRATOR

Born
October 11, 1959, Regina, Saskatchewan

School
Fine Arts, University of Manitoba; BA Economics, University of Winnipeg

Where I live now
Winnipeg, Manitoba

My favourite book when I was young
Alice in Wonderland

My favourite book now
"I have many favourites."

Career
"Children's book illustrator and author. I've also been a community worker and art instructor, a research assistant, and have held odd jobs such as shovelling gravel and doing yard work."

Family
"Husband, Dale; daughter Noni; son Iain; and a house full of pets (cats, birds, fish and a chinchilla)."

The room where I create
"In the summer I spend the early mornings working in my front porch, where the sun streams in through the windows. I have a studio and an office upstairs. The studio has a drafting table, a long trestle table, built-in cupboards and running water. It's the most cluttered room you can imagine, full of paper, canvas, boxes of books, sculpture, children's drawings, photographs, and every type of paint and drawing tool ever invented."

Spare time
"I like to read, walk, canoe, and travel with my family."

When I was growing up
"When I was young, an artist lived in our basement. He allowed me to use some of his materials; we painted on leather and made papier maché masks. We didn't do much art in my elementary school — just a lot of crafts, like gluing tissue paper onto bottles. But someone gave me a book called *How to Draw Horses*. That was the beginning. I spent all my spare time either riding or drawing horses."

My first book (and how it happened)
"I used to live near Pemmican Publications' office. I must have walked past it every day for two years before I got up the nerve to knock on their door. They just happened to need an illustrator for *Jen and the Great One*, written by Peter Eyvindson. They liked my portfolio, a collection of drawings and paintings that I'd done over several years. I've enjoyed working for Pemmican ever since."

Where my ideas come from
"Most of my ideas come from experience or issues that are important to me. If I think about, worry about, and practise drawing something long enough, some kind of light bulb is bound to come on. Eventually, if I play with a problem long enough, I'll get an idea for an interesting piece of the story or illustration."

Who and what influenced me
"I learned a lot from teachers and fellow students in art school. But most of what I've learned has come from teaching art to children and adults. There are always new approaches and ideas to try.

"I also spend time looking at picture books and other artists' work. Books by Anthony Browne and Chris Van Allsburg have taught me about visual jokes and transforming everyday objects. *Animalia*, by Graham Base, has lots to teach about design and detail. Barbara Reid's books have interesting vantage points, humour, and an interesting art medium. I admire the scratchy lines and overlapping colours in Kady MacDonald Denton's illustrations. And then there are Eric Beddows, Eric Carle, Jan Brett, Brian Wildsmith, Maurice Sendak…"

How I work

"First, I read through the text and scribble on it. These are quick, thumbnail sketches — a record of what I'm thinking as I read. Then I begin making storyboards to plan the sequence of illustrations and how they fit together with the text.

"Many of the books have required a lot of research. This might involve finding a model and taking photographs, finding pictures in books in the library, or going through the drawers and cupboards in the archives at the museum.

"When I have all of the pieces of the illustrations and I've practised drawing them, I make decisions about design: will the illustrations have borders, what shape will they be, and so on. Then I choose what medium I'm going to work in: watercolour, pencil, oil paint, tempera, or crayon. Then I can finally start work on the illustrations. A series of illustrations might take from three months to a year to complete."

Something nobody knew about me (until now)

"I'm basically a shy person and I'm never happy with my finished illustrations. Partly this is because of time restrictions, but it is very common for artists to be dissatisfied with their own work.

"Also, I have a degree in economic development."

My favourite book that I've created

"I think *Foster Baby* is my favourite. It was the first book that I wrote as well as illustrated. Not only was I able to speak from experience about the baby who had lived with us for three months, but drawing babies is fun; they have expressive, toothless faces that look like caricatures. I was able to include information in this book too, so it was a useful project as well as a fun one to work on."

Tips for young creators

"Drawing requires 'slowness.' Too much of our time is spent scurrying breathlessly about, or involved in some mindless activity. Things like riding bikes and playing Nintendo are fun; don't give them up. But make sure you leave yourself time to look at things slowly, daydream and draw the things that are important to you."

Rhian Brynjolson

BIBLIOGRAPHY

All books illustrated by Rhian Brynjolson

Brynjolson, Rhian. *Foster Baby*. Winnipeg: Pemmican Publications, 1996 Paper 0-921827-54-7.

—. *Art and Illustration in the Classroom*. Winnipeg: Peguis Publishers, 1998 Paper 1-895411-90-4.

Eyvindson, Peter. *Jen and the Great One*. Winnipeg: Pemmican Publications, 1990 Paper 0-921827-19-9.

—. *The Yesterday Stone*. Winnipeg: Pemmican Publications, 1992 Paper 0-921827-24-5.

—. *The Missing Sun*. Winnipeg: Pemmican Publications, 1993 Paper 0-921827-29-6.

—. *The Night Rebecca Stayed Too Late*. Winnipeg: Pemmican Publications, 1994 Paper 0-921827-39-3.

—. *Red Parka Mary*. Winnipeg: Pemmican Publications, 1996 Paper 0-921827-50-4.

—. *Chubby Champ*. Winnipeg: Pemmican Publications, 1997 Paper 0-921827-59-8.

Klassen, Dale. *I Love to Play Hockey*. Winnipeg: Pemmican Publications, 1994 Paper 0-921827-44-X.

McLellan, Joseph. *Nanabosho Dances*. Winnipeg: Pemmican Publications, 1991 Paper 0-921827-14-8.

—. *Nanabosho, Soaring Eagle and the Great Sturgeon*. Winnipeg: Pemmican Publications, 1993 Paper 0-921827-23-7.

—. *Nanabosho, How the Turtle Got its Shell*. Winnipeg: Pemmican Publications, 1994 Paper 0-921827-40-7.

—. *Nanabosho and the Woodpecker*. Winnipeg: Pemmican Publications, 1995 Paper 0-921827-49-0.

Selected articles about Rhian Brynjolson

Eyvindson, Peter. "Rhian Brynjolson." *Children's Book News* 21.1 (Winter 1998): 17.

Weber, Terry. "Art Won Out Over Banking." *Winnipeg Free Press* 13 Nov. 1997.

From *Red Parka Mary*

Geoff Butler
ILLUSTRATOR

Born
January 13, 1945, Fogo, Newfoundland

School
Art Students League, New York City

Where I live now
Granville Ferry, Nova Scotia

My favourite books when I was young
Treasure Island, *The Count of Monte Cristo*

My favourite book now
Don Quixote

Career
Visual artist, writer and illustrator

Family
Wife, Judi McClare; daughters, Teagan, Kirsten and Leah; son, Sean

The room where I create
"For years, I worked in the small attic of my home. As this space has been taken over by my children, I now work in a studio next door. It is not very far from Port Royal and, as I look across the harbour to Annapolis Royal, I can sometimes see harbour seals, great blue herons, and always lots of seagulls."

Spare time
"I try to keep physically fit by playing sports, mostly soccer, hockey and basketball. I also like to play music on the guitar, fiddle or piano."

When I was growing up
"I did not display any particular interest or talent in art. There were certainly no galleries or art classes in the place I lived. But, during my early years in a small rural area, I did learn to milk cows, drive a tractor, and watch the birth and death of farm animals. As a teenager, I lived in a slightly larger town that had electricity, a jukebox and pinball machines. I mention these things only to point out it would have been difficult to predict from my childhood experiences that I would end up as an artist. It does show that someone who does not have natural artistic talents can learn the techniques of art at a later age."

My first book (and how it happened)
"My first children's book was *The Killick: A Newfoundland Story*. I had been a visual artist for several years, exhibiting my paintings in galleries. Because there was usually a narrative element in my paintings, I thought I'd like to try book illustration, so I sent slides of my work to various publishers across Canada. In the meantime, I had self-published a book on a series of my paintings, called *Art of War*. When May Cutler, then president of Tundra Books, saw this, and also learned I had been brought up in Newfoundland, she asked me if I'd like to write and illustrate a Newfoundland story."

Where my ideas come from
"My ideas can come from anywhere at any time, so I always carry a notepad around with me to jot down things before I forget them. Often when I start a painting, I don't have any idea at all, or only a vague idea, or perhaps just a word or phrase. It is then that I follow the advice of Leonardo da Vinci who stated '...look into the stains of walls, or ashes of a fire, or clouds, or mud or like place, in which you...may find really marvellous ideas.' I make up my own stains, ashes, etc. by applying paint randomly to the canvas. Then I step back to see if these shapes and colours suggest anything to me. I find this approach helpful not only to get ideas, but to develop compositions when I already have an idea in mind."

Who and what influenced me

"One influence on me was a spider I saw on the outside of a sixth-floor window, one lazy afternoon. It occurred to me that the spider was being much more industrious than I was.

"The folk songs of the 1960s have also influenced me, in the sense that they were an example of an art form that tried to raise awareness of social issues and create the mood for change. As for book illustrations, I still fondly remember, when I studied in New York, standing in front of some original N.C. Wyeth illustrations I had seen as a child in such books as *Treasure Island, Robin Hood* and *The Last of the Mohicans.*"

How I work

"It's often asked of songwriters if the words or the music come first. Similarly, one could ask of book writers and illustrators if the words or the pictures come first. It depends. With my children's stories, I write the text first. This guides me to pick out salient parts of the story to illustrate, and try to keep the illustrations interesting in them-selves by varying colours, compositions, points of view, and so on. In my *Art of War* book, I did the paintings first, and then wrote the text. For an unpublished book on the theme of angels, I wrote poems that correlate only loosely with the visual images, and either can stand on its own."

Something nobody knew about me (until now)

"Though I have been a professional artist for about 25 years, I still find painting as difficult as it was when I started. Perhaps I have different problems to confront now, but when I start painting, there is still no guarantee I will complete it successfully. I have learned, however, to be patient and to let the creative process percolate."

My favourite book that I've created

"Perhaps because it was my first book, and a labour of love that I worked on for eight years, I think *Art of War: Painting It Out of the Picture* is the favourite of my own books. I self-published it because I believed in it so strongly, and had to immerse myself in learning the skills necessary to produce a book."

Tips for young creators

"My tips for creators would be the same tips I would give for general living. Learn as much as you can. Keep an open mind. Ask questions. Seek advice. Always do your best."

Geoff Butler

BIBLIOGRAPHY

Wyman, Peter. *Dear Don*. Annapolis Royal: Peter Wyman, 1985 0-88999-291-6. Illustrated by Geoff Butler.

Butler, Geoff. *The Killick: A Newfoundland Story*. Toronto: Tundra Books, 1995 Paper 0-88776-449-5; Cloth 0-88776-336-7. Illustrations by the author.

—. *Art of War: Painting It Out of the Picture*. Granville Ferry: Self-published, 1990 0-9694447-0-2. Illustrations by the author.

—. *The Hangashore*. Toronto: Tundra, 1998 Cloth 0-88776-444-4. Illustrations by the author.

Awards

1996 Ruth Schwartz Children's Book Award for *The Killick: A Newfoundland Story*

Selected articles about Geoff Butler

Day, Karen S. *Across Canada: A Guide to Canadian Children's Literature*. Toronto: Prentice Hall Ginn-Allyn and Bacon, 1998. 2

Poole, Margaret. "Outport is Butler's Canvas." *Halifax Sunday Herald*, 7 June 1998.

From *The Killick: A Newfoundland Story*

Scott Cameron
ILLUSTRATOR

Born
July 3, 1962, Mississauga, Ontario

School
Ontario College of Art

Where I live now
Mississauga, Ontario

My favourite books when I was young
The Lord of the Rings, by J.R.R. Tolkien

My favourite book now
The Complete Short Stories of Mark Twain

Career
Illustrator for magazines, readers, book covers, children's book illustrator. Currently, background painter for Disney Animation, Canada, in Toronto.

Family
Single

The room where I create
"Two rooms actually — my bedroom which has my drawing table where I draw and draw and redraw and figure everything out. And the spare room where I paint the illustrations standing at my easel, because I use oil paints and this room has better ventilation."

Spare time
"I think I had some spare time in the summer of 1974 but that was so long ago I can't quite be sure."

When I was growing up
"Even though I grew up in the suburbs, it was a heavily wooded area. Much of my childhood was spent in the wild ravine behind our house with its stream and marsh and fallen trees, or in the park down the street.

"I think it's one of the reasons I try to paint things loosely instead of being too tight. Whenever I see trees, plants or landscapes that are painted slickly and photographically, they feel dead to me. They don't have the feel or the rugged liveliness I grew up around."

My first book (and how it happened)
"The first was *Beethoven Lives Upstairs*, in 1993. Originally, the publisher wanted to take stills off the video version of the story and have them painted, but the still pictures didn't come out well, so they let me come up with my own ideas for pictures. It was certainly more satisfying that way. I spent two months researching the time period and three months doing the paintings."

Where my ideas come from
"When reading the story I'm going to illustrate, I don't concentrate on just the dramatic action scenes. I stay open to anything that might suggest an interesting image. Sometimes it's an emotional moment or a scene that sets the time and place of the story.

"In *The Root Cellar*, I read the sentence 'she became part of the woods and the water, of the boat and Will' and the image it created in my mind became one of my favourite illustrations."

Who and what influenced me
"Where I've grown up has had a big influence on me and I seem to respond on a gut level to painters whose work has a feeling or energy and life to it — people such as Frank Frazetta, N. C. Wyeth, Frederic Remington, James Reynolds, John Singer Sargent and Claude Monet."

How I work
"Now that I work full-time for Disney, I can only work on my own projects after work, on the weekends and during vacation time. That's why I joked about no spare time. Research is always the first step, trying to find visual reference for the time and place of the story. Then come the sketches for each illustration

trying to find the best composition for each and to make sure the compositions alternate interestingly from page to page. Lastly, the drawings are transferred to canvases that I try to paint loosely enough to give a static image some sense of life."

Something nobody knew about me (until now)

"If I wasn't a painter I would be a veterinarian or working in an animal sanctuary or trying to help animals in some way. I've been around cats and dogs all my life. At one point there were six cats, but now it's down to three. The area of Clarkson in which I live is basically a forest full of trees and various wildlife.

It's a big part of who I am and how I view the world."

My favourite book that I've created

"*The Token Gift*. You try hard to do your best, but there are always flaws and things you could have done better. *The Token Gift* is the one I'm the least unhappy with."

Tips for young creators

"It's an old cliché, but follow the things you love, the things that excite you and make you passionate. It's that passion that will help give whatever you make its value."

Scott Cameron

BIBLIOGRAPHY

Brummel Crook, Connie. *Maple Moon*. Stoddart Kids, 1997 Cloth 0-7737-3017-6. Illustrations by Scott Cameron.

De Regniers, Beatrice S. *David and Goliath*. New York: Orchard Books, 1996 Cloth 0-531-09496-0. Illustrations by Scott Cameron.

Lunn, Janet. *The Root Cellar*. Toronto: Lester Publishing, 1981. 2nd ed. 1994 Cloth 1-895555-39-6. Illustrations by Scott Cameron.

McKibbon, Hugh William. *The Token Gift*. Toronto: Annick Press, 1996 Paper 1-55037-498-2; Cloth 1-55037-499-0. Illustrations by Scott Cameron.

Nichol, Barbara. *Beethoven Lives Upstairs*. Toronto: Stoddart Kids, 1992 Cloth 1-895555-21-3. Toronto: Scholastic, 1995 Paper 0-590-24686-0. Illustrations by Scott Cameron.

From *The Token Gift*

Harvey Chan
ILLUSTRATOR

Born
November 21, 1957, 9:00 p.m.

School
Ontario College of Art and Design

Where I live now
Toronto, Ontario

My favourite books when I was young
"*Children Weekly* magazine and comic books in Hong Kong."

My favourite books now
"Books with great stories and beautiful illustrations."

Career
Illustrator, caricature artist, fine artist

Family
Wife, Labrador retriever, and a corgi

The room where I create
"A small studio at home, plus a larger studio downtown."

Spare time
"Music, movies, basketball, yard sales and sleeping."

When I was growing up
"Chinese New Year in Hong Kong, a long holiday, was the most exciting thing annually. That was the only time I spent a lot of time with my family, had new clothes, ate many big feasts, and became very wealthy with lucky money."

My first book (and how it happened)
"*Roses Sing on New Snow,* published by Groundwood, in 1991. Recommended by *Owl/Chickadee* magazine, I showed my portfolio to Groundwood. After exploring different styles of drawings, both the publisher and I finally agreed on something we were very happy with. It carried the right tone for the book."

Where my ideas come from
"My ideas usually come from the feel of the story and from the characters that carry the flow of the drama. Through research of the subject and historical detail, exciting visual ideas can be triggered."

Who and what influenced me
Harvey is influenced by a variety of art forms. "There is a big list of people and things that have influenced me over the years: illustrators from N.C. Wyeth to Maurice Sendak to Ed Young to Gary Kelly, music from classical to rap to blues to flamenco, Japanese comic books to fine art, sculptures by Rodin to pottery."

How I work
"First I read the story until an emotion is established. Thumbnail sketches are then explored, after which I determine breaks in the story that benefit the layout design and flow of storytelling. Then I do research with the help of hired models. Finally, I do the finished art."

Something nobody knew about me (until now)
"Other than a visual artist in my lifetime, I would also dream of being a musician, dancer and martial artist."

My favourite book that I've created
Harvey's favourite book so far is *Ghost Train,* published by Groundwood Books. "It was exciting to work on an historical story that told a part of Chinese Canadian history. Being of Chinese origin, I am proud to have been involved in the creation of the book."

Tips for young creators

"Explore, imagine, research, draw, draw, draw. Then observe, and draw again. Never give up."

Harvey Chan

BIBLIOGRAPHY

Gillmor, Don. *The Trouble With Justin*. Toronto: Groundwood Books, 1993 Cloth 0-88899-177-0. Illustrations by Harvey Chan.

Jam, Teddy. *The Charlotte Stories*. Toronto: Groundwood Books, 1994 Cloth 0-88899-210-6. 1997 Paper 0-88899-302-1. Illustrations by Harvey Chan.

Lottridge, Celia Barker. *Music for the Tsar of the Sea*. Toronto: Groundwood Books, 1998 Cloth 0-88899-328-5. Illustrations by Harvey Chan.

Ye, Ting-Xing. *Three Monks, No Water*. Toronto: Annick Press, 1997 Cloth 1-55037-443-5; Paper 1-55037-442-7. Illustrations by Harvey Chan.

Yee, Paul. *Roses Sing On New Snow: A Delicious Tale*. Toronto: Groundwood Books, 1991 Paper 0-88899-217-3. 1994 Cloth 0-88899-144-4. Illustrations by Harvey Chan.

Yee, Paul. *Ghost Train*. Toronto: Groundwood Books, 1996 Cloth 0-88899-257-2. Illustrations by Harvey Chan.

Awards

1992 Ruth Schwartz Children's Book Award for *Roses Sing on New Snow: A Delicious Tale*

1997 Amelia Frances Howard-Gibbon Illustrator's Award for *Ghost Train*

1997 Elizabeth Mrazik-Cleaver Canadian Picture Book Award for *Ghost Train*

1997 Ruth Schwartz Children's Book Award for *Ghost Train*

1999 Ruth Schwartz Children's Book Award for *Music for the Tsar of the Sea*

Selected articles about Harvey Chan

Quill and Quire Oct. 1994.

From *Ghost Train*

Veronika Martenova Charles
AUTHOR/ILLUSTRATOR

Born
Prague, Czech Republic

School
Ryerson Polytechnic University (BAA); Ontario College of Art

Where I live now
Toronto, Ontario

My favourite books when I was young
Myths, legends and fairy tales

My favourite books now
"They're still the same…but now I have more of them."

Careers in the past
Rock singer/songwriter, interior designer, art director, author/illustrator.

Family
Husband David, who works in the movies; two sons, Sam and Matt; daughter Alex; and a small Tonkinese cat named Emerald

The room where I create
"I have a studio on the top floor of my house. There are tons of books, CDs and music tapes, toys, a copying machine, a sink, a couch (on which Emerald sleeps), and a huge drawing table underneath a window. Because I like to work at night I often get visited by raccoons."

Spare time
"I like to go to places I haven't been to and discover things. There are two ways I travel. The first is the real way, when I walk and walk for hours, explore and observe. The second is the pretending way, when I let my mind wander and see where it takes me. It's hard to say which way is better, but the second way definitely costs less."

When I was growing up
"I didn't have any brothers or sisters, didn't have TV, didn't go to daycare or babysitters; I hung around my mother who was designing and sewing costumes. She had a radio on and every day there were stories read for children. I would listen to them, and afterwards do my own version of the tales, playing on the ground with scraps of fabric and buttons.

"I always doodled in class and made very good imaginary creatures for classmates in exchange for candybars. Later my parents sent me to an art class with big people. This came to an abrupt end when my grandmother discovered in my sketchbook drawings of naked people from figure-drawing class. I became a singer instead. I didn't draw for a long time, until I came to Canada as a teenager and decided to start all over again"

My first book (and how it happened)
"I was working in an interior design office, drawing plans of shopping malls. So I doodled pictures to a story which I had written and I sent it to a publisher in New York (there weren't too many picture book publishers in Canada then). It was sent back with a long encouraging letter, saying 'send us more of your stuff.'

"This time I mailed a story without pictures and it was sent back without a nice letter. I realized it was because I had sent no pictures. I decided to learn more about illustrating. I went to OCA, assembled portfolio pieces, and sent them to publishers (there were now some in Toronto). A manuscript was sent to me to illustrate. It was called *There's An Alligator Under My Bed* and it was printed in only two colours, and very badly. But it sold lots of copies."

Where my ideas come from
"Ideas are all around us. Just keep your eyes and ears open and they will come. Sometimes I have too many ideas. So I pick only the one that really interests me. That way I can go and find out more about it. This works the other way around too; look into what interests you and ideas will come."

Who and what influenced me

"Growing up in Prague, a city with a long cultural history, was an inspiration to me. I was also influenced by the work of people like painter Paul Klee, Remedios Varo, and composer Antonio Vivaldi.

"Any kind of encouragement I got from my colleagues, teachers, and now from my audiences, keeps me going, makes me try harder."

How I work

"When an idea arrives, I create a little movie in my head. Then I leave it. I'm afraid if I started to write immediately and used the wrong words, I could scare that magic feeling away.

"But every once in a while I replay the movie in my head, to see if the magic feeling persists. When I'm finally sure it won't go away, I start collecting words and images. And then one day I sit down and start to write.

"I already know in my head what the pictures will look like when I start sketching. I draw on tracing paper so I can move things around. Sometimes I act out the characters and my family takes Polaroids of me so I can draw the angles right. When I paint the figures I try to feel the way the characters feel. If the character grins, I draw with a grin on my face. If it's sad, I'm sad... sometimes so sad I can't even draw.

"Now I paint mostly with acrylics, but mix them with whatever media will achieve the effect the picture needs."

Something nobody knew about me (until now)

"From travels to faraway places, I always bring small rocks and pretty stones back home. My friends bring me some too. I have stones in my house from all parts of the world."

My favourite book that I've created

"It's like asking a mother which of her children she loves the best. I like them all but I'm always most concerned about the book I'm working on at the time."

Tips for young creators

"Do what makes you happy and try to get better at it every day. Don't give up no matter what!"

From *Stretch, Swallow and Stare*

Veronika Martenova Charles

BIBLIOGRAPHY

Charles, Veronika Martenova. *The Crane Girl*. Toronto: Oxford University Press, 1992 Cloth 0-19-540877-2. 1995 Paper 0-7737-5718-X. Illustrations by the author.

—. *Hey! What's that Sound?* Toronto: Stoddart, 1994 Cloth 0-7737-2841-4. 1996 Paper 0-7737-5702-3. Illustrations by the author.

—. *Necklace of Stars*. Toronto: Stoddart, 1996 Cloth 0-7737-2967-4. Illustrations by the author.

—. *Stretch, Swallow & Stare*. Toronto: Stoddart Kids, 1999 Cloth 0-7737-3098-2. Illustrations by the author.

Gill, Gail E. *There's An Alligator Under My Bed*. Toronto: Three Trees Press, 1984. Illustrations by Veronika Martenova Charles. Out of print.

Gugler, Laurel D. *Casey's Carousel*. Windsor: Black Moss Press, 1989 Paper 0-88753-186-5. Illustrations by Veronika Martenova Charles.

Mineau, Marion. *The Flowers*. Windsor: Black Moss Press, 1988 Cloth 0-88753-171-7. Illustrations by Veronika Martenova Charles.

Plant, Maria R. *Robin and the Rainbow*. Toronto: Three Trees Press, 1985. Illustrations by Veronika Martenova Charles. Out of print.

Selected articles about Veronika Martenova Charles

Smulders, Marilyn. "Pen Power: Czech Author Veronika Martenova Charles Overcame the Odds to Become A Kids' Writer." *The Sunday Daily News* [Halifax] 2 Nov., 1997: 48.

Mostyn, Richard. "Writer Still Sees World as a Six-Year-Old." *Yukon News* [Whitehorse] Nov. 1996.

Brenda Clark
ILLUSTRATOR

Born
February 10, 1955, Toronto, Ontario

School
Sheridan College, Oakville, Ontario

Where I live now
Port Perry, Ontario

Career
Children's book illustrator

Family
"One husband, one child and one cat."

The room where I create
"A spare bedroom in my home."

Spare time
"Reading, camping, canoeing, hiking, travelling and playing squash."

When I was growing up
"In school, drawing was how I best communicated ideas, told a story, or decorated a workbook. Inspiration came from looking at the richly-coloured animated films and traditionally illustrated books of my childhood.

"Making a living as a full-time artist was always my ambition. I dreamed of working out of my house and raising a family at the same time. The career came quite quickly; the family much later."

My first book (and how it happened)
"After high school, I took a three year illustration course at Sheridan College in Oakville, Ontario where I studied all aspects of illustration including graphic design, advertising, editorial and book illustration. My graduating portfolio was strongest in children's book illustration and that's what helped me begin freelancing for educational publishers, providing art for reading anthologies and textbooks. I have also illustrated for *Chickadee* magazine.

"A few years of experience gave me some published pieces for my portfolio and the confidence to approach publishers of children's books. Fortunately, I was soon able to concentrate most of my energies on producing picture books, eventually completing at least one per year."

Where my ideas come from
"My pictures grow from the words in a manuscript. The words are my starting point. Any part of a story that contains an unfamiliar situation, animal or object sends me off to do research. References can come from real life, books or other pictures. It always helps me to see what things really look like, even if I don't interpret them realistically. The pictures should harmonize and enhance the words of the story even if they carry a separate storyline or contain characters not mentioned in the story."

How I work
"It takes me from seven to ten months to finish a 32-page book, depending on the amount of research and detail required. The *Franklin* books are done much quicker — an average of three months per book. To achieve the same amount of detail and quality as the earlier books requires the help of an underpainter to speed up the process.

"I use mostly watercolours, but my painting style varies from book to book with the exception of the *Franklin* series where it is important to maintain consistency. Different styles of writing require separate painting treatments. The variety keeps me interested and allows more opportunities to work with various authors.

"Although my style often changes, there are some similarities among the books. My characters are never truly realistic. I call this approach 'believable.' Total realism does not inspire me. I do enjoy adding extra details for children to discover over numerous readings.

"I like to work without the

guidance of the author or editor until I've been alone with a manuscript and produced thumbnail sketches (small sketches) for the whole book. Once my first ideas are established I can work easily with suggestions and criticism. A successful book requires lots of input and cooperation from all sides."

My favourite book that I've created

"My favourite character is Franklin, and my favourite book is *Little Fingerling*."

Tips for young creators

"Draw at least once a day. Keep sketchpads and drawing materials handy (in your backpack). Observe everything around you. This saves time later. If you memorize how things look, you'll have less research to do. The more items you can draw, the more freedom you'll have to create. Much like writing, this is improving your vocabulary."

Brenda Clark

BIBLIOGRAPHY

All books illustrated by Brenda Clark

Baillie, Marilyn. *My Cat: A Scrapbook of Drawings, Photos and Facts.* Toronto: Kids Can Press, 1993 Cloth 1-55074-125-X. 1995 Paper 1-55074-206-X.

—. *My Dog: A Scrapbook of Drawings, Photos and Facts.* Toronto: Kids Can Press, 1993 Cloth 1-55074-127-6. 1995 Paper 1-55074-208-6.

Bourgeois, Paulette. *Big Sarah's Little Boots.* Toronto: Kids Can Press, 1987 Paper 0-921103-70-0; Paper (Little Kids Series) 1-55074-141-1. ✢

—. *The Franklin Series.* Toronto: Kids Can Press.✢

Franklin in the Dark. 1986 Paper 0-921103-31-X; Cloth 0-919964-93-1.
Hurry Up, Franklin. 1989 Paper 1-55074-016-4; Cloth 0-921103-68-9.
Franklin Fibs. 1991 Paper 1-55074-077-6; Cloth 1-55074-038-5.

Franklin is Lost. 1992 Paper 1-55074-105-5; Cloth 1-55074-053-9.
Franklin is Bossy. 1993 Paper 1-55074-257-4; Cloth 1-55074-119-5.
Franklin and Me. 1997 Paper 1-55074-335-X; Cloth 1994. 1-55074-211-6.
Franklin is Messy. 1995 Paper 0-155074-245-0; Cloth 1-55074-243-4.
Franklin's Blanket. 1995 Paper 1-55074-278-7; Cloth 1-55074-154-3.
Franklin and the Tooth Fairy. 1995 Paper 1-55074-270-1; Cloth 1-55074-280-9.
Franklin's Bad Day. 1996 Paper 1-55074-293-0; Cloth 1-55074-291-4.
Franklin's School Play. 1996 Paper 1-55074-289-2; Cloth 1-55074-287-6.
Franklin Has a Sleepover. 1996 Paper 1-55074-302-3; Cloth 1-55074-300-7.
Franklin's Halloween. 1996 Paper 1-55074-285-X; Cloth 1-55074-283-3.
Franklin Goes to Day Camp. 1997 Paper 1-55074-396-1.
Fun with Franklin: Trace and Colour Book. 1997 Paper 1-55074-396-1.
Fun with Franklin: Puzzle Book. 1997 Paper 1-55074-394-59.
Franklin's New Friend. 1997 Paper 1-55074-363-5; Cloth 1-55074-361-9.
Fun with Franklin: A Learning to Read Book. 1997 Paper 1-55074-391-0.
Franklin Rides a Bike. 1997 Paper 1-55074-354-6; Cloth 1-55074-352-X.
Fun with Franklin: Activity Book. 1997 Paper 1-55074-392-9.

Finders Keepers for Franklin. 1997 Paper 1-55074-370-8; Cloth 1-55074-368-6.
Franklin and the Thunderstorm. 1998 Paper 1-55074-405-4; Cloth 1-55074-403-8.

Hughes, Monica. *Little Fingerling.* Toronto: Kids Can Press, 1989. 1992 Paper 1-55074-075-X. ✢

McSweeney, Susanne. *The Yellow Flag* (Northern Lights Series). Toronto: PMA Books, 1980. Out of print.

Morgan, Allen. *Christopher and the Dream Dragon* (A Kids Can Read Book). Toronto: Kids Can Press, 1984. Out of print.

—. *Sadie and the Snowman.* Toronto: Kids Can Press, 1985 Paper 0-919964-78-8; Paper (Little Kids Series) 1-55074-167-5.

Staunton, Ted. *Puddleman* (Little Kids Series). Toronto: Kids Can Press, 1994. Out of print.

Awards

1989 IODE Book Award - Toronto Chapter for *Little Fingerling*

Selected articles about Brenda Clark

Lesynski, Loris. "Brenda Clark." *Behind the Story.* Ed. Barbara Greenwood. Markham: Pembroke Publishers, 1995: 24-27.

From *Franklin Is Lost*

Franklin™ Kids Can Press Ltd.© 1986 P. Bourgeois and B.Clark

Sheldon Cohen
ILLUSTRATOR

Born
October 1, 1949, Montreal, Quebec

School
McGill University, Montreal, Quebec (Bachelor of Science degree, 1970): Sheridan College, Oakville, Ontario (Diploma in Art Fundamentals, 1971)

Where I live now
Andover, Massachusetts (temporary residence while teaching Film Animation at Harvard University as Visiting Lecturer)

My favourite books when I was growing up
The Hardy Boys series by Franklin W. Dixon

My favourite book now
The Power of One by Bryce Courtney

Career
Film director/animator, children's book illustrator, painter

Family
Wife, Donna; son, Matt

The room where I create
"I have a small studio in my house arranged with various desks that I've collected over the years. I like to have one desk set aside for each project that I'm working on. Once I complete a project, I'll clean off that particular desk and keep it ready for a new project to come my way."

Spare time
"Watching my son's baseball games; taking long walks with my wife through the neighbourhood letting our dog play with other dogs; and reading good books."

When I was growing up
"I always liked drawing. I remember as a child going through the *Books of Knowledge* and trying to reproduce paintings that I would find there, such as the Mona Lisa. It was a big surprise to discover that it took da Vinci 14 years to complete his masterpiece, and I could draw mine in 20 minutes."

My first book (and how it happened)
"In 1980 I finished animating Roch Carrier's story, *The Sweater*, at the National Film Board of Canada. I decided to submit a proposal to publisher May Cutler at Tundra Books in Montreal, asking if she would be interested in putting out a children's book based on the same story as the film. She immediately said yes, since she had heard the story narrated on CBC Radio and always wanted to do a book on that very story. I remember thinking, 'This is so easy getting a book published.' After the tenth rejection for my next proposal, I eventually realized what it's really like out there and how lucky I was to get a contract the first time I asked."

Where my ideas come from
"I like to take other people's stories and bring them to life on paper (or film if I'm making an animated movie). I begin by reading the author's work and visualizing the characters and settings in my mind. Then I imagine the story unfolding picture by picture, scene by scene."

Who and what influenced me
"It's the author's words that come first and influence what I draw. I feel very lucky to have come across the richness of many gifted writers with whom I've collaborated on books and film (Roch Carrier, Tim Wynne-Jones, Dayal Kaur Khalsa, Wilma Riley and Raymond Souster)."

How I work
"Sometimes I'll sit down and know exactly what I want to draw. Other times, I'm not so certain. When that happens, I'll make a scribble drawing and

pick out images that I see in the lines and curves of the scribble. It gets me started and I work from this very rough outline — hardly readable except by me. Step by step, I clean up each drawing until it's ready to be coloured. One day I'd like to shoot a stop-motion sequence of these stages and watch the illustration come to life within a few seconds of film time."

Something nobody knew about me (until now)

"Until the end of my science studies at McGill University, I was sure I was going to be a dentist — a good example that you can never know for certain the road you may eventually take."

My favourite book that I've created

"I keep very strong attachments to all books I've illustrated, and feel they are all wonderful stories. My first book, *The Hockey Sweater* (written by Roch Carrier), holds a special place for me, along with all of Roch's rich childhood stories. *Pies* (written by Wilma Riley) holds an equally special place for me. I feel it's a very humorous book with a powerful message of bringing people together."

Tips for young creators

"Often, one of the first questions students ask at the end of my school visit is 'how much money do you make?' I answer that there's very little money making children's books in Canada. That's just how it is here, even though we create some of the best books in the world. But I also tell them that it's so much fun to make a book. And it feels good to walk into a bookstore or

library and see your work up on a shelf alongside other people's work. You've put your best into it and now it's out there…Success!

"Then I ask the class if they have any spare change."

Sheldon Cohen

BIBLIOGRAPHY

Carrier, Roch. *The Hockey Sweater.* Toronto: Tundra Books, 1984 Paperback 0-88776-174-7; Cloth 0-88776-169-0. Illustrations by Sheldon Cohen.✤

—. *The Boxing Champion.* Toronto: Tundra Books, 1991 Paper 0-88776-257-3; Cloth 0-88776-249-2. Illustrations by Sheldon Cohen.✤

—. *The Longest Home Run.* Toronto: Tundra Books, 1993 Cloth 0-88776-300-6. Illustrations by Sheldon Cohen.✤

—. *The Basketball Player.* Toronto: Tundra Books, 1996 Cloth 0-88776-367-7. Illustrations by Sheldon Cohen.✤

Riley, Wilma. *Pies.* Regina: Coteau Books, 1991 Paper 1-55050-021-X. Illustrations by Sheldon Cohen.

Awards

1984 Communication Jeunesse Children's Jury Prize for illustration for *The Hockey Sweater*

1985 American Institute of Graphic Arts: Certificate of Excellence for Book Design for *The Hockey Sweater*

1991 Governor General's Literary Award for *Un Champion*

From *The Basketball Player*

Heather Collins
ILLUSTRATOR

Born
July 22, 1946, Montreal, Quebec

School
Ontario College of Art, Toronto, Ontario

Where I live now
Toronto, Ontario

My favourite book when I was young
Anne of Green Gables

Career
Children's book illustrator

Family
Husband, Blair; daughter, Brooke; son, Max

The room where I create
"The attic of our home — a small room which houses the television and a dripping skylight and also serves as a guest room. I have lots of shelves for my pencils, pens, pastels, paints, brushes and my drawings. There are lots of books: books for reference, picture books to inspire me, books I've illustrated, loads of books."

Spare time
"Read books, see friends, ski in the winter, hang out at our cottage on Nottawasaga Bay in the summer."

When I was growing up
Heather started drawing when she was about two. "I used to draw and colour on everything — the wall, my treasured blackboard, scraps of paper, and the covers of my school notebooks." Her interest in art continued through high school where, she recalls, "I thrived on being the best in art class because I certainly wasn't the best at anything else."

My first book (and how it happened)
"I really think of my first book as *Whoosh, I Hear a Sound* which I illustrated in 1984. *Whoosh* was the most exciting because it was my first picture book and it was the first time I'd been given such creative freedom. It still holds delightful memories because the baby in the book is modelled after my daughter, and I still see Brooke when I look at it. *Whoosh* was also the beginning of a change in my career. From 1984 on I did a picture book a year and gradually less and less educational work."

Where my ideas come from
"My ideas are all around me — right here in the house, in the yard, on the street, in the everyday activities of my own children and the children of friends and neighbours... I love drawing children so I'm always watching them, storing up images. I'm always catching myself staring overly long at the people and children around me, at the store, on the bus, in the school yard. It can be embarrassing!"

Who and what influenced me
"The influences are all around, but as well, I am always bringing books home from the library and learning what works and what doesn't. I have had many favourite illustrators over the years whose work I study. The work I admire most always has a foundation of excellent drawing. My current favourites are Shirley Hughes, Chris Van Allsburg, Jim LaMarche, Janet and Allen Ahlberg, Nicola Bayley and Helen Oxenbury."

How I work
Heather works six to eight hours a day. Because an illustrator's life can be isolated, Heather listens to CBC Radio all day to keep in touch with what's happening.

Once she has prepared rough illustrations and made them into a "dummy" book, (a book that's the same size as the real book with the rough illustrations sketched inside) she is ready for some constructive criticism. Her husband Blair, a book designer, often gives her feedback and suggestions. She will also work with suggestions from the editor and art director. For the final illustrations, she may work with pencil, watercolours or chalk, depending on what is appropriate for the text.

Something nobody knew about me (until now)

"Kids always seem most surprised to find out I'm a mom too — that I make breakfast, talk to my kids, do laundry, buy groceries and generally have a rather dull life — they think illustration is very glamorous and that I'm out talking to people all the time. Not exactly! Mostly illustration, like writing, is quite lonely and I, like most creative people, wish I could do it better. But I've come to the conclusion that creative people need to feel this way or they wouldn't constantly challenge themselves to get better."

My favourite book that I've created

"The series of board books I did in 1997 — *Eency Weency Spider; One, Two, Buckle My Shoe; This Little Piggy* and *Hickory Dickory Dock*. I've always loved stuffed animals and these books gave me the opportunity to play at being three years old again and live in the world of pretend. They are happy books and I felt happy doing them."

Heather Collins

BIBLIOGRAPHY

Aldis, Dorothy. *Hiding*. Toronto: Kids Can Press, 1993 Paper 1-55074-342-2. Illustrations by Heather Collins.

Bird, Florence. *Holiday in the Woods*. Don Mills: General Publishing, 1976. 1991 Paper 0-7736-7302-4. Illustrations by Heather Collins.

Collins, Heather. *This Little Piggy*. Toronto: Kids Can Press, 1997 Cloth 1-55074-404-6. Illustrations by the author.

—. *Hickory Dickory Dock*. Toronto: Kids Can Press, 1997 Cloth 1-55074-408-9. Illustrations by the author.

—. *One, Two, Buckle My Shoe.* Toronto: Kids Can Press, 1997 Cloth 1-55074-410-0. Illustrations by the author.

—. *Eency Weency Spider*. Toronto: Kids Can Press, 1997 Cloth 1-55074-406-2. Illustrations by the author.

Drake, Jane and Ann Love. *The Kids Cottage Book*. Toronto: Kids Can Press, 1993 Paper 1-55074-132-2. Illustrations by Heather Collins.

—. *The Kids Campfire Book.* Toronto: Kids Can Press, 1996 Paper 1-55074-275-2. Illustrations by Heather Collins.

—. *The Kids Cottage Games Book*. Toronto: Kids Can Press, 1998 Paper 1-55074-467-4. Illustrations by Heather Collins.

Galloway, Priscilla. *When You Were Little and I Was Big*. (Annick Toddler Series) Toronto: Annick Press, 1984. Illustrations by Heather Collins. Out of print.

Greenwood, Barbara. *A Pioneer Story: The Daily Life of a Canadian Family in 1840*. Toronto: Kids Can Press, 1994 Paper 1-55074-128-4; Cloth 1-55074-237-X. Illustrations by Heather Collins.

—. *Pioneer Crafts*. Toronto: Kids Can Press, 1997 Paper 1-55074-359-7. Illustrations by Heather Collins.

—. *The Last Safe House*. Toronto: Kids Can Press, 1998 Paper 1-55074-509-3; Cloth 1-55074-507-7. Illustrations by Heather Collins.

Hearn, Emily. *Whoosh, I Hear a Sound*. Toronto: Annick Press, 1984. Annikin Paper 0-920303-21-8. Illustrations by Heather Collins.

Hickman, Pam. *The Kids Canadian Tree Book*. Toronto: Kids Can Press, 1995 Cloth 1-55074-198-5. 1996 Paper 1-55074-336-8. Illustrations by Heather Collins.

continued...

From *A Pioneer Story*

—. *The Kids Canadian Bird Book.* Toronto: Kids Can Press, 1995 Cloth 1-55074-196-9. 1996 Paper 1-55074-334-1. Illustrations by Heather Collins.

—. *The Kids Canadian Bug Book.* Toronto: Kids Can Press, 1996 Cloth 1-55074-231-0. 1997 Paper 1-55074-329-5. Illustrations by Heather Collins.

—. *The Kids Canadian Plant Book.* Toronto: Kids Can Press, 1996 Cloth 1-55074-233-7. 1997 Paper 1-55074-331-7; Illustrations by Heather Collins.

—. *A Seed Grows.* Toronto: Kids Can Press, 1997 Cloth 1-55074-200-0. Illustrations by Heather Collins.

—. *Hungry Animals.* Toronto: Kids Can Press, 1997 Cloth 1-55074-204-3. Illustrations by Heather Collins.

—. *A New Butterfly.* Toronto: Kids Can Press, 1997 Cloth 1-55074-202-7. Illustrations by Heather Collins.

Lewis, Amanda. *Writing: A Fact and Fun Book.* Toronto: Kids Can Press, 1992 Paper 1-55074-052-0. Illustrations by Heather Collins.

Polkosnik, George. *Bluetoes, Santa's Special Helper.* Toronto: Clark, Irwin & Co., 1975. Illustrations by Heather Collins. Out of print.

McKay, Jed. *The Big Secret.* Willowdale: Annick Press, 1984. Illustrations by Heather Collins. Out of print.

McKend, Heather. *Moving Gives Me A Stomach Ache.* Windsor: Black Moss Press, 1988. 1990 Paper 0-88753-178-4. Illustrations by Heather Collins.

Merrifield, Margaret. *Come Sit by Me.* Toronto: The Women's Press, 1990 Paper 0-88961-141-6. Illustrations by Heather Collins.

—. *Morning Light.* Toronto: Stoddart, 1995 Cloth 0-7737-5704-X. Illustrations by Heather Collins.

Murphy, Joanne Brisson. *Feelings.* Windsor: Black Moss Press, 1985. Illustrations by Heather Collins.

Plantos, Ted. *Heather Hits Her First Home Run.* Windsor: Black Moss Press, 1989 Paper 0-88753-185-7. Illustrations by Heather Collins.

Stinson, Kathy. *The Bare Naked Book.* Willowdale: Annick Press, 1986 Paper 0-920303-53-6; Cloth 0-920303-52-8. Illustrations by Heather Collins.♣

—. *The Dressed Up Book.* Willowdale: Annick Press, 1990 Paper 1-55037-104-5; Cloth 1-55037-103-7. Illustrations by Heather Collins.

—. *The Fabulous Ball Book.* Don Mills: Stoddart Press, 1993 Paper 0-19-540913-2. Illustrations by Heather Collins.

Heather Collins has also illustrated a number of novels for young adults.

Awards
1995 Ruth Schwartz Children's Book Award for *A Pioneer Story: The Daily Life of a Canadian Family in 1840*

1995 Mr. Christie's Book Award for *A Pioneer Story: The Daily Life of a Canadian Family in 1840*

Selected articles about Heather Collins
Jennings, Sharon. "Heather Collins." *Behind the Story.* Ed. Barbara Greenwood. Markham: Pembroke Publishers, 1995: 31-34.

Sylvie Daigneault
AUTHOR/ILLUSTRATOR

Born
November 28, 1952, Montreal, Quebec

School
University of Quebec in Montreal, for painting

Where I live now
Toronto, Ontario

My favourite books when I was young
Babar l'Eléphant, Peter Pan, La Craie Magique

My favourite book now
"Any book by Chris Van Allsburg."

Career
Animation colourist, commercial illustrator (packaging, posters and ads), children's book illustrator and author

Family
"Husband, Doug, also an illustrator; his children, Rachel and Ben. Two cats, Phoebe and Violet. They are sisters."

The room where I create
"I used to rent a studio but now I prefer to work at home. The third floor of my house is one open space. At one end is my bed, and at the other, my tiny, super-organized work area. There is a flat roof outside my window. I dream that one day I will have a studio built there. I would be surrounded by trees and roof-tops."

Spare time
"Read, sew, knit, garden, bicycle, speedwalk or go to the gym."

When I was growing up
"I used to carve small pieces of wood that I would find on the beach. My mother was always looking for her best kitchen knives. When I was four, I already loved drawing and made many make-believe books. They were small, like my hands — two inches-square. Each page was fastened with Scotch tape. Then I would pretend to write a story and squiggle to the last page.

"My drawings were detailed. Adults around me used to say that I had talent, but for me, drawing was only another way to have fun. It was something I could do without the help of my older brother or sister. When I was drawing, I could create my own world."

My first book (and how it happened)
"I moved to Toronto in 1979 and did illustrations for school books and worked freelance at advertising agencies. When Kids Can Press phoned with an offer to illustrate *Simon's Surprise*, I was thrilled. The story happens in a backyard where many details have to be shown. I decided to take a birds-eye view perspective. It created another challenge for me: learning to draw the same details from other points of view, throughout the rest of the book. I didn't know at the time that this first book was going to plant the seed of my career."

Where my ideas come from
"Nature. As a child, I spent my summers on a lake in Quebec. I have seen many other country-sides since then; but still, I know that the beauty of that place and the fond memories have played a role in my imagination.

"Light, weather and seasons: they change how people behave and feel.

"Animals: they fascinate me."

Who and what influenced me
"Since my teenage years, the works of the great impressionist painters, like Van Gogh, Cézanne, Renoir and Matisse have inspired me. Now, I admire many artists of my time who have created children's book master-pieces, such as Fred Marcellino, Mark Buehner, Nicola Bayley, Chris Van Allsburg. Also, in the advertising world I like the work of Anita Kunz, René Milot and Brad Holland."

How I work

"I have started writing my own stories, and I find that the ideas for the sketches come almost instantly because when I invent the story, I imagine pictures as I go along. I still take time to do research, so I continue learning. This way, I can always add fun details to my drawings. I use colour pencils and a good electric sharpener to keep my pencils at a fine point."

Something nobody knew about me (until now)

"My cats love to sleep on my table under the warm lamp. Sometimes they stretch all across my drawing or papers and play with my pencils. I don't want to chase them away because I like their company when they behave. So I pick up the cat and put her on my lap. I draw like this for a while, until she falls asleep. As soon as I put her on the bed, she returns to my table. By the second time, it usually works."

My favourite book that I've created

"Bruno in the Snow. Even though I love drawing vegetation, winter scenes are special and so cozy. They remind me of my child-hood."

Tips for young creators

"Details and good design can be as important as the drawing. They add flavour and power to your creation."

From *Bruno Springs Up*

Sylvie Daigneault

BIBLIOGRAPHY

Bailey, Lydia. *Mother Nature Takes a Vacation*. Toronto: Alligator Press, 1992. Illustrations by Sylvie Daigneault. Out of print.

Bogart, Jo Ellen. *Sarah Saw a Blue Macaw*. Toronto: North Winds Press, 1991 Paper 0-590-73227-7; Cloth 0-590-73809-7. Illustrations by Sylvie Daigneault.♣

—. *Mama's Bed*. Toronto: Scholastic, 1993 Cloth 0-590-74309-0. 1995 Paper 0-590-74312-0. Illustrations by Sylvie Daigneault.♣

Daigneault, Sylvie. *Bruno in the Snow. Toronto*. HarperCollins, 1994 Cloth 0-00-224261-3. 1997 Paper 0-00-647953-7. Illustrations by the author.♣

—. *Bruno Springs Up*. Toronto: HarperCollins, 1997 Cloth 0-00-224411-X. 1998 Paper 0-00-648124-8. Illustrations by the author.

—. *Bruno and the Bees*. Toronto: HarperCollins, 1998. Illustrations by the author.

Harris, Dorothy Joan. *No Dinosaurs in the Park*. Toronto: North Winds Press, 1990 Cloth 0-590-73210-2. 1992 Paper 0-590-73211-0. Illustrations by Sylvie Daigneault.♣

Staunton, Ted. *Simon's Surprise*. Toronto: Kids Can Press, 1986. Toronto: Scholastic, 1993 Paper 0-590-74823-8. Illustrations by Sylvie Daigneault.

Alan Daniel
ILLUSTRATOR

Born
June 12, 1939, Ottawa, Ontario

School
Elementary and high schools, Hamilton and Belleville; McMaster University, Hamilton; University of Toronto, Toronto; all in Ontario

Where I live now
Kitchener, Ontario

My favourite book when I was young
Horton Hatches an Egg by Dr. Seuss

Career
"I wanted to be a nuclear physicist but luckily, I discovered illustration."

Family
"We have three grown-up children. Our grandsons are just the right ages to enjoy my books and suggest ways to make them better."

The room where I create
"I work in a former bedroom in my house. It's a mess, but I really do know where everything is."

Spare time
"I like to spend time with my wife, Lea, and the rest of the family. We go to movies, read, canoe, swim, and when we travel, we hike and climb a bit. I love museums and art galleries."

When I was growing up
"My dad took me on a long bus ride every week to the downtown library in Hamilton. I learned to read the words and devoured the pictures in their wonderful books. My parents had always read to my sisters and me, but now the world of books was mine. Playing in Cootes Paradise, a nearby swamp, my buddies and I became the characters in those books — pirates, explorers, castaways, wolves."

My first book (and how it happened)
"Art was just my favourite hobby until I visited five illustrators at their studio. 'Like to try?' asked Merle Smith, the senior illustrator. I nodded. 'Sit over there, take off your shoes, and draw them.' As he critiqued my drawing, I understood how much I had to learn. But I was hooked.

"I finished my year in university and the next day, joined the studio. By day, I learned to make a living doing diagrams and maps. By night, I learned to draw and paint. I was lucky to have five generous and patient teachers. After two years — my big break! A rush job of two paintings — a rear view of cows lined up for milking and a pen full of pigs. I worked day and night and then awaited the publisher's verdict. They liked them! I was an illustrator. In time, I moved on to more demanding and more interesting projects, but I was never more excited."

Where my ideas come from
"I sift through the warehouse in my head and spill out scenarios and images to try out on the text. Suddenly, one of them just seems right. On and around it I build with more bits and pieces from my memory until I have a visual story to complement the text."

Who and what influenced me
"Many people helped me to become an illustrator. Mom read me to sleep before I could read. When he travelled, Dad sent us letters interrupted by little pictures. His art was terrible, but that made it even more fun trying to guess what the missing word or phrase was. English and history teachers instilled in me the excitement they felt for their subjects. And Merle Smith shared his passion for illustration and his love of drawing with me.

"Many more have inspired me to improve as an illustrator. But mostly it's the kids. My own children and grandchildren, and all the others who share their stories and illustrations with me."

41

How I work

"When I know a new story almost by heart, I visualize it as a play. And when I want to illustrate it, I freeze the players and become a flying camera, looking at them from every angle to find the best one. I'll scribble the visual storyline down very roughly, often three or four times until I'm satisfied. I've practised until I can draw almost anything I can picture in my head. If I need to know specific details such as how the stripes on a zebra really look, or what Halifax was like in 1840, I'll look in my own library, or go to public libraries, museums or zoos.

"The story dictates the style of drawing I use. I usually do half-size pencil roughs and then project them on to watercolour paper or canvas at the size of the book or larger. The medium for the finished art may be pencil, ink, paints, or collage containing clay, cloth, coloured paper, string, dried grass, or anything else that gives me the effect I want."

Something nobody knew about me (until now)

"My secret weapon has always been Lea, my wife and partner. We share ideas, and her advice, when I take it, often keeps me from making mistakes. For the last 10 years, most of our illustration jobs have been done together. Each job is divided differently, but usually I do the concept and drawing, and Lea does the painting. When I get desperate to paint, we share, or, as in the case of the large oils for *The Story of Canada,* I solo. We have begun to write stories and books together too."

From *Sody Salleratus*

Tips for young creators

"Have fun when you create and never be afraid to try something new. Be self-critical and learn the necessary skills. For more than 10 years, I drew every day and then analyzed my mistakes. It was hard work, but what I learned has made illustration fun for me because I can create a world in pictures just the way I want to."

Alan Daniel

SELECT BIBLIOGRAPHY

Allinson, Beverley. *Dog Power Tower.* Toronto: Methuen, 1977. Illustrations by Alan Daniel. Out of print.

Cameron, Silver Donald. *The Baitchopper.* Toronto: James Lorimer & Co., 1982 Paper 0-88862-598-7; Cloth 0-88862-599-5. Illustrations by Alan Daniel.

Craig, John. *The Wormburners.* Richmond Hill: Scholastic Canada, 1975. Illustrations by Alan Daniel. Out of print.

Daniel, Alan et al. *Cloak of the Winds.* Bothell WA: The Wright Group, 1998 Paper 0-7802-9399-1. Illustrations by Alan Daniel and Lea Daniel.

—. *Letters from the Sea.* Bothell WA: The Wright Group, 1998 Paper 0-7802-9401-7. Illustrations by Alan Daniel and Lea Daniel.

continued...

Davis, Aubrey. *Sody Salleratus.* Toronto: Kids Can Press, 1996 Cloth 1-55074-281-7. Illustrations by Alan Daniel and Lea Daniel.♣

Foster, Dorothy, ed. *In Praise of Cats: An Anthology.* Don Mills: Stoddart, 1982. Illustrations by Alan Daniel. Out of print.

Hinton, S. E. *Big David, Little David.* New York: Doubleday, 1995 Cloth 0-385-31093-5. Illustrations by Alan Daniel.

Howe, Deborah, and James Howe. *Bunnicula: A Rabbit Tale of Mystery.* New York: Atheneum, 1979 Cloth 0-689-30700-4. New York: Avon, 1980 Paper 0-380-51094-4. New Jersey: Simon & Schuster Children's, 1996 Paper 0-689-80659-0. Illustrations by Alan Daniel.

—. *Return to Howliday Inn.* New York: Atheneum, 1992 Cloth 0-689-31661-5. New York: Avon, 1993 Paper 0-380-71972-X. Illustrations by Alan Daniel.

—. *Rabbit-Cadabra.* New York: Avon, 1993 Paper 0-380-71336-5. New York: Morrow Junior Books, 1993 Cloth 0-688-10402-9; 0-688-10403-7 (Library Bound). Illustrations by Alan Daniel.

—. *The Bunnicula Fun Book.* New York: Morrow Junior Books, 1993. Illustrations by Alan Daniel. Out of print.

—. *Bunnicula Escapes: A Pop-Up Adventure.* New York: Morrow Junior Books, 1994 Cloth 0-688-12312-X. Illustrations by Alan Daniel.

—. *Bunnicula's Pleasantly Perplexing Puzzlers.* New York: Little Simon, 1998 Paper 0-689-81664-2. Illustrations by Alan Daniel.

—. *Bunnicula's Wickedly Wacky Word Games.* New York: Little Simon, 1998 Paper 0-689-81663-4. Illustrations by Alan Daniel.

Lee, Dennis. *The Difficulty of Living on Other Planets.* Toronto: Macmillan Canada, 1987. Illustrations by Alan Daniel. Out of print.

Lunn, Janet and Christopher Moore. *The Story of Canada.* Toronto: Lester Publishing, 1992 Cloth 1-895555-32-9. Rev ed. Toronto: Key Porter, 1996 Paper 1-895555-88-4. Illustrations by Alan Daniel.

Munsch, Robert. *Good Families Don't.* Toronto: Doubleday Canada, 1990 Paper 0-385-25267-6. Illustrations by Alan Daniel.

—. *Get Out of Bed!* Toronto: Scholastic, 1998 Cloth 059076977-4. Illustrations by Alan Daniel and Lea Daniel.♣

Naylor, Phyllis Reynolds. *How Lazy Can You Get?* 1979. New York: Dell, 1992. Illustrations by Alan Daniel. Out of print.

—. *The Grand Escape.* New York: Atheneum, 1993 Cloth 0-689-31722-0. Illustrations by Alan Daniel.

—. *The Healing of Texas Jake.* New York: Atheneum, 1997 Cloth 0-689-81124-1. Illustrations by Alan Daniel.

Penner, Jim et al. *Night Music.* Bothel WA: The Wright Group, 1998 Paper 0-7802-9401-7. Illustrations by Alan Daniel and Lea Daniel.

Penner, Jim et al. *Dancing with Jacques.* Bothell WA: The Wright Group, 1998 Paper 0-7802-9400-9. Illustrations by Alan Daniel and Lea Daniel.

Rowe, Erna Dirks. *Flying and Swimming Creatures from the Time of the Dinosaurs.* Richmond Hill: Scholastic Canada, 1980. Illustrations by Alan Daniel. Out of print.

—. *Strange Creatures from the Time of the Dinosaurs.* New York: Scholastic, 1981. Illustrations by Alan Daniel. Out of print.

Rubin, Mark. *The Orchestra.* Toronto: Groundwood Books, 1984 Paper 0-88899-051-0. Illustrations by Alan Daniel.

Schenk de Regniers, Beatrice. *This Big Cat and Other Cats I've Known.* New York: Crown Publishers, 1985. Illustrations by Alan Daniel. Out of print.

Stinson, Kathy. *Writing Your Best Picture Book Ever.* Markham: Pembroke Publishers, 1994 Paper 1-55138-028-5. Illustrations by Alan Daniel and Lea Daniel.

Valley, Timothy. *Bo-Wo-Wones.* Bothell, WA: The Wright Group, 1994. Music by Jim Valley. Illustrations by Alan Daniel. Out of print.

Walker, Eleanor. *Cat Names: The Best Book Ever.* New York: HarperCollins, 1984. Illustrations by Alan Daniel. Out of print.

Awards
1992 IODE Book Award - Toronto Chapter for *The Story of Canada*

Selected articles about Alan Daniel
Greenwood, Barbara, ed. *The CANSCAIP Companion.* Markham: Pembroke Publishers, 1994.

Something About the Author. Detroit: Gale Research, 1994.

The Canadian Who's Who. Toronto: Trans-Canada Press, 1994.

Kady MacDonald Denton
AUTHOR/ILLUSTRATOR

Born
July 22, 1942, Winnipeg, Manitoba

School
Toronto, Ontario

Where I live now
Brandon, Manitoba

My favourite book when I was young
"*Babar* was a favourite and so were the *Madeline* books."

Career
Children's book artist

Family
Husband, two children, one cat.

The room where I create
"My studio in our house."

Spare time
"Reading, stage and costume design, walks, swimming, being with friends."

When I was growing up
"I have always liked to draw. It came as a surprise to me when I started school to find out that everyone didn't draw all the time. My family always had projects in progress, restoring furniture, caning, painting and print-making, so there were lots of supplies around for us children. Creating interesting things was considered important work. We didn't have a television until I was a teenager.

"Books were also a great love of mine. I read almost anything: science, mysteries, fairy tales, pirate stories, magazines, the books my parents read. Just how books were grouped in a library was something I never quite understood, so I would wander around all the shelves picking out anything with an interesting title or spine colour. I loved the pictures in some books. The last picture in E. B. White's *Stuart Little* is a pen illustration by Garth Williams showing Stuart heading off down the road in search of Margalo. That illustration intrigued me."

My first book (and how it happened)
"I began to work on children's books when our family lived in London, England, during my husband's sabbatical. My daughter was learning to read and there seemed to be very few good beginning readers on the market. I met Pam Zinnemann-Hope at the Chelsea School of Art, where I was taking some classes, and we decided to create our own books for young children, the Ned series. It was fortunate that Walker Books in London was interested in early readers just at that time."

Where my ideas come from
"Ideas often come when something seems out of order or when usual things are seen more clearly. What is happening? Why is it that way? Some ideas lead to stories, some don't. Ideas for pictures come from the process of drawing or painting."

Who and what influenced me
"Pictures of any kind have always fascinated me. Perhaps that is why I studied art history at university. Perhaps it is why I create my own pictures."

How I work
"After breakfast I go to my studio. It's a small studio with a very big table in it. On the table I spread out my dishes of paint and the pens or pencils I am using. I lay out the sheets of white paper. I look at my rough sketches and think about what I am going to do. Then I settle in to working most of the day.

"Sometimes an illustration will not be perfect but it will have warmth and a sparkle and so I leave it. Some work takes a long time and some work just seems to spring right out of the paper."

My favourite book that I've created
"My favourite book is always the one I am beginning. I've been lucky to have been given wonderful stories to illustrate, about all sorts of things. They all have been fun. I don't mean that they

have all been easy to do, but just that each is special to me and, I hope, to others."

Tips for young creators
"Find a quiet place to work. Put down your ideas just the way you want. If anyone laughs at your work or criticizes it, tell them to go and do their own. Everyone has their own way of working and with time and practice your own special style will develop."

Kady MacDonald Denton

BIBLIOGRAPHY
All books illustrated by Kady MacDonald Denton

Booth, David, ed. *Til All the Stars Have Fallen: Canadian Poems for Children*. Toronto: Kids Can Press, 1989 Cloth 0-921103-90-5. 1994 Paper 1-55074-143-8.

Denton, Kady MacDonald. *Granny is a Darling*. Toronto: Kids Can Press, 1988. Out of print.

—. *The Picnic*. London: Methuen, 1988. Out of print.

—. *Dorothy's Dream*. Toronto: Kids Can Press, 1989. Out of print.

—. *Janet's Horses*. London: Walker Books, 1990. Rpt. as Janet's Ponies. 1992 Paper 0-7445-2063-0.

—. *The Christmas Boot*. Toronto: Little Brown, 1990. Out of print.

—. *Would They Love a Lion?* New York: Kingfisher Books, 1995 Cloth 1-85697-546-0. 1997 Paper 1-85697-148-1.

—. *Watch Out, William*. New York: Kingfisher Books, 1997 0-7534-0021-9.

— ed. *A Child's Treasury of Nursery Rhymes*. New York: Kingfisher Books; Toronto: Kids Can Press, 1998 Cloth 0-7534-0143-6.

Ellis, Mary. *The Arctic Fox*. Toronto: HarperCollins, 1998 Cloth 0-00-185675-8.

Gibson, Betty. *The Story of Little Quack*. Toronto: Kids Can Press, 1990. Out of print.

Lunn, Janet. *The Umbrella Party*. Toronto: Groundwood Books, 1998 Cloth 0-88899-298-X.

Page, P.K. *The Travelling Musicians*. Toronto: Kids Can Press, 1991. Out of print.

Pilling, Ann. *Before I Go to Sleep*. Toronto: Kids Can Press, 1990 Cloth 0-921103-45-X.

—. *Realms of Gold: Myths and Legends From Around the World*. New York: Kingfisher Books, 1993. Out of print.

—. *The Kingfisher Children's Bible*. New York: Kingfisher Books, 1993 Cloth 1-85697-840-0.

Roddie, Shen. *Toes Are to Tickle*. Toronto: Reed Books Canada, 1997 Cloth 0-433-39868-X.

Zinnemann-Hope, Pam. *Find Your Coat, Ned*. London: Walker Books, 1986. Out of print.

—. *Time for Bed, Ned*. London: Walker Books, 1986. Out of print.

—. *Let's Go Shopping, Ned*. London: Walker Books, 1987. Out of print.

—. *Let's Play Ball, Ned*. London: Walker Books, 1987. Out of print.

Awards
1990 Amelia Frances Howard-Gibbon Illustrator's Award for *Till All the Stars Have Fallen*

1991 Mr. Christie's Book Award for Illustration for *The Story of Little Quack*

Selected articles about Kady MacDonald Denton
Goldsmith, Annette. "Denton's Dictum: Paint Like a Child." *Quill and Quire* Feb. 1990: 13.

Jenkinson, Dave. "Portraits: Kady MacDonald Denton, Watercolorist Extraordinaire." *Emergency Librarian* May-June 1994: 61-64.

Alexander, Wilma. "Kady MacDonald Denton." *Behind the Story*. Ed. Barbara Greenwood. Markham: Pembroke Publishers, 1995: 35-36.

From *A Child's Treasury of Nursery Rhymes*

Hélène Desputeaux
ILLUSTRATOR

Born
July 10, 1959, Quebec City, Quebec

School
Bachelor's degree in Graphic Arts, Laval University, Quebec; Bachelor's degree in Education, UQAM, Montreal

Where I live now
Beloeil, Quebec

My favourite book when I was young
The Princess and the Pea by H.C. Andersen

My favourite book now
Léonie dévore les livres by Laurence Herbert and Frédéric Dubus, published by Casterman

Career
Children's book illustrator, kindergarten and primary school teacher, art teacher

Family
"My husband, children's book author Michel Aubin, my two daughters Marie-Charlotte and Juliette...and lots of other children ...meaning the many characters I've created."

The room where I create
"It's up in my attic. Around me, there's a lot of paper, toys, crayons, pictures, photographs, greeting cards, books and knick-knacks ...all in a big indescribable muddle. I create only in these conditions and in complete silence (if that's possible)!"

Spare time
"Drawing, drawing, drawing!... and fighting for my royalties!"

When I was growing up
"I drew on everything, walls, floors and...on me. I remember when my father used to tape a long piece of paper on a wall and I drew on it until it was full of colours and then he would tape another one. I read and drew all the time, creating my own imaginary world."

My first book (and how it happened)
"I did five illustrations on Michel Aubin's story for the Bologna Book Fair in 1983 and I was selected. The book was never published. My first published book was with Scandinavia Publishing House in Denmark and titled *The Emperor's New Clothes*."

Where my ideas come from
"From my everyday life. From the people I observe on the streets, in the metro or on buses, to the people I know, the people I love. From all of them some distinctive feature or personality will catch my attention and will serve to create a new character. My feelings and emotions are also powerful creative tools."

Who and what influenced me
"My life, people around me, places I've lived in."

How I work
"First I observe, then I do a lot of roughs. The illustrations get constructed step by step. I often start over to really 'feel' my character. I experiment with lines, colours and when the author or publisher loves my dummy book, I do the final colour illustrations. It's at this stage of my work that I'm happiest."

Something nobody knew about me (until know)
"I don't like cats and dogs but I love anything that's miniaturized."

My favourite book that I've created
"*Purple Green and Yellow* by Robert Munsch, because Brigid is just like me when I was little and now it looks like it's my daughter Juliette's turn."

Tips for young creators
"Always be cautious in dealing with your publisher: It's not a friendly affair; it's a business affair. Sign a contract only after a lawyer says 'yes you can.' Never before. Never forget you work for children, not for a publisher."

Hélène Desputeaux

SELECT BIBLIOGRAPHY

All books illustrated by Hélène Desputeaux

Andersen, Hans Christian. *The Emperor's New Clothes.* Copenhagen: Scandinavia Publishing House, 1984.

Aubin, Michel. *Mon Petit Frère Bertrand.* Montreal: Boréal, 1986. Out of print.

—. *Trottinette et crème glacée.* Montreal: Boréal, 1986. Out of print.

—. *Le code secret.* Montreal: Boréal, 1986. Out of print.

—. *The Birthday Party.* Trans. Shelley Tanaka. Toronto: Lorimer, 1987 Paper 1-55028-029-5. ✤

—. *La vraie campagne.* Montreal: Boréal, 1990. Out of print.

—. *Je joue du saxophone.* Montreal: Boréal, 1990. Out of print.

—. *Aujourd'hui je reste chez-moi.* Brussels: Casterman, 1990. Out of print.

Casson, Les. *My Uncle Max.* Toronto: Annick Press, 1990 Annikin Paper 1-55037-130-4.

Chislett, Gail. *Melinda's No's Cold.* Toronto: Annick Press, 1991. Out of print.

Desputeaux, Hélène. The *Caillou* Series. Montreal: Editions Chouette.

  —. *Caillou-Le repas.* 1991 2-921198-23-1.

  —. *Caillou-Les jeux.* 1991 2-921198-21-5.

  —. *Caillou-Les vêtements.* 1991 2-921198-21-5.

  —. *Caillou-La maison.* 1991 2-921198-20-7.

  —. *Lollypop's Zoo.* 1995 2-921198-81-9.✤

  —. *Lollypop's Travels.* 1995 2-921198-83-5.✤

  —. *Lollypop's Music.* 1995 2-921198-82-7.✤

  —. *Lollypop's Farm.* 1995 2-921198-80-0.✤

Frasier, Kathleen. *Follow the Leader.* Toronto: Houghton Mifflin, 1995. Out of print.

Gagnon, Cecile. *Jules Tempête.* St. Lambert QC: Héritage, 1991. Out of print.

MacAulay, Craig. *Ten Men on a Ladder.* Toronto: Annick Press, 1993 Paper 1-55037-340-4; Cloth 1-55037-341-2.✤

McVeity, Den. *The First Day of School.* Toronto: Houghton Mifflin, 1995. Out of print.

Munsch, Robert. *Purple, Green and Yellow.* Toronto: Annick Press, 1992 Paper 1-55037-256-4; Cloth 1-55037-255-6.✤

—. *Where is Gah-Ning?* Toronto: Annick Press, 1994 Paper 1-55037-982-8; Cloth 1-55037-983-6.

Tregebov, Rhea. *The Extraordinary Ordinary Everything Room.* Toronto: Second Story Press, 1991 Paper 0-929005-24-4.

—. *Sasha and the Wiggly Tooth.* Toronto: Second Story Press, 1993 Paper 0-929005-50-3; Cloth 0-929005-51-1.✤

—. *Sasha and the Wind.* Toronto: Second Story Press, 1996 Paper 0-929005-83-X; Cloth 0-929005-84-8.

—. *Sudden Miracles: Eight Women Poets.* Trans. Cécile Gagnon. Toronto: Second Story Press, 1991 Paper 0-929005-26-0.

—. *Tempête et chocolat chaud.* Trans. Cécile Gagnon. Toronto: Scholastic, 1996 Paper 0-590-16018-4.

Awards

1993 Mr. Christie's Book Award for *Caillou – La petite soeur and Le petit pot*

1995 Medaille Rayond Blais from Laval University for her entire body of work

Selected articles about Hélène Desputeaux

Baillargeon, Stéphane. "La maman de Caillou." *Le Devoir* [Montréal] 20 Nov. 1994.

Cornacchia, Cheryl. "Inspired by Children." Montreal *Gazette* 16 Sept. 1996.

From Sasha and the Wind

Suzanne Duranceau
ILLUSTRATOR

Born
August 2, 1952, Montreal, Quebec

School
St-Laurent CEGEP; Quebec University in Montreal for Visual Arts; and a session of Photography at the Parson School of Design in New York

Where I live now
"I live in Westmount, close to downtown Montreal."

My favourite book when I was young
Le Petit Prince by Saint-Exupéry

My favourite book now
Les limbes du Pacifique by Michel Tournier

Career
Freelance illustrator for 25 years

Family
"My daughter Alma has been raised in illustrators' studios, since her father is an illustrator as well. My companion Benoît Aquin is a photo-reporter and fine art photographer. I have two Egyptian Maus (cats), and seven turtles, of which four were born in my house. I am also very close to my 81-year-old father."

The room where I create
"I used to have a studio with a few assistants on the floor beneath my apartment. Since my work space was in the same building, my daughter could come over to see me at work whenever she wanted.

"However, I became tired of the financial pressure of holding together a children's book business. Now my studio is in my apartment."

Spare time
"At my country home I grow perennial flowers. I enjoy sports, especially swimming, hiking, rollerskating, bicycling and scuba diving. As a hobby I breed turtles. I am also a movie fanatic."

When I was growing up
"My primary school was 9/10 of a mile from home. Because it wasn't exactly one mile away from school, I couldn't take the school bus, nor could I stay at school during lunch hour ('rules are rules'). So, during most of my childhood, I had to walk four miles a day to and from school. I was often late, trying to find new short cuts through back alleys and gardens. On my journey, I stopped to look at insects, pets, flowers, and streams of melting snow.

"I spent my summers by a lake, in a remote area with few children. I explored the forest, and became friends with many wild animals in addition to those I was taking care of.

"I would go into the woods with my father to get wood for the winter, so the sound of the roaring chainsaw in the midsummer heat is very familiar to me. But I never liked the sun very much. I was always in the shade, drawing, painting, and creating collages using my grandmother's old-fashioned magazines."

Becoming an illustrator
After university, Suzanne joined the National Film Board as an assistant in animation. She moved to the publishing industry and eventually became a freelance illustrator.

"Illustration was the perfect medium for me, as it enabled me to have one foot in fine arts and the other in the communications industry. I started with school books, political illustrations for small left wing brochures, and university magazines. Then, I illustrated short stories for magazines, book covers, posters and finally, children's books. I have also worked with advertising agencies, graphic design firms and large organizations such as the United Nations, Canada Post and the Royal Canadian Mint.

"In the mid 1970s and early '80s, the cultural industry in Quebec was booming and there were a lot of opportunities for illustrators. We rapidly came to realize that we knew little about business practices, copyright law and contracts.

"In 1982, about 10 of us started the Quebec Illustrators Association. I became its first president and held the position from 1983 to 1985."

How I work

"I read the text many times, using the strongest moments of the story to divide it. I try to avoid putting too much text on a single page, to encourage children to read further.

"I may roughly sketch a two-inch illustration while I'm reading the story, talking on the phone or eating lunch. Then, I take my scribbles back to the dark room, and enlarge them mechanically to find references so I can achieve realism in the drawing. I restructure the image, until I find the right perspective or angle, or until the magic is there and I believe in it.

"I always do extensive research on the subject I am illustrating. When there are one or more characters in the story, I take pictures of models (not professionals but regular kids). I then recreate the scenes as if for a theatre production, searching for accurate gestures and emotions. For the past few years, I have been in the habit of creating a 'dummy' book of 4" x 5" images to get a feeling for the book's atmosphere and unity. This method is very time consuming.

"After the publisher's approval, I transfer the images onto illustration board. I do a detailed black and white drawing as a base for my acrylic paintings, which are done with a water-colour technique, and retouched

later with coloured pencils. I use an airbrush for backgrounds to give depth to the illustration. Even when I work hard to achieve realism in my illustrations, there is always a certain whimsical and naive feeling to the world I create."

Suzanne Duranceau

BIBLIOGRAPHY

All books illustrated by Suzanne Duranceau

Adam, Y., et al. *Crapauds et autres animaux*. Montreal: la courte échelle, 1981. Out of print.

Deschênes, Josseline. *L'autobus à Margo* (Lire Avec Toi). Montreal: Héritage, 1981. Out of print.

Gagnon, Cécile. *Snowfeather*. Trans. by Valerie Hepburn Craig. Toronto: James Lorimer & Co., 1980. Out of print.

Judd, Naomi. *Love Can Build a Bridge*. New York: HarperCollins, 1998 006-027-2066.

Kugler, Marianne. *Jean d'Ailleurs* (Collection Enfantaisie). Montreal: Ovale, 1983. Out of print.

Major, Henriette. *La ville fabuleuse* (Lire Avec Toi). Montreal: Héritage, 1982. Out of print.

Muller, Robin. *Hickory Dickory Dock*. Richmond Hill: Scholastic Canada, 1992 Cloth 0-590-73616-7. 1995 Paper 0-590-73089-4.♣

Munsch, Robert. *Millicent and the Wind*. Toronto: Annick Press, 1984 Paper 0-920236-93-6; Cloth 0-920236-98-7. 1988 Annikin Paper 1-55037-010-3.

Perreault, Denyse. *Des fleurs pour le père Noel*. Montreal: Editions La Presse, 1983. Out of print.

Poupart, Jean-Marie. *Nuits magiques*. Montreal: la courte échelle, 1982. Out of print.

Weeks, Sarah. *Follow the Moon*. New York: HarperCollins, 1995 Cloth 0-06-024-4443-7; Paper 0-06-024442-9.

Awards

1981 Culinar Award for *Les p'tits Crapauds*

1991 Houston Society of Illustrators Annual Show Gold Awards for *City Mouse* and *Country Mouse*

1993 CAPIC Annual Show Gold Award (book cover) for *Hickory Dickory Dock*

Selected articles about Suzanne Duranceau

King, Annabelle. "Animal Attractions." *Montreal Gazette* 31 Oct. 1991: C1.

From *Follow the Moon*

Eugenie Fernandes
AUTHOR/ILLUSTRATOR

Born
September 25, 1943,
Huntington, New York, U.S.A.

School
School of Visual Arts, New York City, New York, U.S.A.

Where I live now
Buckhorn Lake, Ontario

My favourite books when I was young
Picture books illustrated by Gustaf Tenggren

My favourite book now
"I have lots of favourites."

Career
Illustrator, writer

Family
Husband, Henry, illustrator; daughter, Kim, author/illustrator; son, Matt, artist; cat, Smudge

The room where I create
"My studio is glass on three sides and overlooks the lake and the woods, so I'm inside out and outside in. Before this, my studio was the corner of a bedroom, protected only by a strip of tape on the floor that said, 'please knock.' Our two children were quite good about that invisible door. They often sat next to me creating stories and pictures of their own."

Spare time
"Walk barefoot in the sand."

When I was growing up
"My dad is an illustrator, one of the early comic book artists in the 1930s with *D.C.*, *Adventure*, and *More Fun* comics. His studio is at the top of the house where I was born. A picture window looks out over the tree tops to Huntington Bay. I had my own desk next to his. Pop used that ancient desk to create many of the early *Sandman* comic book covers. I used it while I was growing up and now my son is adding his character to the surface. I spent much of my growing-up-time in Pop's studio. The rest of the time... I liked to swim and climb trees and build sand castles and paint and raise baby birds and enjoy the picnic lunches that my mother often brought to the beach."

My first book (and how it happened)
"*Wickedishrag* is a story that I wrote and illustrated for a class project when I was in art school (1965)."

Where my ideas come from
"Feelings and memories from my childhood and from now. Ideas are floating around in the air all the time — sometimes they come from a funny situation, or an angry one, or from some nice visual image. Ideas are the easy part. The hard part is making the story work around the idea."

Who and what influenced me
"The *who's* are my dad who is an artist and my mom who is very enthusiastic. The *what* is life!"

How I work
"My studio is wide open so that while I work kids and other creatures can walk through and look over my shoulder and chat and the cat can jump into my lap. That's when I paint and draw. When I write, I don't like to be interrupted."

Something nobody knew about me (until now)
"I write in my head — in bits and pieces — when I walk, when I wash dishes, wherever I am. But my favourite place for writing is in the bathtub because it's peaceful and quiet there."

My favourite books that I've created
The Tree That Grew to the Moon, Waves in the Bathtub, A Difficult Day, Just You and Me.

Tips for young creators
"Write what you feel. Paint what you love."

Eugenie Fernandes

SELECT BIBLIOGRAPHY

Barnes, Lily. *Lace Them Up* (Step-By-Step Series). Toronto: Somerville House, 1992 Paper 0-921051-64-6. Illustrations by Eugenie Fernandes.

—. *Make It Better* (Lifeskills for Little Ones). Toronto: Somerville House, 1996 Paper 1-895897-29-7. Illustrations by Eugenie Fernandes.

Brimner, Larry Dane. *Elliot Fry's Good-bye*. Honesdale: Boyds Mills Press, 1994 Cloth 1-56397-113-5. Illustrations by Eugenie Fernandes.

Coffey, Maria. *A Cat in a Kayak*. Toronto: Annick Press, 1998 Cloth 1-55037-509-11; Paper 1-55037-508-3. Illustrations by Eugenie Fernandes.

Colbert, Jan. *Good Morning*. Toronto: HarperCollins, 1993. Illustrations by Eugenie Fernandes. Out of print.

—. *Good Night*. Toronto: HarperCollins, 1993. Illustrations by Eugenie Fernandes. Out of print.

Fernandes, Eugenie. *The Little Boy Who Cried Himself to Sea*. Toronto: Kids Can Press, 1982. Illustrations by the author. Out of print.

—. *A Difficult Day*. Toronto: Kids Can Press, 1987. Illustrations by the author. Out of print.

—. *Under the Sea* (Glow in the Dark Series). Racine, WI: Western Publishing, 1991 0-307-06255-4. Illustrations by the author.

—. *Just You and Me*. Toronto: Annick Press, 1993 Cloth 1-55037-324-2; Paper 1-55037-327-7. Illustrations by the author.

—. *Waves in the Bathtub*. Richmond Hill: Scholastic Canada, 1993 Cloth 0-590-74318-X; Paper 0-590-24343-8. Illustrations by the author.

—. *The Tree That Grew to the Moon*. Richmond Hill: Scholastic Canada, 1994 Cloth 0-590-24126-5; Paper 0-590-24936-3. Illustrations by the author.

—. *Little Toby and the Big Hair*. Toronto: Doubleday Canada, 1997 Cloth 0-385-25633-7. Illustrations by the author.

Fernandes, Henry, and Eugenie Fernandes. *Ordinary Amos and the Amazing Fish*. Racine, WI: Western Publishing, 1986. Illustrations by Henry Fernandes. Out of print.

Fraser, Sylvia. *Tom and Francine: a Love Story*. Toronto: Key Porter, 1998 Cloth 1-55013-944-4. Illustrations by Eugenie Fernandes.

Harrison, Troon. *Aaron's Awful Allergies*. Toronto: Kids Can Press, 1996 Cloth 1-55074-299-X. Illustrations by Eugenie Fernandes.

—. *Lavender Moon*. Toronto: Annick Press, 1997 Cloth 1-55037-455-9; Paper 1-55037-454-0. Illustrations by Eugenie Fernandes.

Hayward, Linda. *I Had a Bad Dream: A Book about Nightmares* (Golden Learn About Living Series). Racine, WI: Western Publishing, 1985. Illustrations by Eugenie Fernandes. Out of print.

Korman, Susan. *Wake up Groundhog*. Cambridge: Golden Books, 1998 Paper 0-307-98848-1. Illustrations by Eugenie Fernandes.

Merriam, Eve. *Mommies at Work*. New York: Simon & Schuster, 1989. 1996 Paper 0-689-80999-9. Illustrations by Eugenie Fernandes.

—. *Daddies at Work*. New York: Simon & Schuster, 1989. 1996 Paper 0-689-80998-0. Illustrations by Eugenie Fernandes.

Quinlan, Patricia. *Brush Them Bright* (Step-By-Step Series). Toronto: Somerville House, 1992 Paper 0-921051-65-4. Illustrations by Eugenie Fernandes.

—. *On The Phone* (Lifeskills for Little Ones). Toronto: Somerville House, 1996 Paper 0-895897-24-6. Illustrations by Eugenie Fernandes.

continued...

From *A Cat in a Kayak*

Raffi. *Rise and Shine* (Raffi Songs to Read). Toronto: Random House, 1996 Cloth 0-679-30819-9. Illustrations by Eugenie Fernandes.

Reid, Suzan. *Grandpa Dan's Toboggan Ride.* Richmond Hill: Scholastic Canada, 1992 Paper 0-590-7460-1. Illustrations by Eugenie Fernandes.

Suzuki, David. *Nature In The Home* (Nature All Around). Toronto: Stoddart Publishing, 1993 Paper 0-7737-5586-1. Illustrations by Eugenie Fernandes.

—. *If We Could See The Air* (Nature All Around). Toronto: Stoddart Publishing, 1994 Paper 0-7737-5666-3. Illustrations by Eugenie Fernandes.

—. *The Backyard Time Detectives* (Nature All Around). Toronto: Stoddart Publishing, 1995 Paper 0-7737-5740-6. Illustrations by Eugenie Fernandes.

Thompson, Richard. *Sky Full Of Babies* (The Jesse Adventures). Toronto: Annick Press, 1987 Paper 0-920303-92-7. Illustrations by Eugenie Fernandes.

—. *Foo* (The Jesse Adventures). Toronto: Annick Press, 1988 Paper 1-55037-032-4. Illustrations by Eugenie Fernandes.

—. *I Have To See This* (The Jesse Adventures). Toronto: Annick Press, 1988 Cloth 1-55037-015-4; Paper 1-55037-014-6. Illustrations by Eugenie Fernandes.

—. *Effie's Bath* (The Effie Stories). Toronto: Annick Press, 1989. Illustrations by Eugenie Fernandes. Out of print.

—. *Gurgle, Bubble, Splash* (The Jesse Adventure Series). Toronto: Annick Press, 1989. Illustrations by Eugenie Fernandes. Out of print.

—. *Jesse On The Night Train* (The Jesse Adventures). Toronto: Annick Press, 1990 Cloth 1-55037-093-6; Paper 1-55037-094-4. Illustrations by Eugenie Fernandes.

—. *Maggee and the Lake Minder.* Toronto: Annick Press, 1991. Illustrations by Eugenie Fernandes. Out of print.

—. *Tell Me One Good Thing.* Toronto: Annick Press, 1992 Cloth 1-55037-215-7; Paper 1-55037-212-2. Illustrations by Eugenie Fernandes.

—. *Don't Be Scared, Eleven* (The Jesse Adventure Series). Toronto: Annick Press, 1993 Illustrations by Eugenie Fernandes. Out of print.

Vaughan, Marcia. *Kapoc the Killer Croc* (Animal Fair Series). Morristown, NJ: Silver Burdett Press, 1994 0-382-24075-8. Illustrations by Eugenie Fernandes.

Wark, Laurie. *Katie's Hand-Me-Down Day.* Toronto: Kids Can Press, 1994 Cloth 1-55074-159-4. Illustrations by Eugenie Fernandes.

Wilson, Budge. *The Long Wait.* Toronto: Stoddart Publishing, 1997 Cloth 0-7737-3021-4. Illustrations by Eugenie Fernandes.

Eugenie Fernandes has published two book series in England (*Little Ladybird* Board Books and the *Jolly Book Box Early Learning for Toddlers* Series). She has also illustrated several books for Simon & Schuster and a number of Little Golden Books for Western Publishing.

Kim Fernandes
AUTHOR/ILLUSTRATOR

Born
September 4, 1969, Long Island, New York, USA

School
Ontario College of Art, Toronto

Where I live now
Port Perry, Ontario

My favourite books when I was young
"The whole series of the *Little House On the Prairie*, by Laura Ingalls Wilder; *Little Bear*, by Minarik, illustrated by Maurice Sendak; *Hop on Pop*, by Dr. Seuss."

My favourite books now
"Picture books: my affections change each season. Novels: *A Prayer for Owen Meany*, by John Irving."

Career
Children's book illustrator/ author *and* mom!

Family
Husband, Mike; daughter, Robyn; two cats, Suki and Kisu

The room where I create
"My work space is a 5'x 8' cubby off the dining room. The shelves are full of books, the walls are decorated with knick-knacks from my childhood and the drawers are full of clay (sorted by colour in Tupperware containers) and craft supplies. My room may be small but it's very functional. As I sit working at my desk, I can watch my daughter playing in the living room, make sure dinner isn't burning in the kitchen and see out my window if anyone's coming to visit at the side door."

Spare time
"Play with my daughter, see friends and family, work on the house and yard, do yoga, solve crossword puzzles and read."

When I was growing up
"My earliest memories are of decorating sandcastles with pebbles and shells, and learning to swim in the salty water of Huntington Bay, New York. When I was four, my family moved to Toronto, but we still find ourselves 'Visiting Granny' on Long Island every summer."

My first book (and how it happened)
"The art for my first book started as a grade 13 independent art project. I can't remember the mark I got, but when my 3-dimensional kitchen (made of wood, fabric and Fimo) was complete, my mom suggested I write a story about it. With a lot of help, I came up with a story called *Visiting Granny* and was extremely lucky to have it accepted by Annick Press. At only 19, my career had begun."

Where my ideas come from
"I think I'm subconsciously absorbing images and formulating ideas all the time. Because, when I sit down at my desk, they miraculously seem to be there. My wonderfully creative family is also a sounding board with whom I receive and share many concepts. My daughter is a constant source of reference, reminding me how to play, imagine and learn."

Who and what influenced me
"Growing up, I was always encouraged to express my creative talents. My childhood was filled with crafts. When I was five, I remember sitting next to my mother in her studio and designing my first picture book (unpublished to date). My parents, Eugenie and Henry Fernandes, are both freelance artists and have created many books for children."

How I work
"I go through many stages when creating my 3-D illustrations for a book. First, I do quarter-size thumbnails and lay out the whole book. Then I blow these

up to full size and tighten up the drawings (with much help and advice from my family). Once approved by the publisher, I start working in clay (Fimo). I use the line drawings to help with size and position. It usually takes me a week to ten days to create each illustration which I bake in the oven until it's hard. I paint the backgrounds on a piece of thick illustration board and then glue the baked Fimo piece onto it. When all the art is complete, I work with a professional photographer who captures my 3-D images on transparencies. These are then used to print in the book (phew!!!)."

My favourite book that I've created

"Children ask me this question all the time and I find it so hard to answer. It's like asking a mother which child is her favourite! Of course, she loves them all equally but for very unique and individual reasons… That's how I feel about my books."

Tips for young creators

"All the old clichés are true (with some modifications)! Practice makes perfect (or at least pleasing); there are no mistakes (only milestones); and if at first you don't succeed draw, draw again."

From *One Gray Mouse*

Kim Fernandes

BIBLIOGRAPHY

Burton, Kathy. *One Gray Mouse*. Toronto: Kids Can Press, 1995 Paper 1-55074-225-6; Cloth 1-55074-225-6. Illustrations by Kim Fernandes.

Fernandes, Kim. *Visiting Granny*. Toronto: Annick Press, 1990 Paper 1-55037-084-7; Cloth 1-55037-077-4. Illustrations by the author.

—. *Zebo and the Dirty Planet*. Toronto: Annick Press, 1991 Paper 1-55037-180-0; Cloth 1-55037-183-5. Illustrations by the author.

—. *Gifts to Make with Crayola Model Magic*. Toronto: Scholastic, 1996 0-590-24902-9. Illustrations by the author.

—. *Christmas Crafts with Crayola Model Magic*. Toronto: Scholastic, 1997 0-590-24902-9. Illustrations by the author.

Fernandes, Eugenie. *Just You and Me*. Toronto: Annick Press, 1993 Paper 1-55037-327-7; Cloth 1-55037-324-2. Illustrations by Kim Fernandes.

—. *Little Toby and the Big Hair*. Toronto: Doubleday, 1997 Paper 0-385-25678-7; Cloth 0-385-25633-7. Illustrations by Kim Fernandes.

Moore, Clement C. *A Visit from St. Nicholas*. Toronto: Doubleday, 1998 Paper 0-385-25793-7; Cloth 0-385-25784-8. Illustrations by Kim Fernandes.

Awards

1992 Silver Award for *Zebo and the Dirty Planet* at the 3-Dimensional Art Directors and Illustrators Awards show

Selected articles about Kim Fernandes

"Illustration's New Wave." *Quill and Quire* Feb. 1997

Laura Fernandez & Rick Jacobson
ILLUSTRATOR TEAM

Born
Laura: May 20, 1960, Madrid, Spain

Rick: Nipawin, Saskatchewan, Jan 7, 1959

School
Alberta College of Art

Where we live now
Toronto, Ontario

My favourite book when I was young
Laura: "I had many favourite books — all of them with beautiful illustrations: *Alice in Wonderland, Poucette* and an illustrated version of *1001 Nights.*"

Rick: "I read a lot of sci-fi and fantasy books like *Conan.* The cover art by Frazetta, Boris and others attracted me."

My favourite book now
Laura: "*To Kill a Mockingbird, Little Women*, and all of Chris Van Allsburg's books."

Rick: "*The English Patient* by Michael Ondaatje, *Famous Last Words* by Timothy Findley, *The Book of Secrets* by M. J. Vassanji and *Neuromancer* by William Gibson."

Career
Laura: "My first job was as a bank teller — my first serious job. It put me through art college and I have been an illustrator since then! I worked at a design studio for about six months and quit to become a freelancer, and I still am!"

Rick: "Art director for a business publication for one year, and an illustrator for 15 years."

Family
Illustrating partners Rick Jacobson and Laura Fernandez are married to each other and have three children: Michael, Maria Teresa and Mercedes."

The room where they create
"With the help of Laura's father (an architect), we built a beautiful new studio in our house with skylights, a fireplace, a huge aquarium, and a family area. We have four large desks, and a room for our large canvases and a place to photograph our artwork."

When I was growing up
Laura: "When I was a child I loved to read. I also loved to draw and paint. I loved music and I learned to play the piano. I wrote many songs and considered becoming a musician, but my art was more important to me. I would often sit my sisters down and make them pose for me. I also would sit in front of a mirror and draw self portraits. Now I make my children pose!"

Rick: "I did a lot of canoeing, archery, hunting, horseback riding and helping around the farm."

Our first book (and how it happened)
Laura had done many covers for HarperCollins and they asked if she would consider doing *I Heard My Mother Call My Name*. Laura loved the story and doing a children's book appealed to her "because I was soon to become a mother. It was difficult because we hadn't illustrated a book before, but we did it. And loved doing it. Nancy Hundal wrote a beautiful story!" [*Ed. note:* Although this was a joint work, only Laura was credited as the illustrator.] Says Rick, "After having our first child, children's books seemed very appealing."

Where my ideas come from
Laura: "My ideas come from anywhere! From my life or movies I've seen, books I've read, pictures I see — from my own influences and from my imagination. I also get inspiration from other art I see. I love looking at beautiful art."

Rick: "From everywhere. It is impossible to find a single source because it just comes."

Who and what influenced me

Laura: "Many artists have influenced me, from the great classical artists such as Vermeer, Velazquez, David, Ingres, da Vinci, to the Impressionists — Manet, Degas, Renoir — to Picasso and my own father who also painted and my husband who is a wonderful creative artist!"

Rick: "Frazetta, Boris and painters of fantasy at first, but recently the Pre-Raphaelites, Vermeer, Velazquez."

How I work

Rick: "Reading and re-reading the manuscript. Sketching images that come to me as I read, breaking the manuscript into page breaks, tightening the sketches and finally, final sketches to canvas for painting."

Laura: "I work on books with my partner and husband, Rick Jacobson. We talk about each book and gather a lot of reference to support our initial ideas. We do rough sketches and then go to more finished sketches, which we present to our editors and art directors. These are approved, or maybe slightly modified, before we go to the finished paintings which we do in oil paints and gouache. It takes us at least a year to complete a book — the paintings are painstakingly created."

Something nobody knew about me (until now)

Laura: "When I was three years old I knew the name of any symphony my dad would play for me in a few short bars."

My favourite book that I've created

Laura: "I haven't created it yet — I always think the next one is going to be the biggest and the best and I think each one we do is a little closer to what we are trying to achieve."

Rick: "Each one has merits and problems to me. My favourite book is always the one that is not finished yet. An unfinished book has no mistakes yet."

Tips for young creators

Rick: "Draw a lot, look a lot, read a lot."

Laura: "Learn how to do the basics first — really well; for me it was drawing! It's no good to paint if you don't know how to draw and compose and practice and work at it diligently and consistently."

Laura Fernandez & Rick Jacobson

BIBLIOGRAPHY

Bedard, Michael. *Glass Town.* Toronto: Stoddart Kids, 1997 Cloth 0-7737-2997-6. Illustrations by Laura Fernandez and Rick Jacobson.

Bogart, Jo Ellen. *Jeremiah Learns to Read.* Toronto: Scholastic, 1997 Cloth 0-590-24927-4. Illustrations by Laura Fernandez and Rick Jacobson.

Hundal, Nancy. *I Heard My Mother Call My Name.* Toronto: HarperCollins, 1994 Paper 0-00-647496-9. Illustrations by Laura Fernandez.

Kallman, Esther. *Tchaikovsky Discovers America.* Toronto, Stoddart Kids, 1994 Cloth 1-895555-82-5. Illustrations by Laura Fernandez and Rick Jacobson.

Trottier, Maxine. *Prairie Willow.* Toronto: Stoddart Kids, 1998 Cloth 0-7737-3067-2. Illustrations by Laura Fernandez and Rick Jacobson.

Awards

1998 Ruth Schwartz Children's Book Award for *Jeremiah Learns to Read*

Laura Fernandez has also won numerous advertising awards.

From *Prairie Willow*

Joanne Fitzgerald
ILLUSTRATOR

Born
February 17, 1956, Montreal, Quebec

School
Mount Allison University, Sackville, New Brunswick

Where I live now
Georgetown, Ontario

My favourite books when I was young
Charlotte's Web by E.B. White, *Harriet the Spy* by Louise Fitzhugh

My favourite books now
Running in the Family by Michael Ondaatje, *A Prayer for Owen Meany* by John Irving

Career
Illustrator-on-staff, Royal Ontario Museum; freelance illustrator (1980 to present)

Family
Husband, Robert; daughter, Laura; dog, Zigg E. Dogg (Ziggernaut).

The room where I create
"Upstairs studio in our house — very small, but nice and close."

Spare time
"Bike, cook yummy stuff, knit, crafts... Having no spare time is one of my favourite things."

When I was growing up
"From the earliest time I can remember, I wanted to be an artist. I also loved books — so it is quite natural that these two loves came together. I would like to write and illustrate a book, because I think it would be a new challenge for me. I think about the books we had while growing up, and they were not, for the most part, as captivating as the books of today. Somehow, my own imagination took over and added the visual subtext. I was a doodler — I doodled over everything, and got into a bit of trouble over it at school. Nothing was spared from some sort of 'doodle' and it seemed I couldn't stop."

My first book (and how it happened)
"My first book from Groundwood Books came about in a wonderful kind of storybook way. I had illustrated a piece for *Chickadee* magazine, and a little while after it had been published, I received a call from the book designer at Groundwood asking if maybe I could stop in with my portfolio. I did (nervously) and not long after that, I was offered a book. The book was *Plain Noodles,* and I was astonished by how challenging it was to illustrate 32 pages of

the same characters, especially those babies with all their fingers and toes! I am much more comfortable drawing people now than I was then. I like to think I learn something with each book."

Where my ideas come from
"Some of my ideas come from just doodling. A lot of them just seem to grow out of examining a manuscript for clues about the characters. Often, I do impose my own tastes on the characters, but usually I have a strong sense about the sorts of things they might wear and do from the content of the story. I add details — and sometimes cannot resist adding some details from my family's own life, just for fun."

Who and what influenced me
"This is a hard question to answer! I think just about everything is an influence of some sort. There are phases where one is swept away by the work of one artist or another. For a while, I will love absolutely everything by one artist, and I am sure it affects the way I see things around me, and the way I draw. Some of my ongoing loves are Burne-Jones, the Van Eycks, Dulac, Henri Rousseau, Kate Greenaway, and Carl Larsson. Sometimes what influences me

From *Jacob's Best Sisters*

Joanne Fitzgerald

BIBLIOGRAPHY

Jam, Teddy. *Doctor Kiss Says Yes.* Toronto: Groundwood Books, 1991 Cloth 0-88899-141-X. Illustrations by Joanne Fitzgerald.✤

—. *Jacob's Best Sisters.* Toronto: Groundwood Books, 1996 Cloth 0-088899-229-7. Illustrations by Joanne Fitzgerald.

Lottridge, Celia Barker. *Ten Small Tales.* Toronto: Groundwood Books, 1993 Cloth 0-88899-156-8. Illustrations by Joanne Fitzgerald.

Scharer, Niko. *Emily's House.* Toronto: Groundwood Books, 1992 Paper 0-88899-158-4. Illustrations by Joanne Fitzgerald.✤

Waterton, Betty. *Plain Noodles.* Toronto: Groundwood Books, 1989. 1997 Paper 0-88899-132-0. Illustrations by Joanne Fitzgerald.

Awards
1991 Governor General's Literary Award for *Dr. Kiss Says Yes*

Selected articles about Joanne Fitzgerald
Mahoney, Jeff. *The Hamilton Spectator* 16 Jan. 1992.

Mahoney, Jeff *The Montreal Gazette* 4 Apr. 1992.

is a dream. It is just as though you suddenly see something clearly, and you think 'I must remember this', and eventually it shows up in your work."

How I work
"I try to be self-disciplined and work regular hours. I do some physical exercise first thing every morning because it gives me energy, and helps me to concentrate more intensely. I usually try to set a goal for each day or week. Usually, I just work on one project at a time, giving it my full focus. I often work at night, except that I am tired the next day. I try to go to bed early and get up to work extra early.

"When I get a manuscript, I have to let it sink in a bit before anything comes to me. Gradually, I start having more and more ideas about a book, and then I sit down to put them on paper. Often, when you see how it all looks on paper you have to discard some of those ideas, and expand on other ones. The drawing stage is the problem-solving stage. It can also require a lot of research — when you have to draw things you are not familiar with. I do my research at the local library, although, sometimes, I have to go further afield and even enlist help from friends to find out about some things."

My favourite book that I've created
Dr. Kiss Says Yes

Tips for young creators
"I think no matter how good you are at something today, you can only be better tomorrow if you practice. My biggest tip would be to draw, draw, and draw some more — whether it's making comic strips, drawing from your imagination or from what you see around you, drawing with your computer, or with a pencil and paper."

Laszlo Gal
AUTHOR/ILLUSTRATOR

Born
February 18, 1933, Budapest, Hungary

School
Budapest, Hungary

Where he lives now
Toronto, Ontario

Career
Graphic designer, illustrator

When he was growing up
As a teenager in Hungary, Laszlo was interested in books and illustration, but more than anything else he wanted to be an actor. After high school, he was accepted by the prestigious Academy of Dramatic Arts in Budapest, but was cut from the program after his first year.

Laszlo next tried to pursue his interest in book illustration. That proved equally difficult because the education authorities in Hungary decided he should be an art teacher. He graduated with an art education diploma and taught in Budapest for three years before emigrating to Canada during the Hungarian Revolution.

His first book (and how it happened)
Although Laszlo has lived in Canada since 1956, his career as an illustrator began in Italy. In 1962, he took a selection of his illustrations to the famous publishing house of Arnoldo Mondadori. Mondadori was impressed with Laszlo's work, but not willing to offer him a commission. Instead Laszlo could illustrate a forthcoming children's book, and if the publishing house liked his illustrations, he would be paid for his work. It was a risk, but also a fabulous opportunity.

Back in Canada, Laszlo spent the next year preparing illustrations in whatever time he could spare from his work as a graphic designer for CBC Television. His gamble paid off: his 60 illustrations were accepted by Mondadori, and within three years he was offered a contract to work exclusively on the company's children's books.

It was an unusual arrangement between an illustrator and a publishing house, but it was ideal for Laszlo, giving him both artistic freedom and security. For the next four years, he lived in Verona, illustrating two full-colour books a year for Mondadori and revelling in Italian culture.

His first Canadian book (and how it happened)
Laszlo's first Canadian book, *Cartier Discovers the St. Lawrence* by William Toye, was published in 1970. Over the next seven years, he illustrated six Canadian children's books. At the time, the cost of publishing full-colour books was too expensive for Canadian publishers, but Laszlo produced award-winning books using two-colour and black-and-white illustrations.

Laszlo Gal's first full-colour Canadian book was Janet Lunn's *The Twelve Dancing Princesses*, which took him two years. The rich Renaissance style of the paintings revealed the influence of his years spent in Italy.

How he works
With each book, Laszlo makes a conscious effort to develop a style that will reflect the art of the period in which the story is set. He doesn't copy the style, but allows it to influence his choice of medium, composition, and technique, melding old techniques and styles with new influences.

For example, in Eva Martin's collection *Canadian Fairy Tales*, Laszlo reflected the art of Europe — the source of many of the stories in the book — but placed his work in a Canadian setting, filling it with flowers and plants of the new land. His illustrations for the Chinese legend, *The Enchanted Tapestry* were done in the style of Chinese landscape painting.

Laszlo Gal

SELECT BIBLIOGRAPHY

All books illustrated by Laszlo Gal

Bertelli, Mariella. *The Shirt of the Happy Man.* Toronto: Kids Can Press, 1977. Out of print.

Clenman, Donia Blumenfeld. *The Moon and the Oyster.* Victoria: Orca Book Publishers, 1992 Cloth 0-920501-83-4.

Collins, Meghan. *The Willow Maiden.* New York: Dial, 1985. Out of print.

Downie, Mary Alice. *Scared Sarah.* Scarborough: Nelson Canada, 1974. Out of print.

Engel, Marian. *My Name is Not Odessa Yarker.* Toronto: Kids Can Press, 1977. Out of print.

Erhlich, Amy. *Pome and Peel.* New York: Penguin, 1993; New York: Dial, 1990. Out of print.

Fowke, Edith. *Folklore of Canada: Tall Tales, Songs, Stories, Rhymes, Jokes from Every Corner of Canada.* Toronto: McClelland & Stewart, 1990 Paper 0-7710-3204-8.

Gal, Laszlo. *Prince Ivan and the Firebird.* Toronto: McClelland & Stewart, 1991 Cloth 0-7710-3300-1.

—. *East of the Sun and West of the Moon.* Toronto: 1993 Cloth 0-7710-3301-X. 1994 Paper 0-7710-3302-8.

—. *Merlin's Castle.* Stoddart, 1995 Cloth 0-7737-2852-X.

Gal, Laszlo and Raffaella Gal. *The Parrot: an Italian Folktale.* Toronto: Groundwood, 1997 Cloth 0-88899-287-4. Illustrations by Laszlo Gal and Raffaella Gal.

Lunn, Janet. *The Twelve Dancing Princesses.* Toronto: Methuen, 1979. Out of print.

Maloney, Margaret Crawford. *The Little Mermaid.* Don Mills: Stoddart, 1983 Cloth 0-458-951102.

Maloney, Margaret Crawford, and Laszlo Gal. *The Goodman of Ballengiech.* Don Mills: General Publishing, 1991 Paper 0-7736-7349-0.

Martin, Eva. *Canadian Fairy Tales.* Toronto: Groundwood Books, 1984 Paper 0-88899-030-8.

—. *Tales of the Far North.* New York: Dial, 1987. Out of print.

Mayer, Marianna. *Iduna and the Magic Apples.* New York: Simon and Schuster Kids, 1988 Cloth 0-02-765120-7.

—. *The Spirit of the Blue Light.* New York: Macmillan, 1990. Out of print.

Melzack, Ronald. *Why the Man in the Moon is Happy and Other Eskimo Tales of Creation.* Toronto: McClelland & Stewart, 1977. Out of print.

Page, P. K. *A Flask of Seawater.* Don Mills: Stoddart/Oxford University Press, 1989. Out of print.

Robertson, Joanne. *Sea Witches.* Don Mills: Oxford University Press/Stoddart, 1991. Out of print.

San Souci, Robert D. *The Enchanted Tapestry.* New York: Dial, 1987. 1990 Paper 0-8037-0862-9.

Shakespeare, William. *Hamlet.* Edited by Marilyn Eisenstat. Toronto: Harcourt Brace & Co. Canada, 1988 Paper 0-7747-1268-6.

—. *A Midsummer Night's Dream.* Ed. Harriet Law. Toronto: Harcourt Brace and Co. Canada, 1988 Paper 0-7747-1267-8.

Shaw-MacKinnon, Margaret. *Tiktala.* Toronto: Stoddart, 1996 Cloth 0-7737-2920-8.

Smythe, Anne. *Islands.* Toronto: Groundwood, 1995 Cloth 0-88899-238-6.

Williams, Bert. *Sword of Egypt.* Richmond Hill: Scholastic Canada, 1977. Out of print.

Wynne-Jones, Tim. adapt. *Dracula.* By Bram Stoker. Toronto: Key Porter, 1997 Paper 1-55013-900-2.

Awards

1978 IODE Book Award - Toronto Chapter for *The Shirt of the Happy Man, My Name is Not Odessa Yarker* and *Why the Man in the Moon is Happy*

1979 Canada Council Children's Literature Prize for *The Twelve Dancing Princesses*

1980 Amelia Frances Howard-Gibbon Illustrator's Award for *The Twelve Dancing Princesses*

1983 Canada Council Children's Literature Prize for *The Little Mermaid*

1985 Parents' Choice Award for *The Willow Maiden*

From *Merlin's Castle*

Annouchka Gravel Galouchko
AUTHOR/ILLUSTRATOR

Born
July 26, 1960, Montreal, Quebec

School
University of Quebec in Montreal

Where I live now
St.-Sauveur des Monts, Quebec

My favourite books when I was young
L'Auberge de l'ange gardien, Le Général Dourakine, Les Malheurs de Sophie, Le Bon petit diable by Comtesse de Ségur. Favourite picture books: *Les Aventures de Tintin*

Career
Illustrator, painter, author

Family
"My companion Stephan Daigle (also an illustrator and a painter), a son Sacha, and a small Siamese cat named Doucha."

The room where I create
"Some days, looking through my east window of my studio, I see the Cairo of my childhood with its minarets merged into the orange sunset and its sweet-smelling oleanders. A north window brings me back to the present and the Laurentians. Autumn comes, and they take on vibrant colours."

Spare time
"I use my free time for working because my son takes all my time! But what I like doing: singing, playing flute (I do this with the baby), walking in the woods, swimming in the lake, reading, meeting friends and enjoying new recipes with good company."

When I was growing up
When Annouchka was a child, teachers scolded her for being dreamy, which was true in mathematics and science but not in the creative subjects.

"My parents encouraged me. We had a library full of art books. For Christmas, I received artist's materials and filled up my notebooks with free and colourful drawings. I believe that all this creativity was a major factor in my artistic development."

My first book (and how it happened)
"My first book *The Nutmeg Princess* written by Richardo Keens-Douglas was published in 1992 by Annick Press. It's a story full of magic and warm colours.

"For many years before that, I had worked on the text and illustrations of a children's book called *Le Jardin de Monsieur Préfontaine*. I had no publisher and decided to try my luck at the international children's book fair in Bologna. The publishers found my work interesting, but nobody would sign a contract with me.

"On the evening before my departure, when I was feeling disappointed to have to come back empty-handed, the telephone suddenly rang. It was my husband calling to say that Annick Press would publish a book with me. Which shows that the answer to the invested energy does not always come when we are waiting for it. Six years later, *Le jardin de Monsieur Préfontaine* was published by the Montreal publisher, Les 400 coups."

Where my ideas come from
"My inspiration comes from my own vision of the world, in which every thing is animated. In my illustrations, a tree can walk and a mountain can observe the events around it. I also project human feelings on inanimate objects: a house inhabited by sad people can cry, the spray of a fountain can be transformed into a maternal and soothing figure, singing lullabies."

Who and what influenced me
"When I was a child and a teenager, my father took me to the countries where he worked (Iran, Egypt, Austria and Mexico). I saw many different cultures up close. My experiences and my dual background (my mother is French Canadian and my father is of Russian origin) have enriched me and made my cultural identity more complex. These influences are mirrored in my work as an author and illustrator."

How I work

"When I receive an author's story or when I write my own, a slow gestation begins.

"For *The Nutmeg Princess*, I went many times to the tropical section of the Montreal Garden, to fill myself with the humid and sensual atmosphere of the place and to sketch some species of trees. Music also has an important place in my artistic life. Music from the Caribbean, India or Japan brings a distinctive touch to my illustrations. Reference books play a great part in my work. The book *Shō and the Demons of the Deep* is dedicated to Hokusaï, a seventeenth century Japanese painter. I work in a non-intellectual fashion, using all my feelings and emotions.

"I often reread my books after publication because I need distance to truly appreciate the results of my hard work. Often, after a certain time has passed, the pictures and the story reveal facets that were buried in the subconscious."

My favourite book that I've created

"I loved drawing *Shō and the Demons of the Deep* because of the idea of Shō confronting his fears and changing them to something creative. It forced me to face my own demons."

Tips for young creators

When she studied at the French School in Vienna, Austria, Annouchka rebelled against the severity and intolerance. The vice-principal told her that she was spoiling her life, her parents' life and her future. He turned up at the French School she attended in Teheran, Iran, three years later.

"In 1987, I had an exhibition at the Canadian Cultural Centre in Paris with other illustrators from Quebec. A friend from my school days was with me at a café. Suddenly, she said: 'Annouchka, you will never guess who is sitting behind you!'. I turned around and there was that same vice-principal. He couldn't get over seeing us. He went to the exhibition. I thought back to when he had predicted my failure, and I savoured my victory secretly.

"The advice I would give to young creators is not to be destroyed by people who scorn or condemn you; pursue your own way and be confident in the knowledge of the life that beats in your veins."

Annouchka Gravel Galouchko
BIBLIOGRAPHY

Children's Television Workshop. *The Old Woman in a Shoe.* Chds. Tel. Wkshp. 1998 0-7635-2118-3. Illustrations by Annouchka Galouchko.

Galouchko, Annouchka Gravel. *Shō and the Demons of the Deep.* Toronto: Annick Press, 1995 Paper 1-55037-393-5; Cloth 1-55037-388-6. Illustrations by the author.

—. *Le Jardin de Monsieur Préfontaine.* Laval, QC: Les 400 coups, 1997 Cloth 2-921620-22-7. Illustrations by the author.

Keens-Douglas, Richardo. *The Nutmeg Princess.* Toronto: Annick Press, 1992 Paper 1-55037-236-X; Cloth 1-55037-239-4. Illustrations by Annouchka Gravel Galouchko.✦

Leslie-Spinks, Tim and Alice Andrews. *The Treasures of Trinkamalee.* Toronto: Annick Press, 1993 Paper 1-55037-323-4; Cloth 1-55037-320-X. Illustrations by Annouchka Gravel Galouchko.

Trottier, Maxine. *The Walking Stick.* Toronto: Stoddart Kids, 1998 Cloth 0-7737-3101-6. Illustrations by Annouchka Gravel Galouchko.

Wolf, Gita. *Mala.* Toronto: Annick Press, 1996 Paper 1-55037-490-7; Cloth 1-55037-491-5. Illustrations by Annouchka Gravel Galouchko.✦

Awards

1990 Grand Prize from Salon de l'illustration Québécoise de Montreal for best unpublished illustration

1995 Governor General's Literary Award for *Shō and the Demons of the Deep*

1996 Ontario Silver Birch Award for *Shō and the Demons of the Deep*

From *Shō and the Demons of the Deep*

Luis Garay
AUTHOR/ILLUSTRATOR

Born
September 16, 1965, Granada, Nicaragua

School
Art School, Granada, Nicaragua

Where I live now
Toronto, Ontario

My favourite book when I was young
The Little Prince

Career
Children's book illustrator and fine artist

Family
"My parents and two sisters. I am single."

The room where I create
"I work in a small room at home. In this room I have the books that I use for reference purposes. I have all my materials (art supplies) to create my paintings, a drafting board and a stereo to listen to music when I am painting, because I cannot work without music."

Spare time
"Read books, watch good movies, go out with my friends, and, sometimes, go dancing."

When I was growing up
"One of the things that I enjoyed was playing baseball every single afternoon, and after that, going to the art school where I used to spend no less than five hours. It was a lot of fun for me because I enjoyed drawing. I never imagined that I was going to become an artist and an illustrator."

My first book (and how it happened)
"I never imagined that I would illustrate a children's book, but one day I met a publisher, Gordon Montador. This gentleman saw one of my paintings and liked it, so he asked me to illustrate a book about my experiences as an immigrant. I was afraid of the challenge, because I had never taken any courses in illustration before, but I did it. That was how *The Long Road* was created."

Where my ideas come from
"I like to paint everything related to my roots. I am always thinking about every single aspect of Latin America, but especially the social issues. Now I have the opportunity to go back home every year and spend a few months. I go to see different places, like old houses with broken walls, markets, poorer areas, and poor people in whom I find many expressions."

Who and what influenced me
"I am an admirer of the work of the French painter Paul Cezanne, and the Mexican muralist Diego Rivera. I think that simplicity is one of the most difficult things to achieve in life. Because of this, I consider that everyday life is my most challenging and most wonderful thing to depict."

How I work
"I spent at least eight months working on each book. I normally work six or seven hours every day, except Saturdays. I like to research a lot about each book before I start to do the drawings. I like to work on all the illustration at the same time, because in this way I find better ideas. I also work with my editor to make sure that what I am doing is fine, I am my own critic."

Something nobody knew about me (until now)
"I am a night person. I always work at night because the silence and the tranquility helps me to create better ideas, and I work faster, better, and more confidently."

My favourite book that I've created

"I love all my books, so it's hard to say 'this is my favourite' about any one book. Yet in order to illustrate a book, I have to like it. As a Latin American illustrator, I consider relating my books to my roots to be my big task."

Tips for young creators

"I'm a young illustrator, but I can say that I give my best without expecting anything back. I work with all my heart because I think kids deserve the best from us."

Luis Garay

BIBLIOGRAPHY

Aldana, Patricia. *Jade and Iron: Latin American Tales from Two Cultures.* Toronto: Groundwood, 1996 Cloth 0-88899-256-4. Illustrations by Luis Garay.

Garay, Luis. *The Long Road.* Toronto: Tundra Books, 1997 Cloth 0-88776-408-8. Illustrations by the author.

—. *Pedrito's Day.* Toronto: Stoddart, 1997 Cloth 0-7737-2999-2. Illustrations by the author.

Hughes, Monica. *A Handful of Seeds.* Toronto: Lester Publishing, 1993 Cloth 1-895555-27-2. Illustrations by Luis Garay.

Awards

1996 International Illustrated Children's and Youth Book Prize for *The Long Road*

1997 Blue Ribbon recipient from the Bulletin of the Centre for Children's Books for *Jade and Iron: Latin American Tales from Two Cultures*

From *Pedrito's Day*

Marie-Louise Gay
AUTHOR/ILLUSTRATOR

Born
June 17, 1952, Quebec City, Quebec

School
Institute of Graphic Arts, Montreal, Quebec; Montreal Museum of Fine Arts School, Montreal, Quebec; Academy of Art College, San Francisco, USA

Where I live now
Montreal, Quebec

My favourite book when I was young
Tales of Narnia by C.S. Lewis

My favourite authors now
Colette, Ursula K. LeGuin, Alice Walker, Gloria Kneeler, Gwendolyn Brooks, Torgny Lindgren, Gabriel Garcia Marquez

Career
Illustrator and author of children's books; designer of children's clothing; author and set designer of puppet plays for children

Family
"I have two boys and one cat."

The room where I create
"A many-windowed room overlooking a garden."

Spare time
"Read, travel, play tennis, ride my bicycle, go to the movies and the theatre."

When I was growing up
"I was born in Quebec City, but then we moved to Sherbrooke, Montreal, Oakville, Vancouver and finally back to Montreal. I was an avid reader because we moved around so much and books were easier to find than new friends sometimes. I don't remember any illustrations from the books I read but I vividly remember the stories. I wanted to become an actress or a history teacher and I never even dreamed that I would write and illustrate.

"When I was about 17 years old, I was doing very poorly in school. I started doing strange little bird cartoons, first on my notebooks or textbooks and then on real paper. My mother suggested that I go to a graphic arts school instead of wasting my time. What a revelation for me! I started having fun at school!"

My first book (and how it happened)
"While I was studying animation at the Montreal Museum of Fine Arts, my strange little bird drawings started to move and fly. I decided to show these cartoon drawings to magazine editors and after a lot of hard work redoing my drawings over and over again, I finally got one cartoon strip published.

"I was publishing in different magazines in Montreal when, in 1976, I was asked to illustrate my first children's book. Now, this was even more fun! Pages and pages of illustrations to do! A whole new visual world to create."

Where my ideas come from
"Sometimes from very ordinary things I see: a playground, a funny-looking cat, a child laughing, children telling stories. Other times I remember things I would do or think when I was a child. But mostly it's imagination, fantasy. It's wanting to tell stories to children, to surprise them, to make them laugh, to make them wonder."

Who and what influenced me
"I went to live in San Francisco for three years to pursue my research in illustration. San Francisco was great; it really broadened my outlook."

How I work
"I work mostly at home in a tiny room, on a huge table littered with paper, pens, brushes, inks,

pencils, etc. I am very concentrated when I work and I hate being disturbed; inspiration just flies out the window. I work mostly with watercolours and dyes (concentrated ink) and I am very meticulous, so I often end up redoing a lot of drawings.

"I often work five to seven hours a day, mostly during daylight hours, but if I'm behind schedule I'll work late into the night. It takes from four to five days to complete each illustration, starting with the first idea scribbled on a bit of paper and moving on to pencil roughs, followed by elaborate pencil drawings, black ink lines and finally colour. It can take anywhere from six months to one year to complete a book."

Tips for young creators

"I consider myself, for the most part, self-taught. It's possible to learn the basics and the techniques in illustration and writing, but I find that the creative whimsy, the original concept, in fact your personal style, can only happen after hours and hours and hours of drawing and writing by and for yourself. So, the only advice I would have for future authors or illustrators is: be prepared to work very hard and be sure you love it...I do."

Marie-Louise Gay

BIBLIOGRAPHY

Duchesne, Christiane. *Berthold et Lucrèce*. Montreal: Quebec-Amerique, 1994. Illustrations by Marie-Louise Gay. Out of print.

Gauthier, Bertrand. *Hou Ilva*. Montreal: Editions le Tamanoir, 1976. Illustrations by Marie-Louise Gay. Out of print.

—. *Dou Ilvien*. Montreal: la courte échelle, 1978. Illustrations by Marie-Louise Gay. Out of print.

—. *Hébert Luée*. Montreal: la courte échelle, 1980. Illustrations by Marie-Louise Gay. Out of print.

Gay, Marie-Louise. *De Zéro à Minuit*. Montreal: la courte échelle, 1981. Illustrations by the author. Out of print.

—. *La Soeur de Robert*. Montreal: la courte échelle, 1983. Illustrations by the author. Out of print.

—. *The Garden*. Toronto: James Lorimer & Co., 1985. Illustrations by the author. Out of print.

—. *Moonbeam on a Cat's Ear*. Toronto: Stoddart, 1986 Cloth 0-7737-2053-7. 1992 Paper 0-7736-7365-2. Illustrations by the author.✤

—. *Rainy Day Magic*. Toronto: Stoddart, 1987 Paper 0-7736-7366-0; Cloth 0-7737-2112-6. Illustrations by the author. Out of print.✤

—. *Angel And The Polar Bear*. Toronto: Stoddart, 1988 Cloth 0-7737-2166-5. 1993 Paper 0-7736-7398-9 Illustrations by the author.✤

—. *Fat Charlie's Circus*. Toronto: Stoddart, 1989 Cloth 0-7737-2285-8. 1994 Paper 0-7736-7420-9; Illustrations by the author.✤

—. *Willy Nilly*. Toronto: Stoddart, 1990 Cloth 0-7737-2429-X. 1995 Paper 0-7736-7433-0. Illustrations by the author.✤

—. *Mademoiselle Moon*. Toronto: Stoddart, 1992 Cloth 0-7737-2653-5. Illustrations by the author.✤

—. *Rabbit Blue*. Toronto: Stoddart, 1993 Cloth 0-7737-2750-7. Illustrations by the author.✤

—. *Midnight Mimi*. Toronto: Stoddart, 1994 Cloth 0-7737-28155. Illustrations by the author.✤

continued...

From *Midnight Mimi*

—. *The Three Little Pigs* (Canadian Fairy Tales Series). Toronto: Groundwood Books, 1994 Cloth 0-88999-211-4. 1997 Paper 0-88899-299-8. Illustrations by the author.

—. *Rumplestiltskin.* Toronto: Groundwood, 1997 Cloth 0-88899-279-3. Illustrations by the author.

Gillmor, Don. *When Vegetables Go Bad!* Toronto: Doubleday Canada, 1994 Cloth 0-385-25451-2. 1996 Paper 0-385-25554-3. Illustrations by Marie-Louise Gay.

—. *The Fabulous Song.* Toronto: Stoddart, 1996 Cloth 0-7737-2860-0. Illustrations by Marie-Louise Gay.

—. *The Christmas Orange.* Toronto: Stoddart Kids, 1998 Cloth 0-7737-3100-8. Illustrations by Marie-Louise Gay.

Leblanc, Louise. *That's Enough Maddie!* Trans. Sarah Cummins. Halifax: Formac, 1991 Paper 0-88780-090-4; Cloth 0-88780-091-2. Illustrations by Marie-Louise Gay.✦

—. *Maddie in Goal.* Trans. Sarah Cummins. Halifax: Formac, 1992 Paper 0-88780-202-8; Cloth 0-88780-203-6. Illustrations by Marie-Louise Gay.✦

—. *Maddie Wants Music.* Trans. Sarah Cummins. Halifax: Formac 1992 Paper 0-88780-219-2; Cloth 0-88780-220-6. Illustrations by Marie-Louise Gay.

—. *Maddie Goes to Paris.* Trans. Sarah Cummins. Halifax: Formac, 1994 Paper 0-88780-278-8, Cloth 0-88780-279-6. Illustrations by Marie-Louise Gay.✦

—. *Maddie in Danger.* Trans. Sarah Cummins. Halifax: Formac, 1995 Paper 0-88780-306-7; Cloth 0-88780-307-5. Illustrations by Marie-Louise Gay.✦

—. *Maddie in Hospital.* Trans. Sarah Cummins. Halifax: Formac, 1996 Paper 0-88780-374-1; Cloth 0-88780-375-X. Illustrations by Marie-Louise Gay.✦

—. *Sophie vit un cauchemar.* Montreal: la courte échelle, 1996 2-89021-267-X. Illustrations by Marie-Louise Gay.

—. *Sophie devient sage.* Montreal: la courte échelle, 1997 2-89021-298-X. Illustrations by Marie-Louise Gay.

Lee, Dennis. *Lizzy's Lion.* Don Mills: Stoddart, 1984 Cloth 0-7737-0078-1. 1993 Paper 0-7736-7397-0. Illustrations by Marie-Louise Gay.

Nicolas, Sylvie. *Le Beurre de Doudou.* St. Lambert: Editions Héritage, 1997. Illustrations by Marie-Louise Gay.

Papineau, Lucie. *Monsieur Soleil.* St. Lambert: Editions Héritage, 1997. Illustrations by Marie-Louise Gay.

Wynne-Jones, Tim. *The Last Piece of Sky.* Toronto: Groundwood Books, 1993 Cloth 0-88899-181-9. Illustrations by Marie-Louise Gay.✦

Awards

1984 Alvin Bélisle Prize (Quebec)

1984 Canada Council Children's Literature Prize for *Lizzy's Lion*

1984 Canada Council Children's Literature Prize for *Drôle d'École*

1987 Amelia Frances Howard-Gibbon Illustrator's Award for *Moonbeam on a Cat's Ear*

1987 Governor General's Literary Award for *Rainy Day Magic*

1988 Amelia Frances Howard-Gibbon Illustrator's Award for *Rainy Day Magic*

1993 White Ravens Selection, International Youth Library, Munich for *Mademoiselle Moon*

1997 Mr. Christie's Book Award for *The Fabulous Song*

Selected articles about Marie-Louise Gay

Davis, Marie. "'Un Penchant Pour la Diagonale': An Interview with Marie-Louise Gay." *Canadian Children's Literature* 60 (1990): 52-73.

Jenkinson, Dave. "Portraits: Marie-Louise Gay: Award Winning Picture Book Author and Illustrator." *Emergency Librarian* May-June 1992: 65.

O'Brien, Leacy. "An Interview with Marie-Louise Gay." *Canadian Materials* Mar. 1989: 54-55.

Sarfati, Sonia. "Á en attraper un coup de lune!" *La Presse* [Montreal] 27 Sept. 1992.

Phoebe Gilman
AUTHOR/ILLUSTRATOR

Born
April 4, 1940, New York City, New York, USA

School
Public School 86, Bronx, New York; High School of Art and Design, Manhattan, New York; Hunter College, New York; Art Students League, New York; Bezalel Academy, Jerusalem, Israel

Where I live now
Etobicoke, Ontario

Favourite books when young
Andrew Lang's fairy tales

Favourite book now
"I can't choose one. I am constantly reading. Some of my favourite authors are Jane Urquhart, Isabel Allende and Barbara Kingsolver."

Career
Author and illustrator of children's books

Family
"I am married to Brian Bender. We have three children: Ingrid, Jason and Melissa and two grandchildren, Ariana and Emily. We have a cat, Minoo, a turtle, Dweezil, a budgie, Bernice (he's a boy but we didn't know that when we named him), and two rats, Frodo and Gimley."

The room where I create
"My studio is a room that we built over the garage of our house. It has a skylight, and a balcony that overlooks the garden."

Spare time
"I like to read, watch the water, go for walks, play with friends and family, go to the movies and go ice-skating."

When I was growing up
"My mother chose my name out of a book. She thought it was special and unusual. I didn't like it and tried to get people to give me a nickname. No one did. I guess having an unusual name helped to make me feel different. I don't mind being different now.

"If I didn't share my mother's taste in names, I did share her love of books. My favourites were fairy tales. I remember covering up the pictures with my hands. It used to bother me when the pictures didn't match the images that the author's words painted in my head. I still do that.

"I think of myself as an artist rather than a writer. It was because of my friend Gladys Hopkins, that I became an artist. When we were about to graduate from P.S. 86, she came up with the brilliant idea that we should try out for one of the special high schools in Manhattan. That way we could avoid the terrible fate of attending the all-girls high school, which was right next door to P.S. 86. That is how I happened to go to The High School of Art and Design."

My first book (and how it happened)
"It was because of my daughter, Ingrid, that I wrote my first book, *The Balloon Tree*. It was her balloon that started it all. She let go of it and up, up, up it flew until ... kablam! It popped on the branch of a tree. I wished that tree would magically sprout balloons. It didn't, but I made up a story for Ingrid about a magic tree that blossomed balloons. We liked it so much, I decided to write it down. And that's how I came to write *The Balloon Tree*. It is not how I came to be published. That took 15 years of rewriting and umpty-zillion rejection slips."

Who and what influenced me
"My mother. She loved to read and she loved to write. She believed I was special even when everybody else thought I was crazy, (when I kept rewriting *The Balloon Tree*, trying to get it published)."

How I work
"As Dr. Seuss once wrote, 'A thing my sister likes to do in evenings

after supper, is sit around in her small room and use her thinker-upper.' That's what I do. I turn my thinker-upper on and it thinks up all these things. What I don't do is listen to the little voice in my head that says, 'That idea stinks.' I just keep working away, fixing and changing my picture or story until it's as good as I can make it. Sometimes that takes a month, sometimes that takes a year, sometimes that takes 15 years."

Something nobody knew about me (until now)

"I once vacuumed a chocolate chip cookie. I made it as a surprise for my husband and since I didn't want him to see it, I hid it in the oven. Unfortunately, I forgot it was there when I turned the oven on to make supper. I remembered the cookie too late to prevent the paper that covered it from melting a bit. When I tried to scrape the paper off the top of the cookie it looked messy, all those crumbs and bits of paper. So I figured if I held the vacuum hose over it, not on it, it would smooth it out. Whomp! It sucked up a big hole in the middle of my cookie. Now I had a

doughnut cookie. I filled up the hole with chocolate icing and Brian never knew, but my children knew... and now you know too!"

Tips for young creators

"Get a balloon and let it go. Read. Read. Read! Write. Write. Write! To do anything well takes practice. Don't give up. Keep on trying. Don't be afraid of criticism. Learn from it."

Phoebe Gilman

BIBLIOGRAPHY

Gilman, Phoebe. *The Balloon Tree*. Richmond Hill: Scholastic Canada, 1984 Paper 0-590-71257-8; Cloth 0-590-71410-4. Illustrations by the author.✦

—. *Jillian Jiggs*. Richmond Hill: Scholastic Canada, 1985 Paper 0-590-74875-0; Cloth 0-590-71548-8; Big Book 0-590-71823-1. Illustrations by the author.

—. *Little Blue Ben*. Richmond Hill: Scholastic Canada, 1986 Paper 0-590-73317-6; Cloth 0-590-71692-1; Big Book 0-590-73273-0. Illustrations by the author.

—. *The Wonderful Pigs of Jillian Jigs*. Richmond Hill: Scholastic Canada, 1988 Cloth 0-590-71868-1; Big Book 0-590-71869-X. 1990 Paper 0-590-74847-5. Illustrations by the author.✦

—. *Grandma and the Pirates*. Richmond Hill: Scholastic Canada, 1988. 1990 Cloth 0-590-73221-8. 1992 Paper 0-590-74840-8. Illustrations by the author.✦

—. *Something From Nothing*. Richmond Hill: Scholastic Canada, 1992 Paper 0-590-74557-3; Cloth 0-590-73802-X; Big Book 0-590-72827-X. Illustrations by the author.

—. *Jillian Jiggs to the Rescue*. Richmond Hill: Scholastic Canada, 1994 Paper 0-590-24178-8; Cloth 0-590-74616-2. Illustrations by the author.✦

—. *The Gypsy Princess*. Toronto: Scholastic, 1995 Paper 0-590-12389-0; Cloth 0-590-24441-8. Illustrations by the author.✦

—. *Pirate Pearl*. Toronto: Scholastic, 1998 Cloth 0-590-12495-1. Illustrations by the author.

Little, Jean, and Maggie deVries. *Once Upon a Golden Apple*. Toronto: Penguin Books Canada, 1991 Paper 0-14-054164-0; Cloth 0-670-82963-3. Illustrations by Phoebe Gilman.

Awards

1993 The Ruth Schwartz Children's Book Award for *Something From Nothing*

1993 Vicky Metcalf Award for a body of work

1993 Sydney Taylor Award for *Something From Nothing*

Selected articles about Phoebe Gilman

Gaitskell, Susan. "Phoebe Gilman." *Presenting Canscaip*. Ed. Barbara Greenwood. Markham: Pembroke Publishers, 1990: 122-127.

Greenwood, Barbara, ed. *The Canscaip Companion*. Markham: Pembroke Publishers, 1994.

Perly Rae, Arlene. "Phoebe Gilman (writer illustrator)." *Everybody's Favorites*. New York: Viking, 1997.

From *Pirate Pearl*

Celia Godkin
AUTHOR/ILLUSTRATOR

Born
April 15, 1948, London, England

School
London University, England;
Ontario College of Art, Toronto;
University of Toronto

Where I live now
Toronto, Ontario

My favourite books when I was young
"*Winnie the Pooh* and Beatrix Potter's books, especially her illustrations."

My favourite book now
"*A Fine Balance* by Rohinton Mistry."

Career
"Biologist; then a scientific illustrator and children's author/illustrator. I also teach art at the University of Toronto."

Family
"I live alone with my cat Trixie."

The room where I create
"My office/studio has a sloping drafting table for drawing and painting and a big desk where I write. There are bookshelves with wildlife magazines, field guides and other reference books. There are deeper shelves and drawers for art supplies, filing cabinets full of manuscripts, illustrations, business records and teaching notes.

There's a fax machine, but no computer, as I use the one in my office at the university."

Spare time
"I like to read or paint in oils. I own an old stone church in eastern Ontario, which has been converted to a home. The church is rented out, but there is a cabin at the back where I stay. I love gardening, so I have a flower garden there as well as an allotment garden in Toronto."

When I was growing up
When Celia was two, her family moved to Rio de Janiero, Brazil where they spent most of the next 10 years. "My favourite memories of that time are of the ocean voyages — eight in all — between England and Brazil. We would be two weeks at sea — a week out of sight of land — and we'd stop at places like Lisbon, Portugal, the islands of Madeira or Tenerife and the ports of Recife or Salvador in northern Brazil."

My first book (and how it happened)
"In 1972, friend Arnold Skolnick, a well-known New York illustrator, asked me to write a children's nature book for him to illustrate. So I wrote three stories and he prepared some sample illustrations. We went looking for a publisher but had no luck.

"Years later, I illustrated the adult book *Endangered Species: Canada's Disappearing Wildlife* by Clive Roots. Encouraged by its success, I prepared the illustrations for *Wolf Island*, one of the books I'd written in 1972, and showed it to my publisher. This time the book was accepted and published in 1989 — 17 years after I wrote it."

Where my ideas come from
"Ideas pop into my head when I'm least expecting them. The central idea for my first three books (*Wolf Island, Ladybug Garden* and *Sea Otter Inlet*) came from flipping my original idea about-face. I knew I wanted to write stories which showed how everything in nature is interconnected, and at that time there were lots of news items about introductions — plants or animals arriving in a new location and disrupting everything. The problem with that idea was that it was hard to see how I could arrive at a happy ending. I knew it was important to give children a hopeful message. Then I thought: what if, instead of adding an animal, I take one out? Then I can bring it back at the end to restore the balance. Once I'd hit on that idea, then it was just a question of finding examples of where that had happened."

Who and what influenced me

"Ever since I can remember, I've loved animals, written stories and drawn pictures. In high school I had a wonderfully eccentric biology teacher, Miss Walker, who maintained that she was a drug addict because she drank gallons of tea. Though I was good at a whole range of subjects and not particularly brilliant at biology, I think it was her influence that headed me in that direction initially. But when my career as a biologist landed me in a dead-end job where I spent half my time cleaning out dirty animal cages, I decided to embark on a career as a scientific illustrator and from there it was a short step to illustrating children's nature books."

How I work

"First comes the idea. Then I collect all the background information I can, both for the story and — either then or later — for the pictures. Next I write the story. When that's done, I put it away for weeks or even months so I can come back to it with fresh eyes.

"When it's been revised and polished to my satisfaction, I break it into images and prepare detailed pencil sketches, leaving space for the text, if necessary. I may go on revising the text as I work on the illustrations. Once the texts and sketches are approved by the publisher, I go to final art."

Something nobody knew about me (until now)

"I used to work at the Reptile Breeding Foundation, a non-profit organization which bred endangered snakes, tortoises and charials (Indian crocodiles) to save them from extinction. One of my jobs was to feed the animals. Sometimes they tried to eat me!"

My favourite book that I've created

"I think *Sea Otter Inlet* is my best book in terms of the quality of writing and illustration, but *Flying Lessons*, which I've just completed, was the most fun to do because it was so quick and easy."

Tips for young creators

"Once you've written your story and drawn your pictures, show them to someone who can give you helpful feedback. The person who can help you best will be one who encourages you but who will also make suggestions for improvements. Remember: there is always room for improvement; if you don't agree with others' advice, don't follow it; and never give up."

Celia Godkin

BIBLIOGRAPHY

Godkin, Celia. *Wolf Island*. Markham: Fitzhenry and Whiteside, 1989 Paper 0-7167-6513-6. 1993 Cloth 1-55041-095-4. Illustrations by the author.

—. *Ladybug Garden*. Markham: Fitzhenry and Whiteside, 1995 Cloth 1-55041-083-0. 1997 Paper 1-55041-092-X. Illustrations by the author.

—. *Sea Otter Inlet*. Markham: Fitzhenry and Whiteside, 1997 Cloth 1-55041-080-6. Illustrations by the author.

—. *Flying Lessons*. Markham: Fitzhenry and Whiteside, 1999. Illustrations by the author.

Roots, Clive. *Endangered Species: Canada's Disappearing Wildlife*. Markham: Fitzhenry and Whiteside, 1987. Illustrations by Celia Godkin. Out of print.

Woods, Shirley. *Black Nell: the Adventures of a Coyote*. Toronto: Groundwood Books, 1998 Paper 0-88899-319-6; Cloth 0-88899-318-8. Illustrations by Celia Godkin.

Awards

1990 Children's Literature Roundtable of Canada (best information book) for *Wolf Island*

Selected articles about Celia Godkin

Gale Research Co. *Contemporary Authors: Something About the Author*. Detroit: Gale Research Co., 1991. Vol. 66: 90.

Hirsch et al. *Science Explorations 10*. "Career Profiles: Celia Godkin—Scientific Illustrator." Toronto: John Wiley and Sons, 1987: 184.

From *Sea Otter Inlet*

Georgia Graham
ILLUSTRATOR

Born
October 28, 1959 Calgary, Alberta

School
Alberta College of Art

Where I live now
On a farm north of Lacombe, Alberta

My favourite book when I was young
"*Miss Pickerell and the Geiger Counter* (it's a wonder I became an illustrator)."

My favourite book now
The Bible

Career
"Waitress while I was in Art College (I used to spill on people and *not* get good tips). Commercial artist. Now, as well as writing and illustrating children's books and visiting 40 to 70 schools per year, I make prints (sometimes from my book illustrations) and I sell them."

Family
"Husband and two children: daughter Paige in Grade 7, and son Myles in Grade 5."

The room where I create
"I have an art room that I work in. It's my favourite place to be. I do my illustrations on a drafting table. Beside it, I have ten drawers in which I keep hundreds of colours of pastels and pencil crayons. I like to have a flower beside me when I work. When I type stories, I sit at my computer in a chair shaped like a hand. I call it 'Glovy' — it makes me feel creative."

When I was growing up
"I would draw and draw and draw. My parents and my brothers were not at all artistic, but my sister is a pretty good artist. My mother was a teacher.

"I have many engineers in my family. My dad, sister, brother, brother-in-law and nephew are all engineers. They make more money than an artist like me... but who do you think has more fun?"

My first book (and how it happened)
"My first book was *The Most Beautiful Kite in the World*. Dennis Johnson, from Red Deer College Press, called me up and gave me the manuscript. It was very difficult wanting to be a children's illustrator in Alberta 16 years ago. I wanted to move to Toronto. Then I married a farmer from Central Alberta — so I was here for good. All I can say is thank goodness for the Red Deer College Press. It publishes beautiful quality children's books and is half an hour from where the cows and I live."

Where my ideas come from
"My ideas come from daydreaming. Usually I think of my ideas for a long time before pencil ever touches down on paper."

Who and what influenced me
"One instructor in Art College loved children's books and used to bring them in all the time. That's when I got the bug for it."

How I work
"Daydreaming about my idea. Telling everybody I know my idea, whether they want to hear it or not. Doing small rough sketches and a rough manuscript. Rendering the colour illustrations for 1000 to 1500 hours per book. Then the publisher sends them to the printer (in Hong Kong, Singapore or Mexico), and I pray they don't get lost."

Something nobody knew about me (until now)
"I was reading-disabled as a small child (until about Grade 5). Libraries were the most frightening place to be."

My favourite book that I've created

"My latest, *The Strongest Man This Side of Cremona*. I have illustrated six books but this is the first that I wrote as well. I guess that means I'm an author. I would like to encourage children with reading difficulties that they might just be an author someday too."

Tips for young creators

"In drawing, don't copy cartoon characters, create your own; exercise your imagination. Develop your own personal style, or even a few styles. In writing, think about your own true experiences."

Georgia Graham

BIBLIOGRAPHY

Alderson, Sue Ann. *Comet's Tale*. Edmonton: Tree Frog Press, 1982. Illustrations by Georgia Graham. Out of print.

Fairbridge, Lynne. *We Need a Moose*. Colorado: Victor-Chariot Publications, 1996 Cloth 156-476-565-2. Illustrations by Georgia Graham.

Graham, Georgia. *The Strongest Man This Side of Cremona*. Alberta: Red Deer College Press, 1998 Cloth 0-88995-182-9. Illustrations by the author.

Morck, Irene. *Tiger's New Cowboy Boots*. Red Deer: Red Deer College Press, 1996 Cloth 0-88995-153-5. Illustrations by Georgia Graham.

Spalding, Andrea. *The Most Beautiful Kite in the World*. Red Deer: Red Deer College Press, 1988. Illustrations by Georgia Graham. Out of print.

Vaage, Carol. *Bibi and the Bull*. Edmonton: Dragon Hill Publishing, 1995 Paper 1-896124-00-3; Cloth 1-896124-02-X. Illustrations by Georgia Graham.

Awards

1996 Alberta Children's Title of the Year for *Tiger's New Cowboy Boots*

1996 Alberta Book Illustration Award for *Tiger's New Cowboy Boots*

1996 Western Horseman Christmas Gift Selection for *Tiger's New Cowboy Boots*

From *Tiger's New Cowboy Boots*

Edward (Ted) Harrison
AUTHOR/ILLUSTRATOR

Born
August 28, 1926, Wingate,
County Durham, England

School
Wellfield Grammar School;
Hartlepool College of Art at
King's College, University of
Durham, National Diploma in
Design and Art Teacher's
Diploma; University of Alberta,
B.Ed., Edmonton, Alberta

Where I live now
Victoria, British Columbia

My favourite book when I was young
The Sandalwood Traders by R.M.
Ballantyne

My favourite book now
London by Edward Rutherford

Career
Teacher of art, 1951 to 1979;
fulltime artist, writer and illustrator, 1979 to present

Family
"Wife, Nicky, and son, Charles.
My present pet is Maggie, a dear
fluffy Paisley terrier with a good
yap and a loving nature to all."

The room where I create
"My studio."

Spare time
"Gardening, feeding many bird
species, cooking exotic dishes
and breads, and watching the
History Channel on TV. I also
enjoy reading novels and non-
fiction on many topics, and
surfing the net."

When I was growing up
"I was a keen Cub and Boy Scout.
I loved camping and hiking, also
youth hostelling with my bicycle
and close school friends. I
played a lot of soccer, rugby and
cricket. I loved reading fiction
and non-fiction books, especially those about art and
history."

My first book (and how it happened)
"I was teaching native children
on a reserve in Alberta and
found that no book mirrored
their culture. So, with the
assistance of the Grade 2 class, I
wrote and illustrated A *North-
land Alphabet*. It was distributed
free to native schools in 1968."

Where my ideas come from
"My ideas come from everyday
life around me, and from extensive travel. I am extremely
interested in other cultures,
especially those of the First
Nations and those of Southeast
Asia."

Ted's careers have taken him
around the world. From 1945 to
1948, he served in the British
Army Intelligence Corps and was
posted in India, Egypt, Kenya,
Uganda and Somaliland. From
1951 to 1980, Ted was a teacher
in England, Malaysia, and Northern Alberta.

Ted was the first non-Asian
artist to decorate the Sam Poh
Tong Buddhist Temple in Ipoh,
Malaysia, with a mural of Buddha
receiving enlightenment under
the Boh Tree. He also received a
commission to decorate the King
and Queen of Thailand's Malayan
residence with a paper sculpture
of the Thai regal coat-of-arms.

Who and what influenced me
"My teachers Ben Bailey and
Freddie Grice. My mother and
father. My painter friend,
Norman Cornish and my old
Scout master, Jerry Gordon."

How I work
"Concentrated stretches of hard
intense work and study followed
by periods of absolute idleness
and daydreaming. I believe that
controlled daydreaming is the
clue to inventive creativity."

Ted's books begin as pictures
in his mind. He works out scenes
and incidents and then creates a
story around the images; the
visual image is crucial to him.

His writing and illustrating is done in his painting studio and the chair he uses is important to him, because the round casters enable him to move quickly and easily. In the past, Ted preferred to work with a fountain pen. These days, however, he "finishes off" his work with his word processor. Ted loves to use paper without lines, as it gives him a greater sense of freedom. "Lines indicate other people's guidance to me."

Something nobody knew about me (until now)

"I have a working knowledge of the German language and once studied both Urdu and Kiswahili while serving with the British Intelligence Corps.

"As a student, I worked as an assistant chef in an English hotel and can turn out bread, cookies and desserts. I love cooking Chinese stir-fry and turning out a full-course meal on special occasions."

My favourite book that I've created

"*O Canada* and *The Last Horizon*, equally."

Tips for young creators

"Always be curious, observant, and interested in whatever you do. Read informative books and practise your skills to the best of your ability."

Ted Harrison

BIBLIOGRAPHY

Harrison, Ted. *Children of the Yukon*. Montreal: Tundra Books, 1977. 1988 Paper 0-88776-163-1. Illustrations by the author.

—. *The Last Horizon*. Toronto: Merritt Publishers, 1980. Illustrations by the author. Out of print.

—. *A Northern Alphabet*. Montreal: Tundra Books, 1982. Rev. ed. 1989 Paper 0-88776-233-6. Illustrations by the author.

—. *The Blue Raven*. Toronto: Macmillan Canada, 1989. Illustrations by the author. Out of print.

—. *O Canada*. Toronto: Kids Can Press, 1992 Cloth 1-55074-087-3. Illustrations by the author.

Service, Robert W. *The Cremation of Sam McGee*. Toronto: Kids Can Press, 1986 Cloth 0-919964-92-3. Illustrations by Ted Harrison.

—. *The Shooting of Dan McGrew*. Toronto: Kids Can Press, 1988 Cloth 0-921103-35-2. 1989 Paper 0-88839-224-9. Illustrations by Ted Harrison.

From *The Cremation of Sam McGee*

Awards

1984 IBBY Certificate of Honour for Illustration for *A Northern Alphabet*

1987 Order of Canada

1987 Parents' Choice Award for *The Cremation of Sam McGee*

1991 Honorary Doctor of Athabasca University

1998 Made Honorary Admiral of HMCS *Whitehorse* by the City of Whitehorse

Stéphane Jorisch
ILLUSTRATOR

Born
Brussels, Belgium, 1956; arrived Montreal, 1957

School
BFA in graphic design

Where I live now
"I live in St. Lambert, Quebec, very close to the St. Lawrence River."

Career
"Jobs held in the past: dishwasher; hardware clerk; ski repairman; library clerk; sailing instructor; industrial designer; architectural illustrator etc."

Family
"My wife: Monique (36); three kids: Edith (8), Antoine (5), Clara (3); and me. Our goldfish just died recently. We babysit our neighbour's cat every other weekend; he is called Jule."

The room where I create
"I work in a large studio on the fourth floor, surrounded by windows from which I have an incredible view of the city. I share this space with five other designers and illustrators. We have a lot of fun and we converse on almost every possible topic. Holding a grudge or being unsociable is not allowed and one is quickly brought to terms with collective witty remarks.

"I work from 9 to 6 every day, mainly making pictures for books, magazines, ads and articles for museums. I also direct two collections of fairy tales for Les 400 coups. One is a collection of fairy tales, witches and monsters for ages 4–7. The other is a collection of whimsical pictures and words. I order the work from other writers and artists."

Spare time
"When I was very small my parents were really scared I could get hurt so I wasn't even allowed to have a bike. So, you guessed it, I read a lot. One of my favourite titles was *The Wind in the Willows* and the C.S. Lewis *Narnia* series. Later we moved by the St. Lawrence River, where I spent a great amount of time in anything that floated: motorboats, sailboats, skiffs, and canoes (I also bought a bike). Now, I also ski, windsurf, cross-country ski, and I have even practised rock climbing (my parents are growing less worried)."

Who and what influenced me
"My dad who draws very well and used to illustrate comic strips in Europe. I also have a weakness for Flemish painters before the sixteenth century, the great photographers of the first 30 years of this century, and sculpture."

My first book (and how it happened)
"Philip Béha, who is himself an illustrator, was a director of a collection and he offered me my first book to illustrate. It was a long tedious process and a 'mess.' Luckily, by coincidence, another editor asked me to illustrate a remake of the same title 12 years later, and it ended as finalist for the Governor General's Award.

"I have one or two copies of the 'mess' edition hidden away and I pull it out to make sure I am getting better."

How I work
"I think about the project in question for a while. When visual images begin to take shape, I make very quick sketches for the project. I decide on the one I prefer and adjust it to the layout. I then retrace the sketch on watercolour, gouache and sometimes a little acrylic paint. Et voilà, fini."

Where my ideas come from
"I love looking at photographs of people and places. I buy a lot of photo albums of famous photographers. Somehow they help create the images I want. I also have a very good visual memory which helps enormously in putting the facts on paper."

My favourite book that I've created

"*Charlotte et l'isle du destin*. It is a 48-page picture book which was published in September 1998. It was co-written by Olivier Lasser and myself. It is the story of a little girl who lives on a strange island who seeks adventure, and is helped by her friend the dragon-dog, Zigg."

Something nobody knew about me (until now)

"Sometimes when I think up stories, when no one is looking, I act out what happens."

Tips for young creators

"Sometimes, a doodle says more than a drawing we have spent several days to produce. Time is not always a factor in the quality of the work."

Stéphane Jorisch

BIBLIOGRAPHY

Baker, Barrie. *The Village of a Hundred Smiles and Other Stories.* Toronto: Annick Press, 1998 1-55037-522-9. Illustrations by Stéphane Jorisch.

Jorisch, Stéphane and Olivier Lasser. *Charlotte et l'île du destin.* Laval: Les 400 coups, 1998 Cloth 2-921620-13-8. Illustrations by Stéphane Jorisch.

Papineau, Lucie. *Casse-Noisette*. St. Lambert: Héritage jeunesse, 1996 Cloth 2-7625-8407-8. Illustrations by Stéphane Jorisch.

Soulières, Robert. *Le baiser maléfique*. Laval: Les 400 coups, 1995 2-921620-06-5. Illustrations by Stéphane Jorisch.

Vandal, André. *Le monde selon Jean de* (traditional). Montreal: DV éditeurs, 1992 2-89410-149-X. Illustrations by Stéphane Jorisch.

Awards

1993 Governor General Literary Award for *Le monde selon de Jean de...*

From *The Village of a Hundred Smiles and Other Stories*

Murray Kimber
ILLUSTRATOR

Born
April 11, 1964

School
Alberta College of Art and Design, Calgary

Where I live now
Pahuca, Hidalgo, Mexico

My favourite books when I was young
"Comic books, virtually all of them but in particular *Batman* and *The Incredible Hulk.*"

My favourite books now
"All-time favourite: *Without Feathers*, Woody Allen. Current favourite: *Into Thin Air*, Jon Krakauer. Favourite children's book: *The Polar Express*, Chris Van Allsburg."

Career
A full-time artist; previously, a graphic designer in an advertising agency in Regina.

Family
Wife, Kari; daughter, Kristin; dog, Sam Chavez

The room where I create
"My studio is in a large spare room on the second floor of our house in Mexico. One side of the room is entirely made up of windows so the quality of light in the studio is excellent. I have photos and pictures pasted all over one wall of things that I think are interesting or samples of artists work that I admire."

Spare time
"At the moment my largest spare time activity is discovering Mexico and the countless interesting places to visit. After that, learning Spanish. My next door neighbour, Pepé, is my tutor. I also play on a volleyball team and this year I am going to teach myself the guitar."

When I was growing up
"My fantasy was to be a professional hockey player or something equally glamorous. However, nothing could hold my interest the way drawing did. It was simply something that I really felt comfortable with, even though I was constantly getting frustrated because I could not always draw exactly what I wanted to. That is what drove me to become better. With things like sports I was competitive to impress other people. With art, I was competitive to impress myself.

"As a kid, I was fortunate enough to live in a neighbourhood with a lot of other kids, so we all hung out together playing street hockey or riding our bikes through the coulees near Lethbridge. I couldn't believe it when one day a city crew dug up our entire street to replace the water lines and left mountains of dirt and a huge trench all along our street. We had the best dirt lump flights ever."

My first book (and how it happened)
"My first book was *Josepha: A Prairie Boy's Story*, by Jim McGugan. I had not been looking to illustrate a book but the publisher had been referred to me by another artist who thought my work suited the feel of this prairie story. I began work on it having no idea what was involved or that it would take me nearly two years to complete 16 paintings and six small drawings. I don't think the publisher had any idea it would take me over two years either.

"When the book came out I had an exhibition of all the original paintings hung in the order that they appear in the book with sections of the story under each painting so you could follow the story as you looked at the paintings."

Where my ideas come from
"In the case of a book, my inspiration comes from the author. If I am inspired by the way they write, a certain character, or the way they describe the setting, my ideas grow from that. I translate their inspiration into my own and run with it.

"Also, I think your mind is like

a huge storage bin of images, places, bits of information, memories of moments from your life that you can continually revisit and rummage through like a trunk in the attic to apply to new pictures you are making. Your memories are like photos that are charged with your own emotion."

Who and what influenced me

"As a child, the illustrations in comic books, *MAD* magazine, and political cartoons in magazines and newspapers (remember, this was before computer animation). Now, as an adult, I still love comic books though my tastes are different. I also love the work of the French painter Edgar Degas, the Austrian painter Gustav Klimt, and Edward Hopper of the United States. I am influenced by other artists, but there are too many to mention."

How I work

"I make numerous rough drawings on a pad or in my sketchbook that represent different solutions or variations for what will become a single illustration. At this point I am only interested in the idea or the concept and not so much how it looks. Then I take the idea I think is strongest and work at perfecting the composition, the look of the figure, put in details, do research and find reference if I need to, and essentially push and pull the drawing until it is as strong as I can make it. At this point I can usually see it in my head as a painting and can tell if it will be a good illustration. Next, I redraw the sketch onto canvas that has been primed with gesso. I loosely block in general areas of colour using acrylic paint and when I have covered the entire canvas, I begin to work in oil paint to finish the illustration."

From *Fern Hill*

Something nobody knew about me (until now)

"In Mexico my favourite food is tacos, which taste much better than tacos I have had in Canada. If I could, I would eat them for breakfast."

My favourite book that I've created

"I have only done two books so far, so fast. I really don't have much to choose from. Honestly I don't have a favourite."

Tips for young creators

"For young artists, draw a lot and draw often. Keep a sketchbook of your work so that you can see how your drawing has changed and progressed. If you do this you will find that you have an easier time getting ideas and being able to express them because you won't get hung up about not being able to draw. Like any pursuit of excellence you may always wish to draw better, but one of the most important skills for an illustrator is to be able to get the ideas out of your head and onto paper."

Murray Kimber

BIBLIOGRAPHY

McGugan, Jim. *Josepha: A Prairie Boy's Story*. Red Deer: Red Deer College Press, 1994 Cloth 0-88995-101-2. 1995 Paper 0-88995-142-X. Illustrations by Murray Kimber.

Thomas, Dylan. *Fern Hill*. Red Deer: Red Deer College Press, 1997 Cloth 0-88995-164-0. Illustrations by Murray Kimber.

Awards

1994 Governor General's Literary Award for Children's Illustration for *Josepha: A Prairie Boy's Story*

1995 Elizabeth Mrazik-Cleaver Canadian Picture Book Award for *Josepha: A Prairie Boy's Story*

1998 R. Ross Annett Award for Children's Literature for *Fern Hill*

Maryann Kovalski
AUTHOR/ILLUSTRATOR

Born
June 4, 1951, Bronx, New York

School
St. Martin of Tours; Public School 19; St. Barnabas High School; The School of Visual Arts; all in New York

Where I live now
Toronto, Ontario

My favourite book when I was young
Babar by Jean de Brunhoff

My favourite book now
"Anything by William Steig."

Career
Illustrator and writer

Family
Husband, Gregory Sheppard; daughters, Genevieve and Joanna; one dog, Max, and a rabbit, Lucy

The room where I create
"I have a studio in my house."

Spare time
"Go to movies, exercise, write, play with my kids, walk my dog, ride horses, travel and read. I like to read a lot."

When I was growing up
"We lived across the street from a big laundry factory. One of my favourite things to do was have my brothers push me down the alley where the trucks picked up and delivered stuff in a large canvas bag on wheels. I also loved sitting on the roof of my building and looking off at the distant buildings of Manhattan."

My first book (and how it happened)
"A mutual friend told the publisher of Kids Can Press how much I wanted to do children's books and they gave me a call. I had six weeks to do the book. I guess they liked what I did because they gave me another. I wrote *Brenda and Edward* and they liked that and then my career started to take off with offers from other publishers."

Where my ideas come from
"I get my ideas from the things I see and hear all around me. I also remember my childhood well, and the things that intrigued me then. I remember a couple who ran what we called an ice cream parlour. They lived above the store and I was deeply curious to know what their apartment looked like. I wanted to know what the back room of the restaurant looked like too. Aladdin's cave could not have intrigued my imagination more. I suppose my ideas come from my own curiosity about people."

Who and what influenced me
"Though there were many picture books that I adored as a child, I think the person who most influenced me was Arnold Lobel. I met him when a partner and I were running a gallery that sold originals from children's books. Before the meeting, I went out and looked at as many of his books as I could. I looked closely. And I realized how very good he was. When you see someone doing something so well, it's often very influential in helping you decide what you want to do. I knew, after I looked at those books that I wanted to do children's books."

How I work
"I sketch and doodle. Then I polish my rough sketch by using tracing paper to trace over everything I like and redraw what I don't. When the rough looks the way I want it to look, I transfer it to a good watercolour paper. This I do either by using a light box or covering the back of the tracing paper with pencil and taping it down to good paper — like carbon paper. I use gouache (opaque watercolour paint), coloured pencils, anything I can find."

My favourite book that I've created
"For story, I think it's *Frank and Zelda* and for pictures, maybe *The Wheels on the Bus*. There are always bits I like in my books and bits I don't like."

Tips for young creators

"Don't try to get published too soon. Have a stash of secret writings that you don't show anybody. Write every embarrassing detail. You'll learn how to write honestly. Doodle and draw constantly. Make drawing as natural a thing to do as breathing. It will loosen your hand and make you feel less nervous about drawing well when it comes time to actually draw a picture. If you're right handed, make some drawings with your left hand and vice versa. Try to draw badly. You'll make yourself laugh and find that what comes out isn't half bad. Draw really big. Copy some drawings you like. Draw your room and what's in it. Draw your ceiling — there's more up there than you ever imagined. Get a mirror and draw yourself. Use a Xerox machine. Draw a tiny thing and blow it up and up and up. Trace it and turn it over. Draw circles, cubes, triangles, ovals and cylinders."

Maryann Kovalski

BIBLIOGRAPHY

Atwood, Margaret. *Princess Prunella and the Purple Peanut*. Toronto: Key Porter, 1997; Paper 1-55013-789-1. Cloth 1-55013-732-8. Illustrations by Maryann Kovalski.

Booth, David, ed. *Doctor Knickerbocker and Other Rhymes: A Canadian Collection*. Toronto: Kids Can Press, 1993 Cloth 1-55074-079-2. 1995 Paper 1-55074-253-1. Illustrations by Maryann Kovalski.

Bourgeois, Paulette. *Grandma's Secret*. Toronto: Kids Can Press, 1989. 1991 Paper 1-55074-034-2. Illustrations by Maryann Kovalski.✣

Fitch, Sheree. *Mabel Murple*. Toronto: Doubleday, 1995 Cloth 0-385-25480-6. 1997 Paper 0-385-25634-5. Illustrations by Maryann Kovalski.

Gelman, Rita Golden. *I Went to the Zoo*. Richmond Hill: Scholastic Canada, 1993 Cloth 0-590-74619-7. 1995 Paper 0-590-24533-3. Illustrations by Maryann Kovalski.

Green, John F. *Alice and the Birthday Giant*. Richmond Hill: Scholastic Canada, 1989 Cloth 0-590-73139-4. 1991 Paper 0-590-73138-6. Illustrations by Maryann Kovalski.

—. *Junk-Pile Jennifer*. Richmond Hill: Scholastic Canada, 1991 Cloth 0-590-73873-9. 1993 Paper 0-590-73680-9. Illustrations by Maryann Kovalski.

Harber, Frances. *My King Has Donkey Ears*. Richmond Hill: Scholastic Canada, 1986 Paper 0-590-71521-6; Cloth 0-590-71522-4. Illustrations by Maryann Kovalski.

Kovalski, Maryann. *The Wheels on the Bus*. Toronto: Kids Can Press, 1987 Paper 0-921103-92-1; Cloth 0-921103-09-3. Illustrations by the author.✣

—. *Jingle Bells*. Toronto: Kids Can Press, 1987. Illustrations by the author. Out of print.

—. *Brenda and Edward* (Little Kids Series). Toronto: Kids Can Press, 1984. 1997 Paper 0-919964-59-1; Cloth 0-919964-77-X. Illustrations by the author.✣

—. *Frank and Zelda*. Toronto: Kids Can Press, 1990 Cloth 0-9211-3-98-0. Illustrations by the author.✣

—. *Take Me Out to the Ballgame*. Richmond Hill: Scholastic Canada, 1992 Paper 0-590-74030. Illustrations by the author.

—. *Queen Nadine*. Victoria: Orca Book Publishers, 1998 Cloth 1-55143-093-2. Illustrations by the author.

Lanteigne, Helen. *The Seven Chairs*. Toronto: Key Porter, 1998 Cloth 1-55013-959-2. Illustrations by Maryann Kovalski.

Morgan, Allen. *Molly and Mr. Maloney* (A Kids-Can-Read Book). Toronto: Kids Can Press, 1981. Illustrations by Maryann Kovalski. Out of print.

Mother Goose. *Sharon, Lois and Bram's Mother Goose*. Toronto: Groundwood Books, 1985 Paper 0-88894-487-X. Illustrations by Maryann Kovalski.

Robart, Rose. *The Cake That Mack Ate*. Toronto: Kids Can Press, 1986. Illustrations by Maryann Kovalski. Out of print.✣

Tregebov, Rhea. *The Big Storm*. Toronto: Kids Can Press, 1992 Paper 1-55074-081-4, 1993 1-55074-117-9. Cloth 1-55074-117-9. Illustrations by Maryann Kovalski.✣

Wynne-Jones, Tim. *I'll Make You Small*. Toronto: Groundwood Books, 1986. 1990 Paper 0-88899-105-3. Illustrations by Maryann Kovalski.

Selected articles about Maryann Kovalski

Bildfell, Laurie "The Art of the Children's Book Illustrator." *Quill & Quire* 51.10 (Oct. 1985): 8-9.

Wagner, Dale. "Maryann Kovalski." *Presenting Canscaip*. Ed. Barbara Greenwood. Markham: Pembroke Publishers, 1990: 182-186.

From *The Seven Chairs*

Vladyana Langer Krykorka
ILLUSTRATOR

Born
June 29, 1945, Prague, Czech Republic

Where I live now
Toronto, Ontario

My favourite book when I was young
Alice in Wonderland (with illustrations by Jiří Trnka)

My favourite book now
"I have too many favourites to list!"

Career
"I started as an illustrator of educational textbooks, such as math books, and reading anthologies. Now, I am mainly a picture book illustrator, graphic designer and clothing designer (hand painting on silk)."

Family
"Two children, Zuzanna and Ian, and three animals: a dog, a cat, and a turtle, named Darth Webber."

The room where I create
"I work in my study, a converted attic. My walls are covered with posters and pictures of my own work, as well as the work of other artists. I also have a bird feeder right outside a large sliding door, and I often watch pigeons, blue jays and the occasional squirrel eat while I draw. In the corner I have an old radio, and I listen to the CBC all day while I work."

Spare time
"I like to paint, read, play sports (volleyball, tennis), travel, spend time at our log cabin, and garden."

When I was growing up
"I was an only child and was rather spoiled. My mother was a teacher, storyteller and a wonderful craftswoman. My father was an opera buff and had a thousand hobbies. I grew up in Prague, studying art and architecture there, and came to Canada in 1968, after Czechoslovakia was invaded by the Soviet Union."

My first book (and how it happened)
"I was offered the chance to illustrate my first book when I was 18 years old and was an art student in Prague. It was called *The Magic Umbrella*. When I look back at this first summer job, I'm sure glad that I'm the proud owner of what is probably the only existing copy!"

Where my ideas come from
"My ideas are a combination of imagination and research. For the books I did with Michael Kusugak, I spent time in the Arctic so I could get to know the people that live there and research the northern setting. I couldn't believe how colourful the tundra was in the summer. Even in the winter when everything was supposed to be white, it was blue — light blue, soft blue, pink blue and all other shades of blue."

Who and what influenced me
"Jiří Trnka (a Czech illustrator and filmmaker), Gennadij Spirin (a Russian illustrator), and Paul O. Zelinsky."

How I work
"First, I do rough sketches in black and white, playing with ideas and ways of conveying the words in a visual format. I put these sketches into a 'dummy' book: a book of rough sketches that gives a general idea of the overall design and look of the finished product. Then, I show this book to the author and the publisher. Together, we look it over, and decide if any changes need to be made. Sometimes they suggest that I modify something, in which case I go back and do another rough illustration. When the final illustrations are done, I hand them over to the publisher, and design the typography. Then everything goes to the printer, first to be scanned and colour-separated, and then printed and bound into books.

"Most of my illustrations are done using watercolours, temperas and collages, but sometimes I also use scratchboard, a piece of white paper covered by a thin layer of black ink. When the black ink is scratched away, it reveals the white paper underneath, and voilà — the shapes and patterns you create form the illustration. The entire process, from the rough dummy book to the final illustrations takes about half a year."

Something nobody knew about me (until now)

"My last name means seaweed in the Inuktitut language."

My favourite book that I've created

"My favourite book is always the one I am working on. At the moment it is *Seeing and Believing* by Eliza Clark."

Tips for young creators

"Draw everywhere you can — except on the walls, your parents might get upset!"

From *Baseball Bats for Christmas*

Vladyana Krykorka

BIBLIOGRAPHY

All books illustrated by Vladyana Krykorka

Ackland, S. *Doodle the Poodle*. Toronto: Holt, Rinehart & Winston, 1976. Out of print.

Carefoot, D. *The Big Yellow Frog*. Stratford: Three Trees Press, 1976. Out of print.

Chislett, Gail. *Whump* (Annick Toddler Series). Willowdale: Annick Press, 1989 Paper 1-55037-040-5; Cloth 1-55037-041-3; Annikin Paper 1-55037-253-X.

Clark, Eliza. *Butterflies and Bottlecaps*. Toronto: HarperCollins, 1996 Cloth 0-00-224365-2. 1997 Paper 0-00-648153-1.

Crystal, Nancy. *Are We There Yet?* Richmond Hill: Scholastic Canada, 1991 Paper 0-590-46125-7.

Goodman, Michelle. *Vanishing Cookies: Doing OK When a Parent Has Cancer*. Downsview: Benjamin Institute, 1990 Paper 0-9694724-0-4.

Hochban, Ty. *Hear My Roar: Lungin's Broken Family*. Willowdale: Annick Press, 1994 Cloth 1-55037-969-0.

Kerven, Rosalind. *The Weather Drum*. Cambridge U.K.: Cambridge University Press, 1996.

Kusugak, Michael Arvaarluk. *Baseball Bats for Christmas*. Willowdale: Annick Press, 1990 Paper 1-55037-144-4; Cloth 1-55037-145-2.

—. *Hide and Sneak*. Willowdale: Annick Press, 1992 Paper 1-55037-228-9; Cloth 1-55037-229-7. —. *Northern Lights: The Soccer Trails*. Willowdale: Annick Press, 1993 Paper 1-55037-338-2; Cloth 1-55037-339-0.

—. *My Arctic 1,2,3*. Toronto: Annick Press, 1996 Paper 1-55037-504-0; Cloth 1-55037-505-9.

—. *Arctic Stories*. Toronto: Annick Press, 1998 Paper 1-55037-452-4; Cloth 1-55037-453-2.

Martin, Rafe. *Dear as Salt*. Richmond Hill: Scholastic Canada, 1993 Cloth 0-590-74306-6. ✤

Morgan, Allen. *Megan and the Weather Witch*. Toronto: Oasis Press, 1993 Paper 1-895092-03-5.

—. *Celebrate the Season: Fall*. Toronto: Oasis Press, 1994 Paper 1-895092-04-3.

—. *Celebrate the Season: Winter*. Toronto: Oasis Press, 1995 Paper 1-895092-05-1.

Munsch, Robert, and Michael Arvaarluk Kusugak. *A Promise is a Promise*. Willowdale: Annick Press, 1988 Paper 1-55037-008-1; Cloth 1-55037-009-X.

Quinlan, Patricia. *Planting Seeds*. Willowdale: Annick Press, 1988 Paper 1-55037-006-5; Cloth 1-55037-007-3.

Awards

1983 Kenneth R. Wilson Memorial Award – Design

1987 Kenneth R. Wilson Memorial Award – Design

1994 Ruth Schwartz Children's Book Award for *Northern Lights: The Soccer Trails*

Darcia Labrosse
AUTHOR/ILLUSTRATOR

Born
March 18, 1956, Montreal, Quebec

School
"I went to school in Montreal, but when I was older, I also studied in Vancouver and in San Francisco, California."

Where I live now
"I now live in Montreal, but I like to spend half the year in Europe, particularly in London, England where I work sometimes."

My favourite book when I was young
"*Thumbelina*. I remember how I loved the fact that Thumbelina could sleep in a flower, she was so small."

Career
"My career is based on the fact that I can stay in my pyjamas all day and draw."

Family
"My family are my pets: two cats, Beige and Mats. They give me love and affection and they don't make a big fuss around Christmas. My real family is very nice, but my cats are more stable and dependable."

The room where I create
"...is filled with images, photographs, notes, books, pencils, papers, and my two cats. I have three desks covered with sketches for new books and a computer that I use to write with. I also have a sound system and 247 cassettes. I love music when I draw, but not when I write."

Spare time
"Basically, I love to be lazy. But being lazy can also be a waste of time so I like being lazy a little, then I like to swim, read, and cook new things like Thai food. I love to go to the movies with my friends and I also love to think about new ideas and books."

When I was growing up
"I was either in a bad mood or very funny. I loved to make people laugh. I still do. It's like wearing a mask, and it's a good way to hide yourself. I loved to make things with my hands: little puppets, little books that I used to bind with real leather. I also loved animals of any kind, but my favourite animals were cats.

"When I was a kid, my head was always in the clouds. I'm sure now that all that dreaming gave me the chance to be an artist. My parents were very silly people with a funny way of looking at the world. They always encouraged me to think my own thoughts and they taught me that dreams can come true."

My first book (and how it came to be)
"My first book was an art school project. I was 18 years old and it was called *Where is the Cat?* I had a lot of fun doing it, but my teacher didn't like it and gave me a very low mark. Years later, a publisher saw it and liked it. He decided to turn it into a real book and it was in print for over 10 years."

Where my ideas come from
"The trick with ideas is that they are all around us, and we don't always let them inside our heads. Allowing yourself to dream is a good way to get ideas. Even if they are silly or impractical, let them in, play with them, look at them or try writing them down. I sometimes get a teeny, weeny, little idea that slowly grows inside my head because I give it a lot of space."

Who and what influenced me
"My biggest influence has been my parent's taste. They both loved painting, dance, theatre and music. My mother had an art gallery and, when I was very young, I spent hours looking at pictures and enjoying their company. Pictures make you think and they can also make you feel like you are travelling to other worlds.

"I have also been inspired by all the fantastic children's book illustrators around the world: Tony Ross, David McKee, Max Velthuis, Carme Sole Vendrell and Leo Lionni."

How I work

"I like to draw my ideas while I lie in my bed, the sheets a mess. Then, after doing lots of sketches and receiving lots of approval from publishers, authors and friends, I do colour sketches. Then I take a deep breath and I attack the final artwork. I always find this part nerve-racking because when I'm done, everything gets printed. How would you like to have 10,000 copies of your homework printed and distributed all across Canada? Well, this is how making a book feels sometimes! But it's fun."

Something nobody knew about me (until now)

"When I went to Kenya and Somalia in Africa, I went on a real safari where I saw a baby giraffe with the umbilical cord still dangling from his navel. I saw a lion eat a wildebeest (that was truly disgusting and scary), and a baboon came to sit next to me just to steal my lunch. Don't ever trust monkeys."

Tips for young creators

"Buy yourself a notebook, something you like, and start writing your ideas down. Ideas are like feathers, a little wind and they are gone! After you've written your ideas down, read them, think about them and let those ideas bring you more ideas. Also, anybody can make a book. All you need is an idea, a bit of confidence, and pencils and paper."

Darcia Labrosse

BIBLIOGRAPHY

Fitch, Sheree. *If You Could Wear My Sneakers!* Toronto: Doubleday, 1997 Paper 0-385-25597-7. Illustrations by Darcia Labrosse.

Gagnon, Cécile. *Hello, Tree!* (Leon Series 1). Trans. Patricia Claxton. Toronto: McClelland & Stewart, 1989. Illustrations by Darcia Labrosse. Out of print.

—. *I'm Hot* (Leon Series 2). Trans. Patricia Claxton. Toronto: McClelland & Stewart, 1989. Illustrations by Darcia Labrosse. Out of print.✤

—. *I'm Hungry* (Leon Series 3). Trans. Patricia Claxton. Toronto: McClelland & Stewart, 1989. Illustrations by Darcia Labrosse. Out of print.

—. *A New House* (Leon Series 4). Trans. Patricia Claxton. Toronto: McClelland & Stewart, 1989. Illustrations by Darcia Labrosse. Out of print.

Hébert, Marie-Francine. *My Body Inside Out.* Trans. Linda Gaboriau. Montreal: Héritage and la courte échelle, 1989. Illustrations by Darcia Labrosse. Out of print. (Title available in French only)

—. *Welcome to the World.* Trans. David Homel. Montreal: Héritage and la courte échelle, 1989. Illustrations by Darcia Labrosse. Out of print. (Title available in French only)

—. *The Amazing Adventure of Littlefish.* Trans. Sarah Cummins. Toronto: Second Story Press, 1990 Paper 0-929005-15-5. Illustrations by Darcia Labrosse.

Labrosse, Darcia. *Greg's My Egg!* London: Andersen Press, 1992 Cloth 0-86264-411-9. Illustrations by the author.

Swede, George. *Time is Flies.* Stratford, ON: Three Trees Press, 1984. Illustrations by Darcia Labrosse. Out of print.

Awards

1982 Canada Council Children's Literature Prize for *Agnès et Le Singulier Bestiaire*

1987 Governor General's Literary Award for *Venir au Monde*

1989 Alvine Bélisle Award for *Venir au Monde*

From *If You Could Wear My Sneakers!*

Kim LaFave
ILLUSTRATOR

Born
January 12, 1955, Vancouver, British Columbia

School
Capilano College, North Vancouver, British Columbia; Alberta College of Art, Calgary, Alberta

My favourite book when I was young
How to Draw by John Nagy

My favourite book now
The Little Prince by Antoine de Saint-Exupéry

Career
Illustrator

Family
Wife, Carol; children, Jeffrey and Cameron

The room where I create
"My studio is in a big room over the garage."

Spare time
"... is spent in the garden, or swimming in the ocean."

When I was growing up
"I always knew I'd do artwork on some level. But when you're a kid, you're not sure where or how you fit into the whole scheme of things. The youngest of four children, I started drawing to fill the time after the others went to school. I'd fill page after page with whatever came to mind.

"At school, I was a little anxious about talking because I had a bit of a stutter. I eventually grew out of the stutter, but the shyness stuck. Drawing saved me, because it gave me a role. I was the one who could draw so I got to work on the sports day banners and the school newspaper."

My first book (and how it happened)
"The first book I did was based on a traditional Maritime folk tale, *The Mare's Egg*. I worked with oil paints which seemed consistent with the time the story took place and the feeling I was trying to evoke. Oil is a very slow medium to work in. *The Mare's Egg* took about a year and a half to complete and that too seemed in keeping with the slower pace of life back then."

Where my ideas come from
"If I feel very close to a story and its characters, the ideas come very quickly. I'll doodle in the margins as I read and re-read the manuscript. These are vague little sketches, just enough to capture the essence of the story. From these sketches, the characters develop, the settings emerge around them, and so it builds, layer by layer.

"Whenever possible, it's a big help to work directly with the author of the story. Who better to talk to when you get off track! As we begin to understand each other, our visions dovetail to tell one story."

Who and what influenced me
"As a kid I was enthralled with cartoons on television (Bugs Bunny, Daffy Duck) and movies like *Pinocchio* and *Dumbo*. I was absolutely amazed that they could make a whole universe come to life with pencils and paint."

How I work
"I work at a very big table, most of which is a clutter. I listen to the radio, stoke the fire in the woodstove, doodle, think and weed the garden. That's when I'm stuck on a problem. But when I've got a clear idea of what I want to do, time flies by. Furious spurts of energy, interspersed with quiet days of puttering around. It's a pattern I've come to accept. I can't rush a book. As I move through a story, from rough sketches to final pencil drawings to finished paintings, the energy and ideas ebb and flow."

Something nobody knew about me (until now)
"I've made it to this point in my life without having to buy a suit."

From Doggerel

My favourite book that I've created

"*Amos's Sweater.* Janet Lunn was a wonderful person and a wonderful writer to work with. I learned a lot from her and I never got bored of drawing Amos."

Tips for young creators

"The most important thing to remember is that drawing a picture is not like a math quiz. There are no right or wrong answers. Sometimes what I might think is a mistake at first, turns out to be the very best part of a picture. That is how you grow as an artist, by experimenting and by being open to whatever happens as you create a piece of art."

Kim LaFave

BIBLIOGRAPHY

All books illustrated by Kim LaFave

Andrews, Jan. *Pumpkin Time.* Toronto: Groundwood Books, 1990 Paper 0-88899-112-6.

Bourgeois, Paulette. In My Neighbourhood Series. Toronto: Kids Can Press, 1991.✤
    Canadian Fire Fighters. Paper 1-55074-137-3.
    Canadian Garbage Collectors. Paper 1-55074-138-1.
    Canadian Police Officers. Paper 1-55074-133-0.
    Canadian Postal Workers. Paper 1-55074-135-7.

Cumbaa, Stephen. *The Bones Book and Skeleton.* Toronto: Somerville House, 1991 Paper and Skeleton 0-921051-26-3.

Cumbaa, Stephen, and Karen C. Anderson. *The Bones and Skeleton Gamebook.* Toronto: Somerville House, 1993 Paper 0-921051-54-9. Illustrations also by Bill Kimber and Steve MacEachern.

Cumbaa, Stephen and Kathlyn Stewart. *The Neanderthal Book and Skeleton.* Toronto: Somerville House Publishing, 1997 Paper 0-921051-32-8.

Dalton, Sheila. *Doggerel.* Toronto: Doubleday Canada, 1996 0-385-25533-0.

—. *Catalogue.* Toronto: Doubleday Canada, 1998 0-385-25703-1.

Evans, Hubert. *Bear Stories.* Gibsons, BC: Nightwood Editions, 1991 Paper 0-88971-153-4.

—. *Silversides: The Life of a Sockeye.* Gibsons, BC: Nightwood Editions, 1991 Paper 0-88971-152-6.

Fitch, Sheree. *I Am Small.* Toronto: Doubleday Canada, 1994 Cloth 0-385-25455-5. 1997 Paper 0-385-25589-6.

Hamilton, Mary. *The New World Bestiary.* Vancouver: Douglas & McIntyre, 1986 Cloth 0-88894-485-3.

Henry, Tom. *Paul Bunyan on the West Coast.* Madeira Park, BC: Harbour Publishing, 1995 Paper 1-55017-109-7.

Lines, P. *Cyril the Seagull.* Gibsons, BC: Nightwood Editions, 1991 Cloth 0-88971-048-1.

Little, Jean and Claire Mackay. *Bats About Baseball.* Toronto: Penguin Books, 1995 Cloth 0-670-85270-8.

Lunn, Janet. *Amos's Sweater.* Toronto: Groundwood Books, 1988 Cloth 0-88899-074-X. 1994 Paper 0-88899-208-4.✤

—. *Duck Cakes for Sale.* Toronto: Groundwood Books, 1989 Cloth 0-88899-094-4. 1992 Paper 0-88899-157-6.

APL, Kenneth. *Follow That Star.* Toronto: Kids Can Press, 1994 Cloth 1-55074-134-9.

Saltpan, Judith. *Goldie and the Sea.* Toronto: Groundwood Books, 1987 Cloth 0-88899-060-X. 1991 Paper 0-88899-133-9.

Spray, Carole, ed. *The Mare's Egg.* Camden East: Camden House, 1980 Paper 0-920656-07-2.

Sharon, Lois & Bram. *Sharon, Lois & Bram Sing A-Z.* Toronto: Groundwood Books, 1991 Cloth 0-88894-845-X.

Wilson, Budge. *Duff the Giant Killer.* Halifax: Formac Publishing, 1997 Paper 0-88780-382-2; Cloth 0-88780-383-0.

Wiseman, Adele. *Puccini and the Prowlers.* Gibsons, BC: Nightwood Editions, 1992 Cloth 0-88971-154-2.

Awards

1989 Governor General's Literary Award for *Amos's Sweater*

1989 Ruth Schwartz Children's Book Award for *Amos's Sweater*

1989 Amelia Frances Howard-Gibbon Illustrator's Award for *Amos's Sweater*

1992 Parents' Choice Award for *The Bones Book and Skeleton*

Marie Lafrance
ILLUSTRATOR

Born
July 21, 1955, Quebec City, Quebec

School
CEGEP du Vieux Montreal, Graphic Arts

Where I live now
Montreal, Quebec

My favourite books when I was young
"Comtesse de Segur books: *Les petites filles modeles, Les malheurs de Sophie*, etc."

My favourite books now
"Wide variety, with a preference for the classics in literature."

Career
"Illustrator of children's books, but I also work for designers, in publicity, editorial, packaging, whatever. I love the challenge of tackling very different jobs. But it's with the children's books that I have the most fun and liberty."

Family
"I live with my beau, Pierre, our almost-six-year-old, Beatrice, and Chloe the cat, 14 years old."

The room where I work
"I work in a huge loft-studio with five other illustrators. We all help each other out and laugh a lot. We have a big bookcase with tons of books for references, and a large couch to take breaks on."

Spare time
"My spare time is sparse. I generally do kid stuff with my daughter — occupations evolve as she ages! We ice skate, go to the park, the beach, and the museums."

When I was growing up
"When I was growing up, my parents used to move every year or so, back and forth between Quebec and Montreal, so I never could keep any friends that long. So I was quite solitary as a child.

"I used to read all the time. When my mother wanted me to play outside, I'd sneak a book. I would read my books 20 times over, until I discovered the library. Then, I could read seven books a week. I also drew a lot, and I always was the worst in drawing classes at school."

My first book (and how it happened)
"The first book I illustrated, *Matthew Prince Charming*, was the story of a little boy who wished he could marry his mother. I did it one summer, at a beach house, drawing Philou, son of our friends, three years old, and modelling Matthew on him."

Where my ideas come from
"Well, from my head! It's like staring at the inside of my head, sometimes seeing nothing for the longest time. But really, I guess I watch people a lot, I always did.

"Some ideas come in my sleep. I can agonize over an idea, and find it as soon as I wake up. Sometimes, I also get ideas in the bathtub. Generally when I don't think of it any more, they just pop up!"

Who and what influenced me
"When I started getting serious about producing pictures, I was most impressed by Cezanne, Matisse, Brad Holland, Jean-Michel Folon, Magritte. But now, I get influenced from what I look at every day, even from stuff I don't like much."

How I work
"I first read the text. Then I let it sit and grow in my head, for the longest time. I may look for references, or at other books to determine which way I may go. Then I realize how much time I've lost, freak out and process the roughs, generally quite fast, since it's already mapped out in my mind. After, I get it approved and proceed with finals, at which point I usually have about two months left.

"I work in acrylics, and the technique is not fast. I work on all the pages at the same time and, as I try to get them out from gray dullness to screaming colours, I get into a frenzied state. Then I send it away and fall into a stupor that can last a month."

Something nobody knew about me (until now)

"Everybody knows a lot about me since I talk a lot; I talk entirely too much."

My favourite book that I've created

"Isn't it always the last one? Mine is *The Miss Meow Pageant,* by Richard Keens-Douglas, for Annick Press, because I felt more free doing it. I allowed myself more freedom, and that seems to be the toughest thing to learn."

Tips for young creators

"Work *a lot.*"

Marie Lafrance

BIBLIOGRAPHY

Comissiong, Lynette. *Mind Me Good Now.* Toronto: Annick Press, 1997 Paper 1-55037-482-6; Cloth 1-55037-483-4. Illustrations by Marie Lafrance.

Keens-Douglas, Richardo. *La Diablesse and the Baby.* Toronto: Annick Press, 1994 Paper 1-55037-992-5; Cloth 1-55037-993-3. Illustrations by Marie Lafrance.

—. *The Miss Meow Pageant.* Toronto: Annick Press, 1998 Paper 1-55037-536-9; Cloth 1-55037-537-7. Illustrations by Marie Lafrance.

MacDonald, Anne Louise. *Nanny Mac's Cat.* Charlottetown: Ragweed Press, 1995 Paper 0-921556-54-3. Illustrations by Marie Lafrance.

Sanschagrin, Jocelyne. *Matthew Prince Charming.* Montreal: Editions Chouette, 1990. Illustrations by Marie Lafrance. Out of print.

From *The Miss Meow Pageant*

Michèle Lemieux
AUTHOR/ILLUSTRATOR

Born
May 29, 1955, Quebec City, Quebec

School
Laval University, Quebec City, Quebec

Where I live now
Montreal, Quebec

My favourite book when I was young
Le Petit Prince and *Tintin.*

My favourite book now
Le Petit Prince and *Tintin.*

Career
Illustrator, fine art teacher at the University of Quebec in Montreal.

The room where I create
"I have two apartments right beside each other; one where I live and the other where I work. I have a big window and a balcony with flower pots on it where songbirds come and play."

Spare time
"I love to travel."

When I was growing up
"For Christmas and birthdays, I received presents of art materials like coloured pencils and paper. My parents never thought it was silly or a waste of time to draw.

"I grew up with the St. Lawrence River. In the winter we lived in Quebec City and in the summer we would move to Charlevoix where the river is very wide. I was always a nature fan — I would spend hours looking for animals in the countryside."

My first book (and how it happened)
"I have three 'first' books. I created my first 'first' book when I was really young, about eight or nine. I made it for my aunt for Christmas. I took it very seriously and spent a lot of time working it.

"My second 'first' book was a not a good experience. I had graduated from Laval and was working on a book with a Quebec publisher. It didn't work out very well and after that experience I decided to go to Europe for a while.

"My third 'first' book happened while I was in Europe. I had heard of the children's book fair held every year in Bologna, Italy. I worked for a year painting and drawing so I could take my work to show publishers there. When I went to Bologna, a Japanese publisher liked my work and wanted me to do a book. I consider that book my real first book. I had time to do a good job and they gave me lots of feedback."

Where my ideas come from
Ideas for her books come to her at all hours — "at night when I dream, during the day when I work, while I take a walk or go to the grocery store, or when I meet friends." She loves to travel and to settle into a different country for a couple of months, during which time she often gets more ideas for her stories and pictures.

But Michèle believes that you don't have to travel to get ideas, just concentrate on yourself and what is around you. "Inspiration doesn't come from the sky, it comes from being aware."

Who and what influenced me
"At Laval, I had a drawing teacher from Czechoslovakia named Miloš. Miloš was new to Canada and his French wasn't very good so he communicated through drawing. Every week, he came from Montreal to teach three three-hour classes. Students were only supposed to go to one of his classes, but he let me go to all of them. For three years, I was like a piece of furniture in his studio, always there. We became friends and sometimes he would bring me books from Montreal. We've stayed in touch all these years and I dedicated my book, *There Was an Old Man* to him."

How I work

"I make lots and lots of sketches. It's the best part of the book. I've made 400 sketches for the book I'm working on now. I always carry a sketchbook with me."

Michèle surrounds herself with books she enjoys: children's books, art books, encyclopedias, books about animals, plants and nature. She enjoys listening to music while she works, especially classical music and opera. "I sing along with the music. It sounds horrible but it makes it fun and since I work alone, it doesn't disturb anyone."

Something nobody knew about me (until now)

"Miloš introduced to me to painting designs on ceramic tiles. We did that for several years. Miloš said he painted enough ceramic tiles to pave a road between Montreal and Toronto. I don't think I did that many, but I think I could probably pave a road between Montreal and Kingston."

My favourite book that I've created

"*Stormy Night* is the book to which I am the most attached. It's also the one that says the most about me."

Tips for young creators

"Accept yourself and how you draw. Don't worry if your drawings don't exactly reflect the image you have in your mind. If you try your best, and are drawing for yourself, you will get better and better. For most of my life I wanted to draw like Michelangelo and Leonardo da Vinci and I was always disappointed in myself because my drawings never turned out like theirs. It took me a long time to accept the way that I draw, but now I have so much fun drawing that I don't want to stop."

Michèle Lemieux

SELECT BIBLIOGRAPHY

Booth, David, ed. *Voices on the Wind: Poems for All Seasons.* Toronto: Kids Can Press, 1990 Paper 1-55074-180-2. Illustrations by Michèle Lemieux.

Cole, Joanna. *A Gift from St. Francis: The First Creche.* Toronto: Kids Can Press, 1989 Cloth 0-921103-59-X. Illustrations by Michèle Lemieux. ♣

Grimm, Jacob, and Wilhelm Grimm. *Lucky Hans* (Methuen Fairy Tale Series). Toronto: Methuen, 1985. Illustrations by Michèle Lemieux. Out of print.

Hasler, Eveline. *Winter Magic.* Toronto: Kids Can Press, 1989 Paper 0-921103-71-9. Illustrations by Michèle Lemieux. ♣

Lear, Edward. *There Was an Old Man...: A Collection of Limericks.* Toronto: Kids Can Press, 1994 Cloth 1-55074-213-2. Illustrations by Michèle Lemieux.♣

Lemieux, Michèle. *Le Raton-Laveur.* Tokyo: Gakken, 1982. Illustrations by the author.

—. *What's That Noise?* Toronto: Kids Can Press, 1989 Paper 0-921103-69-7. Illustrations by the author. ♣

—. *Peter and the Wolf.* Toronto: Kids Can Press, 1991 Paper 1-55074-174-8; Cloth 1-55074-011-3. Illustrations by the author.

—. *The Pied Piper of Hamelin.* Toronto: Kids Can Press, 1993 Cloth 1-55074-124-1. Illustrations by the author.♣

—. *Stormy Night.* Toronto: Kids Can Press, 1999. Illustrations by the author.♣

Menotti, Gian Carlo. *Amahl and the Night Visitors.* Toronto: Kids Can Press, 1991 Paper 1-55074-043-1. Illustrations by Michèle Lemieux.♣

Awards

1988 Communication Jeunesse Concours Culinar 1st prize

1990 Studio Magazine Award

1991 Studio Magazine Award

1991 Grand Prize from l'Association des illustrateurs du Quebec

1993 Canadian Association of Photographers and Illustrators in Communication Award

1996 Grand prize from l'Association des illustrateurs du Quebec

1997 Bologna Ragazzi Award for *Gewitternacht* (*Stormy Night*)

Selected articles about Michèle Lemieux

Sarrasin, Françinc. *Double Espace.* Montreal: les 400 coups, 1997.

From *Amahl and the Night Visitors*

Loris Lesynski
AUTHOR/ILLUSTRATOR

Born
"I was born in Sweden March 16, 1949, my parents were from Finland and Poland, and they told me 'Loris' is an Italian name. But I've been in Canada since I was two so I feel 100% Canadian."

Where I live now
"In a little cottage just north of Toronto, near Lake Simcoe."

My favourite books when I was young
"Anything British."

My favourite book now
"My notebook! Or else whatever I'm reading at the moment."

Career
"I've always been a graphic designer (I designed *this* book), and an illustrator. Starting out, I did many of the 'spot' drawings in your spellers, French books and math books for school. I always wanted to write and illustrate my own books for kids. It took me a very long time to learn how. Many rough drafts and revisions are necessary for just about everyone, but I kept thinking if it didn't work right away it meant it wasn't going to be any good *ever* and I'd keep stopping. I'm not very patient.

"Now finally my 'work' is almost all about writing, illustrating and designing picture books and books of poems for kids. I get to go all kinds of places to talk to kids and teachers about how children's books are created, and how kids can get into their own creativity. I show them artwork from the rough sketches to the final stage, and sometimes do quick drawings on the spot."

The room where I create
"…is the one between my ears. The place where I keep *that* room most of the time is my miniscule studio, which is crammed with bulletin boards, watercolours, books, coloured pencils, pictures, cat (asleep on the computer keyboard), and 4,000 bits of paper. It overlooks a little pond and a large country garden. I love working 'at home.' You just have to learn not to sound as if you're still in your pajamas when you answer the phone at noon — even if you are."

Spare time
"My spare time, work time and play time are all kind of mixed up together. My favourite way to spend time aside from drawing and writing is talk talk talking with people I really like — the kind of talking where you laugh a lot and ideas bounce back and forth. I also like reading a lot, and music, writing letters, taking photographs."

When I was growing up
"I drew pictures for other kids all the time, such as cartoon portraits on the backs of their clipboards. I liked writing anything — letters, diaries, poems, stories. I really liked comic books and copied pictures from them a lot.

"From the time I was a kid, I always loved art supplies. If I were rich today what I'd most like to be able to do is give each of the schools I go to an 'art cart' full of the best pencils, paper, and paint (not the cheap crummy stuff!)"

My first book (and how it happened)
"One day the title *Boy Soup* came into my head and I thought it was such a funny title, I started right away, writing:
   'The boys cooked the carrots,
   the boys boiled the peas.'
I really liked how 'boys' and 'boiled' sounded together. That's a line in the middle of the book. I then wrote backwards to the front and frontwards to the end, making dozens of sketches of Giant. It was really fun to draw his nose (he has a terrible giant cold.)

"I especially enjoy creating and drawing the characters in my books. After I gave Giant multi-coloured hair, I put coloured hair on Gronny the ogre boy in *Ogre Fun,* on Arabelle the witch in *Catmagic,* and of course the dancing dog on the cover of *Dirty Dog Boogie.* (By the way, I drew that dog *50 times* before he felt right to me!) I want to draw these characters so they look like somebody you'd really like to spend time with (even if they're an ogre, or a dog). The materials I like best are watercolours and coloured pencils on Arches watercolour paper."

Where my ideas come from
"Not so much 'where' as 'how.' By trying to stay open-minded and open-hearted. Often by looking for a way to avoid boring chores. Sometimes by connecting things that don't go together (like *boy* and *soup*). Mainly by trying to make myself laugh."

Who and what influenced me
"All the wonderful artwork there is in children's books has been like a feast for me since I was a kid myself. My friends who are illustrators dazzle me with their splendid talents, the magic they can make on a piece of watercolour paper or from a couple of blobs of Plasticine. We have absolutely outstanding children's book illustrators in Canada."

How I work
"I'm usually working on a whole bunch of different drawings, sketches, poems, stories and ideas at the same time. This isn't very organized but it's exciting."

Something nobody knew about me (until now)
" I thing it would be fun to do voices for animated cartoons."

Tips for young creators
"If you like to draw, see if you can find art lessons somewhere while you're still a kid, just to learn the basics and get a chance

From Dirty Dog Boogie

to try out different materials.

"Oh – and save some of your favourite drawings in a safe place. You'll enjoy looking at them when you're older. (My own favourite keepsake is a picture I did in crayon of my cat when I was six — drawn on a brown paper bag that my Mum ironed for me beause we were out of drawing paper that day.)"

Loris Lesynski
BIBLIOGRAPHY

Lesynski, Loris. *Boy Soup, or When Giant Caught Cold.* Toronto: Annick Press, 1996 Paper 1-55037-416-8; Cloth 1-55037-417-6. Illustrations by the author.

—. *Ogre Fun.* Toronto: Annick Press, 1997 Paper 1-55037-446-X; Cloth 1-55037-447-8. Illustrations by the author.

—. *Catmagic.* Toronto: Annick Press, 1998 Paper 1-55037-532-6; Cloth 1-55037-533-4. Illustrations by the author.

—. *Dirty Dog Boogie.* Toronto: Annick Press, 1999 Paper 1-55037-572-5; Cloth 1-55037-573-3. Illustrations by the author.

Ashton Shimkofsky, Wendy. *Brainstorm!* Markham: Pembroke Publishers, 1997 Paper 1-55138-031-5. Illustrations by Loris Lesynski.

Awards
"Nobody has given me any prizes or awards yet. If you would like to be the first, please call."

Selected articles about Loris Lesynski
Ceballo, Valerie. "Soup's On!" *The Lazy Writer* 1.3 (Fall 1997): 22-24.

Mireille Levert
AUTHOR/ILLUSTRATOR

Born
December 20, 1956, St-Jean sur Richelieu, Quebec

Education
Visual arts, University of Quebec in Montreal

My favourite book when I was young
"Why one book? Every book was my favourite. I was like a very small but enthusiastic book-ogre."

My favourite book now
"It's difficult to choose but I will try! Among adult books, my favourite is *Soie*, by Alessandro Barrico. In children's books, it is *The True Story of the Three Little Pigs* by Jon Scieszka, illustrated by Lane Smith."

Career
"I had a short career as a children's bookseller. I am now mostly an illustrator, but increasingly, I also create and write my own children's books."

Family
"Unfortunately I have no kids. I greatly value friendship and my friends with whom I have formed a kind of small, happy family, linked by common interests and creativity."

The room where I create
"My studio is separate from my house. In the morning, after going cycling or taking a short walk, I'm always delighted when I open the studio door.

"I work in a large, bright room. On the walls are my own pictures, and also the pictures of my favourite illustrators. I also have plenty of little trinkets and funny toys. In the middle of the room, there's a tree. Of course, I must not forget the corner where I nap.

"During the winter, I love drawing while I look through a very large window at the falling snow."

Spare time
"I like all the arts: film, music, literature, etc. Montreal has a particularly dynamic artistic life. I also like bicycling very much. I have an old bike for the city that makes a lot of little, funny noises and another one for bicycling joyfully on country roads. I have developed a passion for gardening. Right now, my only gardening is on my little balcony; but it does have lots of flowers."

When I was growing up
"I had the same friends as I do today. First of all, Pierre, whom I wished to marry when I was six years old, and his two little brothers. I thank them for lending me all their boyish toys which I liked so much (at home, I was one of three sisters). Another friend was Nicole who had a pool in her yard. I spent two years playing with her and inventing thousands of aquatic games.

"When I was 12 years old, adolescence arrived. I started writing a diary and guess what it contained: a short story with an illustration."

My first book (and how it happened)
"My first book dates back to when I was an 18-year-old visual arts student. My literature professor was a Quebec author who liked my writing, which was always illustrated. He gave me my first work illustrating *Drôle de pique-nique pour le roi Craquelin*.

"That's the historical fact, but, in my heart, my first real book is *Jeremiah and Mrs. Ming* by Sharon Jennings, published by Annick Press. Bravely, I had come to Toronto with my portfolio, and finally, I was offered a job to illustrate a picture book."

Where my ideas come from
"The ideas come from everywhere, and they don't necessarily come when I am looking for them. It's like trying to catch butterflies: you have to catch them when they pass in front of you.

"This said, I strongly believe in the virtues of work. The more one looks, the more one finds. Inspiration can also come from a drawing or scribble which was done without thinking; a character comes from the subconscious and suddenly starts scampering along, telling small bits of stories."

Who and what influenced me

"First of all, I was attracted by the famous illustrators. I was also particularly interested in the work of children's book authors and illustrators such as Maurice Sendak, Chris Van Allsburg, Tony Ross and, closer to us, Marie-Louise Gay. What I like in their work is the powerful relationship between the text and pictures."

How I work

"For projects which I both write and illustrate, I first need to get a feeling of the pencil in my hand, and to scribble. Bits of sentences are mixed with sketches of drawing, all in a joyful chaos. I like the disorganized side of this stage. Then, in a completely different frame of mind, I work on the text using my computer. I polish and I construct; it's like organizing the bricks of a house. For the drawings, I go through the same stages, but with different tools: I draw, I redraw, I refine and add some elements."

Something nobody knew about me (until now)

"When I was younger, I often dreamed of flying in the sky. When I am awake, I always keep this wish with me. Once, to treat myself, I paid for a flight on a glider. Awesome!"

My favourite book that I've created

"*Rose By Night*. It was the first book where I created both the text and the illustrations, and I am very proud of it."

Mireille Levert

BIBLIOGRAPHY

Cloutier, Cécile. *La Giraffe.* Montreal: Pierre Tisseyre, 1984. Illustrations by Mireille Levert. Out of print.

—. *Le Train.* Montreal: Editions Ovale, 1984. Illustrations by Mireille Levert. Out of print.

Jakob, Donna. *Tiny Toes.* New York: Hyperion, 1995 Cloth 0-7868-0013-5. Illustrations by Mireille Levert.

Jennings, Sharon. *When Jeremiah Found Mrs. Ming.* Toronto: Annick Press, 1992 Paper 1-55037-234-3; Cloth 1-55037-237-8. Illustrations by Mireille Levert.✤

—. *Sleep Tight, Mrs. Ming.* Toronto: Annick Press, 1993 Paper 1-55037-325-0; Cloth 1-55037-322-6. Illustrations by Mireille Levert.✤

Levert, Mireille. *Little Red Riding Hood.* Toronto: Groundwood Books, 1995 Cloth 0-88899-226-2. Illustrations by the author.✤

—. *The Molly Bear* Book Series. Toronto: Annick Press.✤
   Molly's Breakfast. 1997 Paper 1-55037-422-2.
   Molly's Clothes. 1997 Paper 1-55037-424-9.
   Molly's Toys. 1997 Paper 1-55037-426-5.
   Molly's Bath. 1997 Paper 1-55037-428-1.
   Molly Draws. 1998 Paper 1-55037-546-6.
   Molly Counts. 1998 Paper 1-55037-547-4.

—. *Rose by Night.* Toronto: Groundwood Books, 1998 Cloth 0-88899-313-7. Illustrations by the author.

—. *Felix and the Atties* (contained within the game-book "Winter Games"). Montreal: Editions Chouette, 1988. Illustrations by the author.✤

l'Heureux, Christiane. *Passing Time.* Montreal: Editions Chouette, 1987. Illustrations by Mireille Levert. Out of print.✤

—. *Les deguisements D'Amelie.* Montreal: la courte échelle, 1986. Illustrations by Mireille Levert. Out of print.

Nicolas, Sylvie. *Dans le ventre du temps.* St-Lambert: Heritage, 1996 Cloth 2-7625-8118-4. Illustrations by the author.

Awards

1992 Communication Arts Magazine Award of Excellence

1993 Governor General's Literary Award for *Sleep Tight Mrs. Ming*

1994 Studio Magazine Merit Award for *Sleep Tight Mrs. Ming*

Selected articles about Mireille Levert

"About Mireille Levert." *Illustration Quebec Repertoire* 1997-1998: vii.

Lecomte, Anne-Marie. "Des images pour grandir." *La Gazette des femmes* 18.1 (1996): 5.

From *Rose by Night*

Ron Lightburn
ILLUSTRATOR

Born
June 24, 1954, Cobourg, Ontario

Where I live now
Coldbrook, Nova Scotia

My favourite book when I was young
"*Rupert the Bear* annuals from England."

My favourite book now
"Too many to list — but I still like Rupert!"

Career
"I illustrate book covers and picture books. Also, I give presentations and workshops about illustration."

Family
"I have two brothers, two sisters and 18 nieces and nephews (and one wife)."

The room where I create
"I have taken over the living room of our house as my studio; it has the largest windows."

Spare time
"Go for long walks, see movies, read about creative people and the creative process, travel, study and collect old toys, books and ceramics."

When I was growing up
"I feel so lucky to have lived near the ocean as a kid. I have fond memories of spending summer days at the beach, swimming, making sand castles, enjoying picnic lunches and reading comic books. I played soccer and rode my bike a lot. When I reached junior high school, I played golf, tennis and ran cross-country. I boated and camped in and around the Gulf Islands. I always made time for drawing."

My first book (and how it happened)
"The original offices of Orca Book Publishers were in a building that I passed on my way to the local art supply store. I read their sign every time I walked by and wondered 'What do they publish?' A year (and hundreds of walks) later, I made an appointment to meet with the owner of Orca. He looked at my portfolio and said he would let me know if they had any children's book projects that would be suited to my drawing style. A few weeks later, he showed me the manuscript for *Waiting for the Whales*, which I loved. And that was my first book."

Where my ideas come from
"I observe people and nature and study the work of other artists, past and present. Most of my ideas are a result of my attempts to be as true to the story as possible, but at the same time contribute something new."

Who and what influenced me
"When I was a kid, I read and collected comic books and picture books (such as *Rupert*). I drew my own comic books and sold them to my classmates in elementary school. As I grew older, I became interested in book and magazine illustration, and illustrators such as Frank Frazetta and Norman Rockwell. At art college I studied art history and was influenced by the work of Edgar Degas, Claude Monet, Mary Cassat and the Group of Seven.

"Over the years I've studied films and the techniques that filmmakers use to tell a story: lighting and composition of a frame; editing of a scene and camera angles. Filmmakers that have influenced me include Stanley Kubrick (*2001*), Alfred Hitchcock (*North by Northwest*) and Walt Disney (*Fantasia*). The common link between most of my influences is the use of pictures to tell a story. Narrative imagery is my main interest as an artist."

How I work
"Since 1982, my principal medium for making artwork has been coloured pencils, usually on a toned or coloured paper. Now I am also using oil paints. Before I start the drawing that will appear

in print, I make a series of rough sketches or 'studies' to work out content, colour and composition. This process also allows for input from the publisher, editor and art director. I spend quite a bit of time doing research at the library and finding models for the characters in my drawings so that the images are as true to the manuscript as possible."

Something nobody knew about me (until now)

"I have not thrown away a coloured pencil stub since 1982."

My favourite book that I've created

"I thoroughly enjoyed illustrating *Driftwood Cove*, a story about two children from the city who become lost on the rugged western shore of Vancouver Island and encounter a family of squatters. It was a wonderful experience collaborating with the author, my wife Sandra (it's her first picture book) and having our friends model as the characters."

Tips for young creators

"Observe people and nature. Study the work of other artists, past and present. Find subjects for your artwork that really interest you. Make lots and lots of pictures. Try different styles and mediums until you find the one that is right for you. And, most importantly, have fun!"

Ron Lightburn

BIBLIOGRAPHY

Farmer, Patti. *I Can't Sleep!* Victoria: Orca Book Publishers, 1992. Illustrations by Ron Lightburn. Out of print.

Gregory, Nan. *How Smudge Came*. Red Deer: Red Deer College Press, 1995 Paper 0-88995-161-6; Cloth 0-88995—143-8. Illustrations by Ron Lightburn.

Lightburn, Sandra. *Driftwood Cove*. Toronto: Doubleday Canada, 1998 Cloth 0-385-25626-4. Illustrations by Ron Lightburn.

McFarlane, Sheryl. *Waiting for the Whales*. Victoria: Orca Book Publishers, 1991. 1993 Paper 0-920501-96-6. Illustrations by Ron Lightburn.

—. *Eagle Dreams*. Victoria: Orca Book Publishers, 1994 Paper 1-55143-125-4. Illustrations by Ron Lightburn.

Sherman, Gisela. *The King of the Class* (Shooting Star Series). Richmond Hill: Scholastic Canada, 1994 Paper 0-590-74768-1. Illustrations by Ron Lightburn.

Awards

1984 Western Magazine Award

1992 Governor General's Literary Award for *Waiting for the Whales*

1992 Amelia Frances Howard-Gibbon Illustrator's Award for *Waiting for the Whales*

1992 Elizabeth Mrazik-Cleaver Canadian Picture Book Award for *Waiting for the Whales*

1996 Sheila A. Egoff Children's Literature Prize for *How Smudge Came*

1996 Mr. Christie's Book Award for *How Smudge Came*

Selected articles about Ron Lightburn

The Best of Colored Pencil Two. Rockport Publishers, 1994.

Collins, Janet. "Meet the Man Behind the Pictures: Ron Lightburn." *CM* Sept. 1994: 104-106.

Guptill, Watson. *Illustrators* 40. 1998.

Print's Regional Design Annual 1991. RC Publications, 1991.

The Very Best of Children's Book Illustration. North Light, 1993.

From *Driftwood Cove*

Sheena Lott
ILLUSTRATOR

Born
Glasgow, Scotland

School
University of British Columbia

Where I live now
Sidney, British Columbia

My favourite book when I was young
Rupert the Bear, *The Secret Garden*, and *The Borrowers*

My favourite book now
Far from the Madding Crowd by Thomas Hardy

Career
"Physiotherapist, fine artist and children's book illustrator. I also teach watercolour workshops on cruise ships."

Family
Husband, Nick; sons Nathan and Fraser; daughter Chelsea; and pet hedgehog Aphrodite

The room where I create
"I am fortunate to live by the Pacific Ocean. My studio is built into the upper floor of our house. It is always bright and welcoming. On the dullest days, I am inspired by passing sailboats, eagles, seagulls, herons, seals, otters and other wildlife."

Spare time
"Creating an English country garden, cycling, kayaking, backpacking, tennis, skiing, playing bridge, and reading."

When I was growing up
"I was eight when I knew I wanted to be an artist. I spent many days going to the beach and park doing pen and ink sketches. As a child, I entered a lot of art competitions. This forced me to develop as an artist. Mural painting was popular at the time. My art teachers gave me a lot of encouragement. I once had a painting stolen from an art class. My teacher gave me an A+ because he said it must have been good enough to steal."

My first book (and how it happened)
"Orca Publishers saw my artwork in a local gallery and felt it would translate well into children's book illustrations. Many of my paintings featured children playing at the beach. It is difficult to break into illustrating and I felt very fortunate to be chosen. The ability to draw people is important. I studied anatomy in university."

Where my ideas come from
"A combination of many things: past experiences, people, places, objects, art shows, and art books. Images flash through my head at any time. I don't know where they come from — outer space perhaps!"

Who and what influenced me
N.C. Wyeth *(Treasure Island, Kidnapped)*; Jill Barkley (the Brambly Hedge series); Arthur Rackham; Walter Phillips; the Impressionist painters; Winslow Homer.

How I work
"I read the story very thoroughly and start to visualize what the illustrations should look like. This process takes the most amount of time. It is important that the book be interesting and balanced. What will the characters look like and wear? Is there a good mixture of close ups and longshots? Are some pages quiet and some busy? Are any faces stuck in the 'gutter' of the book? Is there a colour and shape balance? All these decisions are critical.

"I then gather my models and choose locations. We go and take many photographs. From these I do a storyboard of rough sketches. I then do the final illustrations in watercolour. It takes me a year to complete a book."

Something nobody knew about me (until now)

"Any resemblance between myself and the comic cartoon character Sheena, Queen of the Jungle is purely coincidental.

"I studied real cadavers in anatomy class."

My favourite book that I've created

"*Midnight in the Mountains,* written by Julie Lawson."

Tips for young creators

"Draw, draw, draw! Keep your best work, sign and date it. I guarantee you will improve."

Sheena Lott
BIBLIOGRAPHY

Lawson, Julie. *A Morning to Polish and Keep.* Red Deer: Red Deer College Press, 1992 Cloth 0-88995-082-2. Illustrations by Sheena Lott.

—. *Midnight in the Mountains.* Victoria: Orca Book Publishers, 1998. Illustrations by Sheena Lott.

McFarlane, Sheryl. *Jessie's Island.* Victoria: Orca Book Publishers, 1992 Paper 0-920501-76-1. Illustrations by Sheena Lott.

—. *Moonsail Song.* Victoria: Orca Book Publishers, 1994 Paper 1-55143-008-8. Illustrations by Sheena Lott.

—. *Going to the Fair.* Victoria: Orca Book Publishers, 1996 Paper 1-55143-062-2. Illustrations by Sheena Lott.

From *Midnight in the Mountains*

Selected articles about Sheena Lott

Freeman, Evelyn et al. "Spanning the Literature Globe, Books from Australia and Canada." *The Reading Teacher* 49.5 (1996): 396.

McNaughton, Janet. *Quill and Quire* Mar. 1994.

Morys-Edge, Derek. *Artists of British Columbia* 1986: 73

Michael Martchenko
AUTHOR/ILLUSTRATOR

Born
August 1, 1942, Carcassonne, France

School
Cambridge, Ontario; Ontario College of Art, Toronto, Ontario

Where I live now
Toronto, Ontario

My favourite book when I was young
Treasure Island

Career
Advertising agency art director; art studio creative director; illustrator of children's books

Family
Wife, Patricia; daughter, Holly; stepdaughters Janet and Susan; cat, Smurfy

The room where I create
"Too small! Sunroom at the back of the house, full of books, artboard and supplies, hats and stuff!"

Spare time
"Watch movies and documentaries, go to book stores, antique shows and flea markets, walk, collect old military uniforms, badges etc., ride my bike and listen to music."

When I was growing up
Michael loved comic books and he read all he could find in Carcassonne. He was equally enthralled by Superman, cowboys and Bugs Bunny. Among his first attempts at design were new covers for his Porky Pig comic books.

When he moved to Canada as a young child, his interest in drawing continued. "I drew all the time. Before we got a television (we were late) I'd listen to the radio and draw the characters that I heard. I'd fill my notebooks with drawings. In high school, in Cambridge, I would do cartoons for the school papers as well as lampoon literary and historical characters in my class notes, except in math — that, I didn't find very funny!"

My first book (and how it happened)
"The studio I worked for had a show so people could see what we did. I put in one of my illustrations to fill a space. Robert Munsch, Anne Millyard and Rick Wilks from Annick Press came to see the show because they were looking for a new illustrator. They saw the piece I had done, liked it, and offered me *The Paper Bag Princess.*"

Where my ideas come from
"As I read the story I get pictures in my mind and I do little sketches to record them. Then I redraw and refine the ones that work the best.

Who and what influenced me
"Cartoons and comic books when I was a kid. Visual humour in movies, including silent movies."

How he works
Michael reads the text several times to become thoroughly familiar with it. He draws thumbnail sketches of the situations he thinks would make good illustrations. Next come the full size sketches. The characters are the result of many sketches until Michael is satisfied with the personality which emerges. "Thomas (in *Thomas' Snowsuit*) was not really any one child, but he's just the way I imagined him. Tough but cute, with a shock of hair that you can't comb no matter what, because it won't go where you want it to."

For backgrounds and locations, "I just use things around me or things I've seen." The objects which surround Michael in his studio range from piles of books, army caps, flying helmets and other 'pieces of junk' he has collected. If he needs to take artistic license to create a funny effect, he will do so. "The point is to make drawings which will be fun for children to look at."

"In 1993 I decided to illustrate full time. I had my studio renovated and managed to squeeze an extra three feet out of it. I work at my drawing board which is set on an angle. This helps to save my back. I use a swivel chair which allows me to reach for things around the room. It's great working in the morning when the light is good. I listen to the radio and CDs while I work. Sometimes, when I look at a drawing, I'll remember a program or a song that was playing when I was working on it."

Something nobody knew about me (until now)
"I do realistic aviation art. I've had six limited prints published that depict various events in aviation history."

My favourite book that I've created
"Allen Morgan and I did a book called *Matthew and the Midnight Pirates*. I had a great time creat-

ing the landlocked pirates who are afraid of water, the pirate bus complete with fan-powered sails and of course the mad turkeys."

Tips for young creators
"For artists — draw! And keep on drawing. Look at other artists' work and learn from them. Your work will look a bit like theirs in the beginning, but you will develop your own style. If you're really serious about a career in art, I would suggest studying at an art school."

Michael Martchenko
BIBLIOGRAPHY

Brott, Ardyth. *Jeremy's Decision*. Don Mills: Stoddart, 1990 Cloth 0-19-540775-X. 1993 Paper 0-19-540969-8. Illustrations by Michael Martchenko.

Martchenko, Michael. *Bird Feeder Banquet*. Toronto: Annick Press, 1990 Paper 1-55037-146-0; Cloth 1-55037-147-9. Illustrations by the author.

Morgan, Allen. *Matthew and the Midnight Tow Truck*. Toronto: Annick Press, 1984 Cloth 0-920303-00-5; Paper 0-920303-01-3. 1991 Annikin Paper 1-55037-192-4. Illustrations by Michael Martchenko.

—. *Matthew and the Midnight Turkeys*. Toronto: Annick Press, 1985 Cloth 0-920303-36-6; Paper 0-920303-37-4. 1991 Annikin Paper 1-55037-193-2. Illustrations by Michael Martchenko.

—. *Matthew and the Midnight Money Van*. Toronto: Annick Press, 1987 Cloth 0-920303-75-7; Paper 0-920303-72-2. 1991 Annikin Paper 1-55037-194-0. Illustrations by Michael Martchenko.

—. *The Magic Hockey Skates*. Toronto: Stoddart, 1991. 1994 Paper 0-7737-56973. Illustrations by Michael Martchenko.

—. *Jessica Moffat's Silver Locket*. Toronto: Stoddart, 1994 Cloth 0-7737-28406. 1996 Paper 0-7737-5701-5. Illustrations by Michael Martchenko.

—. *Matthew and the Midnight Pilot*. Toronto: Stoddart, 1997 Paper 0-7737-5852-6. Illustrations by Michael Martchenko.

—. *Matthew and the Midnight Ballgame*. Toronto: Stoddart, 1997 Paper 0-7737-5853-4. Illustrations by Michael Martchenko.

—. *Matthew and the Midnight Pirates*. Toronto: Stoddart Kids, 1998 Paper 0-7737-5940-9. Illustrations by Michael Martchenko.

—. *Matthew and the Midnight Flood*. Toronto: Stoddart Kids, 1998 Paper 0-7737-5941-7. Illustrations by Michael Martchenko.

Munsch, Robert. *The Paper Bag Princess*. Toronto: Annick Press, 1980 Paper 0-920236-16-2; Cloth 0-920236-82-0. 1981 Annikin Paper 0-920236-25-1. Illustrations by Michael Martchenko.

—. *Jonathan Cleaned Up – Then He Heard a Sound or Blackberry Subway Jam*. Toronto: Annick Press, 1981 Paper 0-920236-20-0; Cloth 0-920236-22-7; Annikin Paper 0-920236-21-9. Illustrations by Michael Martchenko.

continued...

From *Stephanie's Ponytail*

—. *The Boy in the Drawer.* Toronto: Annick Press, 1982 Paper 0-920236-36-7; Cloth 0-920236-34-0. 1986 Annikin Paper 0-920303-50-1. Illustrations by Michael Martchenko.

—. *Murmel Murmel Murmel.* Toronto: Annick Press, 1982 Paper 0-920236-31-6; Cloth 0-920236-29-4. 1988 Annikin Paper 1-55037-012-X. Illustrations by Michael Martchenko.✦

—. *David's Father.* Toronto: Annick Press, 1983 Paper 0-920236-64-2; Cloth 0-920236-62-6. 1988 Annikin Paper 1-55037-011-1. Illustrations by Michael Martchenko.

—. *Mortimer.* Rev. ed. Toronto: Annick Press, 1982. 1983 Annikin Paper 0-920236-68-5. 1985 Paper 0-920303-11-0; Cloth 0-920303-12-9. Illustrations by Michael Martchenko.

—. *Angela's Airplane.* Toronto: Annick Press, 1983 Annikin Paper 0-920236-75-8. 1988 Paper 1-55037-026-X; Cloth 1-55037-027-8. Illustrations by Michael Martchenko.

—. *Thomas' Snowsuit.* Toronto: Annick Press, 1985 Paper 0-920303-33-1; Cloth 0-920303-32-3. Illustrations by Michael Martchenko.

—. *50 Below Zero.* Toronto: Annick Press, 1986 Paper 0-920236-91-X; Cloth 0-920236-86-3. Illustrations by Michael Martchenko.

—. *I Have to Go!* Toronto: Annick Press, 1986 Annikin Paper 0-920303-51-X. 1987 Paper 0-920303-74-9; Cloth 0-920303-77-3. Illustrations by Michael Martchenko.

—. *Moira's Birthday.* Toronto: Annick Press, 1987 Paper 0-920303-83-8; Cloth 0-920303-85-4. 1995 Annikin Paper 1-55037-389-7. Illustrations by Michael Martchenko.

—. *Pigs.* Toronto: Annick Press, 1989 Paper 1-55037-038-3; Cloth 1-55037-039-1. 1995 Annikin Paper 1-55037-388-9. Illustrations by Michael Martchenko.

—. *Something Good.* Toronto: Annick Press, 1990 Paper 1-55037-100-2; Cloth 1-55037-099-5. 1995 Annikin Paper 1-55037-390-0. Illustrations by Michael Martchenko.

—. *Show and Tell.* Toronto: Annick Press, 1991 Paper 1-55037-197-5; Cloth 1-55037-195-9. Illustrations by Michael Martchenko.

—. *The Fire Station.* Toronto: Annick Press, 1983 Annikin Paper 0-920236-77-4. 1991 Paper 1-55037-171-1; Cloth 1-55037-170-3. Illustrations by Michael Martchenko.

—. *Wait and See.* Toronto: Annick Press, 1993 Paper 1-55037-334-X; Cloth 1-55037-335-8. Illustrations by Michael Martchenko.

—. *From Far Away.* Toronto: Annick Press, 1995. Illustrations by Michael Martchenko. Out of print.

—. *Stephanie's Ponytail.* Toronto: Annick Press, 1996 Paper 1-55037-484-2; Cloth 1-55037-485-0. Illustrations by Michael Martchenko.

—. *Alligator Baby.* Toronto: Scholastic, 1997 Paper 0-590-12387-4; Cloth 12386-6. Illustrations by Michael Martchenko.

—. *The Dark.* Toronto: Annick Press, 1986 Annikin Paper 0-920303-47-1 (illus. by Sami Suomalainen). Rev ed. 1997 Paper 1-55037-450-8; Cloth 1-55037-451-6. Illustrations by Michael Martchenko.

Munsil, Janet. *Where There's Smoke.* Toronto: Annick Press, 1993 Paper 1-55037-290-4; Cloth 1-55037-291-2. Illustrations by Michael Martchenko.

Parry, Caroline, comp. *Zoomerang-a-Boomerang: Poems to Make Your Belly Laugh.* Toronto: Kids Can Press, 1991. Illustrations by Michael Martchenko. Out of print.

Skrypunch, Marsha. *Silver Threads.* Penguin, 1996 Cloth 0-670-86677-6. Illustrations by Michael Martchenko.

Staunton, Ted. *Anna Takes Charge.* Toronto: Yorkdale Shopping Centre; Scarborough: Scarborough Town Centre; Brampton: Bramalea City Centre, 1993. Illustrations by Michael Martchenko. Out of print.

Trottier, Maxine. *Alison's House.* Don Mills: Stoddart, 1993 Paper 0-19-540968-X. Illustrations by Michael Martchenko.

von Königslöw, Andrea Wayne. *Frogs.* Toronto: HarperCollins, 1993 Cloth 0-00-223895-0. 1996 Paper 0-00-648057-8. Illustrations by Michael Martchenko.

Williams, Felicity. *A Pocketful of Stars.* Toronto: Annick, 1997 Paper 1-55037-386-2. Illustrations by Michael Martchenko.

Walsh, Alice. *Uncle Farley's False Teeth.* Toronto: Annick Press, 1998 Paper 1-55037-542-3. Illustrations by Michael Martchenko.

Awards
1986 Ruth Schwartz Children's Book Award for *Thomas' Snowsuit*

1993 Canadian Information Services Institute Award for *Where There's Smoke*

1994 International Council of Shopping Centres Award for *Anna Takes Charge*

1994 Palmares Livromagie Award for *Bird Feeder Banquet*

1994 Palmares Livromagie Award for *Portus Potter Was Loose*

1994 Palmares Livromagie Award for *Wait and See*

Selected articles about Michael Martchenko
Granfield, Linda. "Michael Martchenko." *Behind the Story.* Ed. Barbara Greenwood. Markham: Pembroke Publishers, 1995: 60-62.

Nodelman, Perry "The Illustrators of Munsch." *Canadian Children's Literature* 71 (1993): 5-24.

Vanderhoof, Ann "The Art of the Children's Book Illustrator." *Quill & Quire* 51.10 (Oct. 1985): 12.

Jirina Marton
AUTHOR/ILLUSTRATOR

Born
April 19, 1946, Liberec, Czech Republic

School
School of Applied Art-Prague, Czech Republic

Where I live now
Toronto, Ontario

My favourite books when I was young
Garden by Jiří Trnka, *Literary Lapses* by Stephen Leacock

My favourite book now
Garden by Jiří Trnka

Career
Flower vendor, cleaning lady, factory worker, assistant seamstress, painter, graphic designer, picture framer, guide in a gallery, layout artist, freelance illustrator and writer

Family
Partner Leonardo; daughter Michelle; Matzos the cat

The room where I create
"The biggest and the lightest room in the house where we live is the master bedroom. So, of course, I took it for my studio, persuading my partner that the bedroom is not so necessary. He eventually agreed (anyway, he had no choice)."

Spare time
"Observing (or as others call it, wrongly, staring); walking (if possible, in nature), meeting friends, listening to music and thinking (from time to time)."

When I was growing up
"When I was about five years old I wanted to be a prima ballerina, so my mother took me to a ballet school. The teacher, after observing my natural dancing ability, told my mother not bring me any more, since it would be lost time. Undisturbed I started to think about how to become an opera singer (like my mother) or a violinist. This dilemma was resolved when I spent a month in hospital. I loved it so much that I wanted to be a doctor. Then I wanted to be an actor, an Indian, a teacher and finally an artist."

My first book (and how it happened)
"When I decided that I would like to be an illustrator, I started to knock on doors of different publishing houses. Finally, one little publishing house gave me 'the book' to do. I was so happy and immediately started to work. When I saw this first book of mine published, I was very disappointed. I didn't like it at all. But it was good. I learned how not to do books."

Where my ideas come from
"From anywhere. Once I was walking near the Jardin du Luxembourg. It was a nice, summer evening and I suddenly imagined a little boy being closed up in this garden and what could happen to him. My daughter did inspire some of my books, [as did] a simple photo of my aunt."

Who and what influenced me
"We are influenced by the world we live in. When I was young, I lived and studied in Czechoslovakia, so I was influenced by Czech artist Jiří Trnka. When, in 1978, I escaped to France, I discovered all the beautiful illustrations by S. Zavřel, J. Capek, I. Gantchev, S. Eidrigevicius etc. My favorite illustrators from Canada are W. Kurelek, L. Zeman, S. Poulin, M. Lemieux, L. Gal, to name a few of them."

How I work
"Very often both (text and illustrations) are born together. But sometimes, the text is far behind the illustrations. Each book needs its own time. Sometimes it goes very quickly (five to six months), sometimes you need much more time for research etc. But once I decide what to do and how to do my illustrations, it goes by itself."

Something nobody knew about me (until now)

"When I escaped from Czechoslovakia to France, the first movie I went to see was Disney's *Snow White*. I saw it for the first time in my life, in my thirty-second year."

My favourite book that I've created

"*Lady Kaguya's Secret*. It took me more than one year to do this book. I learned lots of things about Japan and its culture. It was a challenge, but I loved it."

Tips for young creators

"Be open to everything. Don't let people discourage you. If you feel your story or illustrations are good, continue to do it. You must trust yourself. Write and draw, draw and write. It is marvelous."

Jirina Marton

BIBLIOGRAPHY

Barnes, Maryke. *Setting Wonder Free*. Toronto: Annick Press, 1993 Paper 1-5037-238-6; Cloth 1-55037-241-6. Illustrations by Jirina Marton.

Buchanan, Joan. *Nothing Else but Yams for Supper*. Toronto: HarperCollins, 1989 Paper 0-88753-182-2. Illustrations by Jirina Marton.

Genouvrier, Emil. *Petit Benjamin*. Tokyo: Gakken, 1986. Illustrations by Jirina Marton.

Marton, Jirina. *La Ville Grise*. Tokyo: Gakken, 1986. Illustrations by the author.

—. *Midnight Visit at Molly's House*. Toronto: Annick Press, 1988. Illustrations by the author. Out of print.

—. *I'll Do it Myself*. Toronto: Annick Press, 1990 Paper 1-55037-062-6; Cloth 1-55037-063-4. Illustrations by the author.

—. *Mitzy*. Tokyo: Gakken, 1990. Illustrations by the author.

—. *Flowers for Mom*. Toronto: Annick Press, 1991. Illustrations by the author. Out of print.

—. *Amelia's Celebration*. Toronto: Annick Press, 1992 Paper 1-55037-220-3; Cloth 1-55037-221-1. Illustrations by the author.

—. *You Can Go Home Again*. Toronto: Annick Press, 1994 Paper 1-55037-990-9; Cloth 1-55037-991-7. Illustrations by the author.

—. *Lady Kaguya's Secret*. Toronto: Annick Press, 1997 Cloth 1-55037-441-9. Illustrations by the author.

Morgan, Allen. *Nicole's Boat*. Toronto: Annick Press, 1986. Illustrations by Jirina Marton. Out of print.

Quinlan, Patricia. *Kevin's Magic Ring*. Toronto: Black Moss Press, 1989 Paper 0-88753-188-1. Illustrations by Jirina Marton.

—. *Emma's Sea Journey*. Windsor: Black Moss Press, 1991. Illustrations by Jirina Marton. Out of print

Awards

1995 Grand Prize, Itabashi Picture Book Contest for *Amelia's Celebration*

Selected articles about Jirina Marton

Books in Canada. May 1992: 59.

School Library Journal Nov. 1994: 84-85.

Schwartz, Bernard. "Reprise: A Select Group." *Canadian Children's Literature* 60 (1990): 135-137.

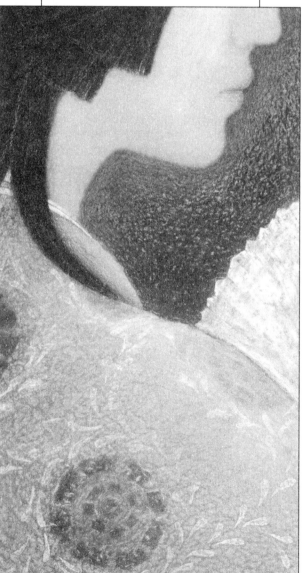

From *Lady Kaguya's Secret*

Marc Mongeau
ILLUSTRATOR

Born
Summerside, Prince Edward Island

School
College Ahuntsic, Montreal

Where I live now
Farnham, Quebec

My favourite book when I was young
Le capitaine de Quinzes Ans, by Jules Verne

My favourite book now
Tournee d'automne, Jacques Poulin

Career
Illustrator for magazines, posters, theatres, children's books etc.

Family
"My son David, and my daughters Matilde and Rosalie."

The room where I create
"I work in the attic. It is a huge room in an old house, and I climb there with a ladder. There is a small window where I can see over the roofs, the fields, the farms, the mountains and the river."

Spare time
"Bicycling with my family, reading, playing guitar and looking at wind blowing through my toes."

When I was growing up
"When I was young, I lived along the St. Lawrence River. It was a great playground. I remember the shore, the fields with wild grass higher than a man where we made mazes, and the huge willow trees in which we built houses. I also remember the herons, the turtles that we collected, and finally, the boats on the river coming from as far as we could imagine."

My first book (and how it happened)
"My first book was *La machine à rêves* written by Henriette Major. It was a small paperback book printed in black and white. I was very nervous, but it is a nice book. Henriette and I also did a theatre play for giant puppets called *Dream Catchers* for théâtre sans fils based on that book."

Where my ideas come from
"Everyday observations, like a bird carrying a worm over a yellow field, a cent rolling on the sidewalk, and other little details."

Who and what influenced me
"Marc Chagall, a great painter. I have admired his painting since my youth. I especially remember a painting in which two people are floating over the floor in a bedroom. The man has no arms and is kissing a lady who is holding a bunch of flowers. It is very poetic."

How I work
"After reading the manuscript, I do very small 2 x 2 cm sketches of each page. At this scale it is easier to have strong composition and balance. I do as many sketches as possible, and then I make a choice. Then, I develop the small sketches into bigger ones by adding details."

My favourite book that I've created
"It's always the last one. I'm now working on a book that I've written called *La dinde aux écrevisses*, to be published by Les 400 coups."

Tips for young creators
"Work, work, work…"

Marc Mongeau

Selected Bibliography

Beaudin, Louise and Marc Mongeau. *Les animaux et leurs petits*. Waterloo QC: Quintin Publishers, 1987. Illustrated by Marc Mongeau. Out of print.

Corrin, Ruth. *His Majesty the King*. Reading, MA: Scott Foresman, 1996. Illustrations by Marc Mongeau.

Dixon, Glenn. *A Billion Building Blocks*. Nashville TN: Nelson, 1990. Illustrations by Marc Mongeau. Out of print.

continued...

Fear, Sharon. *The Greatest Juggler in the World.* Brown Publishing, 1994. Illustrations by Marc Mongeau. Out of print.

Fitch, Sheree. *There Were Monkeys in my Kitchen!* Toronto: Doubleday, 1992 Paper 0-385-25470-9. Illustrations by Marc Mongeau.

Floyd, Lucy. *All I Did.* San Diego CA: Harcourt Brace, 1996. Illustrations by Marc Mongeau.

Goodwin, Stu. *Jin and Lin.* Old Tappan NJ: Macmillan, 1995. Illustrations by Marc Mongeau. Out of print.

Hajdusiewicz, Babs Bell. *Jack and More Jacks.* Reading, MA: Scott Foresman, 1993. 1995 Cloth 0-673-36281-7. Illustrations by Marc Mongeau.

Kushner, Donn. *The Dinosaur Duster.* Toronto: Stoddart Kids, 1992 Cloth 1-895555-38-8. Illustrations by Marc Mongeau.

Major, Henriette. *La machine à rêves.* St. Jerome QC: Mondia, 1984 2-89114-221-7. Illustrated by Marc Mongeau. Out of print.

Melfi, Mary. *Ubu, the Witch Who Would be Rich.* Toronto: Doubleday, 1994 Paper 0-385-25448-2. Illustrations by Marc Mongeau.

Mongeau, Marc. *Quotable Cat.* (Traditional) Philadelphia PA: Running Press, 1997 Cloth 0-7624-0152-4. Illustrations by the author.

—. *La Dinde aux écrevisses.* Laval QC: Les 400 coups, 1998. Illustrations by the author.

Quinn-Harkin, Janet. *Septimus Bean and his Amazing Machine.* Nashville TN: Nelson, 1990 0-17-603043-3. Illustrations by Marc Mongeau.

Richer, Marielle. *Les Perroquets Tralalère.* Radio-Quebec, 1988. Illustrated by Marc Mongeau. Out of print.

Sylvestre, Louise. *C'est tout comme.* Waterloo QC: Quintin Publishers 1987. Illustrated by Marc Mongeau. Out of print.

Vandal, Andre. *Le cheval du désert.* Montreal: Ovale, 1991. Illustrations by Marc Mongeau. Out of print.

Awards

1991 Studio Magazine Merit Award

1991 AXIOM Award of Excellence

1991 Communication Arts Award of Excellence

1993 Studio Magazine Merit Award

1993 Communication Arts Award of Excellence

1994 Signet d'or from Union des Ecrivains du Quebec et le Salon du Livre de Montreal

Selected articles about Marc Mongeau

Studio Magazine 12.3 (1994): 36-42.

Lurelu 14.3 (1992): 49.

From *There Were Monkeys in my Kitchen!*

Paul Morin
ILLUSTRATOR

Born
January 14, 1959, Calgary, Alberta

School
Grant McEwen College, Edmonton, Alberta; Sheridan College, Brampton, Ontario; Ontario College of Art, Toronto, Ontario

Where I live now
"At the edge of a forest near Rockwood, Ontario."

My favourite book when I was young
One River by Wade Davis

My favourite book now
"The Power of Myth and many Joseph Campbell titles."

Career
Children's book illustrator, lecturer, musician, designer

Family
"My partner, Janine, and I have a beautiful baby boy named Palmer."

The room where I create
"My studio is large with lots of windows and skylights. It looks out over a pond and forest. A small creek flows in from a marsh in the back of the property and wildlife abounds."

Spare time
"I have built a recording studio in my house and my friends and I enjoy collecting and playing instruments from around the world. Our band Handprints has many releases including a new CD titled Animal Dreaming. I also make documentary videos about my travels."

When I was growing up
"I always enjoyed hiking and camping. Nature has always fascinated me."

Becoming an illustrator
"My decision to enter art school was based on my employment until then and the fact that I knew I'd have to enjoy work to succeed at it. To pursue art as a career? But, as the author Joseph Campbell says, 'If you follow your bliss, doors will open where there were no doors before.' I interpret this to mean that if you have faith in your intuitions and rely on them, chances are those can be some of the most influential decisions a person can make, and the confidence obtained from this will help you face the opportunities which you come upon."

My first book (and how it happened)
"Kathryn Cole of Oxford University Press had seen a painting I had done of a West African village and when she received the manuscript for The Orphan Boy (which is set in Africa), she felt that I would be a good choice to illustrate it.

"I thought that The Orphan Boy would make an interesting series of paintings and could satisfy my interest in travel, music and anthropology. So, I set out for Africa to do research. All of a sudden I was travelling with a purpose, not just as a tourist. As soon as I arrived I set about arranging transport to the Great Rift Valley on the border of Maasai Mara and Tanzania where the Maasai still live a simple (and complex) life amongst the spectacular backdrop of the African savannah.

"The experiences I had over the following six weeks were the most profound I've had. All of a sudden this project was becoming much more than a commission. It would involve all my thought and attention for the next five months. For me the magical feeling I felt from the Maasai and the passion which I incorporated into the paintings were, in fact, a new branch on my path."

Where my ideas come from

"Everywhere, everything. If I can absorb and observe experiences, I am in a better position to translate those experiences into images. I incorporate some of my own experiences into the essence of the images I create."

Who and what influenced me

"Nature has perhaps been my single biggest influence and my travels have shown me many things that have stimulated my imagination. John Wood, who was my illustration teacher, helped me.

"But most important has been my personal search for truth and the projects I've done over the last five years of following my bliss. I am constantly in search of mystical encounters."

How I work

"I usually begin a project by doing extensive research. Frequently this involves travels to different countries and cultures where I 'soak up' atmosphere. While I'm there, I record the music and sounds of the country and when I get home, my friends and I improvise musical compositions from these recordings. I then listen to this music while I do the artwork. This helps me stay very focused towards the mood of a project."

Something nobody knew about me (until now)

"Every time I sit in front of a blank canvas, I hesitate for an instant in fear that I don't know where to start."

Tips for young creators

"Observe nature, study the way you look at things — experience life!"

From
Animal Dreaming

Paul Morin

Bibliography

Bruchac, Joseph. *Fox Song*. Don Mills: Stoddart/Oxford University Press, 1993 Cloth 0-19-541000-9. Illustrations by Paul Morin.

—. *Lasting Echoes*. New York: Silverwhistle/Harcourt Brace, 1997 Cloth 0-15-201327-X. Illustrations by Paul Morin.

James, Betsy. *The Mud Family*. Toronto: Stoddart, 1994 Cloth 0-19-541075-0. Illustrations by Paul Morin.

Lawson, Julie. *The Dragon's Pearl*. Toronto: Stoddart/Oxford University Press, 1992. 1995 Paper 0-07737-5717-1; Cloth 0-0-7737-2882-1. Illustrations by Paul Morin.

McLerran, Alice. *The Ghost Dance*. Toronto: Stoddart Kids, 1995 Cloth 0-7737-2898-8. Illustrations by Paul Morin.

Mollel, Tololwa. *The Orphan Boy*. Toronto: Stoddart/Oxford University Press, 1990. 1995 Paper 0-7737-5710-4; Cloth 0-19-540783-0. Illustrations by Paul Morin.

Morin, Paul. *Animal Dreaming*. Toronto: Stoddart Kids, 1998 Cloth 0-7737-3062-1. Illustrations by the author.

Whetung, James. *The Vision Seeker*. Toronto: Stoddart Kids, 1996 Cloth 0-7737-2966-6. Illustrations by Paul Morin. 1997 Video 0-7737-5872-0. Produced and directed by Paul Morin.

Awards

1990 Governor General's Literary Award for *The Orphan Boy*

1991 Elizabeth Mrazik-Cleaver Picture Book Award for *The Orphan Boy*

1991 Amelia Frances Howard-Gibbon Illustrator's Award for *The Orphan Boy*

1993 Amelia Frances Howard-Gibbon Illustrator's Award for *The Dragon's Pearl*

1993 Society of Illustrators Award

Paul Morin has received 25 international awards for his book illustrations.

Robin Muller
AUTHOR/ILLUSTRATOR

Born
October 30, 1953, Toronto, Ontario

School
Toronto, Ontario

His favourite books when he was young
Fairy tales, Greek mythology and history

Career
Writer and illustrator of children's books

The room where he creates
Robin likes to work in a small room that has a window overlooking trees.

Spare time
Robin's hobby is rescuing old or damaged toys from junkstore shelves. He once found a wooden dog with ball joints. It was cracked, its paint was chipped, and one of its paws was missing. "But the toy filled me with such a wonderful sense of it having been loved, that I could almost see a child playing with it."

Months later as he was looking through some old family photographs, he came across a picture of himself when he was five holding the same toy. Its body wasn't cracked, and the paint was still bright, but one of its paws was missing — the same paw that was missing on the dog he had bought!

When he was growing up
When Robin was a child he had very little exposure to children's books. "There were no bookstores or libraries near my home at that time. In fact, the only library that we had was a mobile one (a library on wheels) that came once every two weeks, and even then we were only allowed to withdraw one book at a time."

Because there were so few children's books available, Robin's father would read passages from plays by Shakespeare to him in place of bedtime stories. "I think it was listening to Shakespeare as a child that first sparked my interest in language and history."

When he was in public school, Robin started a little publishing house. He was only eight years old. When he was in high school, Robin started a school newspaper to compete with the existing one. Called *Exodus*, the paper featured short stories, poems, book reviews and even paid advertisements.

His first book (and how it happened)
As a teenager, Robin had a job working in the warehouse of a large children's publishing house. He found the books so exciting, he decided to try his hand at book writing. He wrote and illustrated a story called *Rupert's Star*, about a boy trying and failing to capture a star. The book was turned down by every publisher he sent it to, and he was so disappointed by the experience that it was ten years before he tried to get something published again. His second attempt was successful, and he dedicated a later book, *The Sorcerer's Apprentice*, to *Rupert's Star*.

How he works
Robin likes to use pencils and he prefers to print instead of write his words. When working on a story, he likes to use school workbooks instead of loose sheets of paper.

Robin both writes and illustrates his own books.

Working between ten and twelve hours a day means it can take roughly a year for Robin to write and illustrate a book. *The Sorcerer's Apprentice* took Robin eight months to illustrate, *The Magic Paintbrush* took a full year, and *The Angel Tree* took two years. When he illustrates a book he works on nothing else.

"There's a great commitment of time involved, and I don't really have the ability to do anything else until I'm finished. I've often thought it would be nice to have a nine to five job."

Where his ideas come from

Memories of stories that excited him as a child, adventures and games he played out in cardboard forts, and castles he and his friends built in a ravine near his house. He also uses collections of stories for his research. For instance, *Mollie Whuppie and the Giant* is a Gaelic story and *Tatterhood* is from Finland. Robin likes to think of folk and fairy tales as a river of stories running through the centuries.

"The stories we hear today are, for the most part, the same stories that people listened to hundreds of years ago, and in all that time they have lost none of their power to delight or move us."

Robin Muller

Bibliography

Muller, Robin. *Mollie Whuppie and the Giant*. Richmond Hill: Scholastic Canada, 1982 Cloth 0-590-71106-7. 1983 Paper 0-590-71170-9. 1993 Paper 0-590-74036-9. Illustrations by the author.

—. *Tatterhood*. Richmond Hill: Scholastic Canada, 1984 Paper 0-590-71446-5; Cloth 0-590-71411-2. Illustrations by the author.

—. *The Sorcerer's Apprentice*. Toronto: Kids Can Press, 1985 Paper 0-919964-84-2. Illustrations by the author.

—. *The Lucky Old Woman*. Toronto: Kids Can Press, 1987. Illustrations by the author. Out of print.

—. *Little Kay*. Richmond Hill: Scholastic Canada, 1988 Cloth 0-590-74887-8. 1989 Paper 0-590-71886-X. 1990 Paper 0-590-73757-0. Illustrations by the author.✢

—. *The Magic Paintbrush*. Toronto: Doubleday Canada, 1989. 1993 Paper 0-385-25373-7. Illustrations by the author.

—. *The Nightwood*. Toronto: Doubleday Canada, 1991 Cloth 0-385-25305-2. 1995 Paper 0-385-25544-6. Illustrations by the author.

—. *Hickory Dickory Dock*. Richmond Hill: Scholastic Canada, 1992 Cloth 0-590-73616-7. 1995 Paper 0-590-73089-4. Illustrations by Suzanne Duranceau.

—. *Row, Row, Row, Your Boat*. Richmond Hill: Scholastic Canada, 1993 Cloth 0-590-74584-0. 1996 Paper 0-590-24667-4; Illustrations by the author.

—. *Little Wonder*. Richmond Hill: Scholastic Canada, 1994 Cloth 0-590-24225-3. 1997 Paper 0-590-24988-3. Illustrations by the author.

—. *The Angel Tree*. Toronto: Doubleday, 1997 Cloth 0-385-25560-8. Illustrations by the author.

Awards

1985 IODE Book Award – Toronto Chapter for *The Sorcerer's Apprentice*

1989 Governor General's Literary Award for *The Magic Paintbrush*

Selected articles about Robin Muller

Greenwood, Barbara. "Robin Muller." *Behind the Story*. Ed. Barbara Greenwood. Markham: Pembroke Publishers, 1995: 66-68.

"Hope for Outsiders: Frieda Wishinsky Speaks with Robin Muller." *Books in Canada* May 1998: 36

From *The Magic Paintbrush*

Ruth Ohi
ILLUSTRATOR

Born
September 25, 1964, Don Mills, Ontario

School
Earnscliffe Public School, Bramalea Secondary School, University of Toronto, Ontario College of Art

Where I live now
Toronto, Ontario

My favourite books when I was young
"*Snow* by McKie and Eastman and *The Snowy Day* by Ezra Jack Keats."

My favourite book now
"Any book with Alfie and Annie Rose in it (by Shirley Hughes)."

Career
Illustrator

Family
"Husband, Kaarel (pronounced Karl) and two daughters."

The room where I create
"A room in desperate need of renovations. Lots of different wall surfaces, exposed pipes, Lots of windows, live water faucet hovering over computer terminal (we tore out the sink and counters)."

Spare time
"Not renovating. Being with my family."

When I was growing up
"I considered each sheet of blank paper a challenge. I'd take my crayons (later on I graduated to coloured pencils and markers) and fill all that white space with pictures of princesses, castles, trees, cats — anything I could think of. My sister, brother and I used to spend hours putting together a weekly newsletter for our family, full of stories, coloured pictures, puzzles, and even comic strips."

Where my ideas come from
"Nowadays I keep a sketchbook with me all the time. Whenever I see something that catches my fancy, like a young person with an interesting face, I'll take out my book and do a quick sketch. I get a lot of ideas for my pictures from this sketchbook, but I also get a lot of ideas from just paying attention to what's going on around me."

My first book (and how it happened)
"When I was in my final year at the Ontario College of Art, I made copies of my best pictures and mailed them to Annick Press.

"Two days later there was a message on my answering machine from the editor of Annick Press, inviting me to come for an interview. I was so excited! I played that message over and over again. That interview resulted in my very first picture book, *Maybe a Monster*, written by Jill Creighton."

Who and what influenced me
"The houses in my books are like the one I grew up in — comfortably cluttered. It was a bit of a zoo with three children running around screaming and playing and leaving trails of smudgy fingerprints and stepped-on crayons behind them, two hermit crabs, fish, zebra finches, an Australian terrier, and a gerbil who escaped his cage so many times we changed his name to 'Houdini.' In the middle of this commotion were my parents — two loving, patient people who would just gaze at all the chaos and smile at each other contentedly. It was a very happy household in which to grow up, and whenever appropriate I like to instil that kind of feeling into my books."

How I work
"I work on each book pretty much the same way. First I read the story at least three times. Then I start doodling. As I make more doodles, I tear bits of

6000

paper and paste them over the parts I want to change in my drawings.

"As you might imagine, the first pictures I do are pretty messy-looking and are more like collages than drawings. I keep on cutting and pasting until I'm happy with the collage. Next, I place a fresh sheet of layout paper over everything and make a more polished drawing by tracing over it. This is the rough layout copy that I will show to the editor. From that point, I do a little bit of cutting and pasting to make any required changes until I get the approval to begin the final painting."

Tips for young creators

"Keep a sketchbook journal with you all the time and draw every day. Read a lot. Think how you would have illustrated the book to make it better (novel or picture books) and then do it. Try different materials — pencil, pastels, crayons, collage — and different styles. Keep an open mind and don't be afraid of making mistakes."

Ruth Ohi

Bibliography

All books illustrated by Ruth Ohi

Creighton, Jill. *Maybe a Monster.* Toronto: Annick Press, 1989. Out of print.

—. *One Day There Was Nothing To Do.* Toronto: Annick Press, 1990. Out of print.

Cutler, L. W. *Baggage to London.* Toronto: Annick Press, 1994 Annikin Paper 1-55037-345-5.

Hutchins, Hazel. *Norman's Snowball* (Annick Toddler Series). Toronto: Annick Press, 1989 Cloth 1-55037-053-7; Paper 1-55037-050-2. 1996 Annikin Paper 1-55037-494-X.

—. *Nicholas at the Library.* Toronto: Annick Press, 1990 Paper 1-55037-132-0; Cloth 1-55037-134-7.

—. *Katie's Babbling Brother.* Toronto: Annick Press, 1991 Paper 1-55037-156-8; Cloth 1-55037-153-3. 1996 Paper 1-55037-496-6.

—. *A Cat of Artimus Pride* (Annick Young Novels Series). Toronto: Annick Press, 1991 Paper 1-55037-199-1.✤

—. *And You Can Be the Cat.* Toronto: Annick Press, 1992 Paper 1-55037-216-5; Cloth 1-55037-219-X. 1996 Annikin Paper 1-55037-495-8.

—. *The Catfish Palace.* Toronto: Annick Press, 1993 Paper 1-55037-317-X; Cloth 1-55037-316-1.

—. *The Best of Arlie Zack* (Annick Young Novels Series). Toronto: Annick Press, 1993 Paper 1-55037-315-3.

—. *Within a Painted Past* (Annick Young Novels Series). Toronto: Annick Press, 1994 Paper 1-55037-989-5; Cloth 1-55037-369-2.

Lamm, C. Drew *Anniranni and Mollymishi the Wild-Haired Doll.* Toronto: Annick Press, 1990. Out of print.

Orr, Wendy. *Aa-Choo!* Toronto: Annick Press, 1992 Paper 1-55037-208-4; Cloth 1-55037-209-2.

—. *Pegasus and Ooloo Mooloo* (The Micki and Daniel Series). Toronto: Annick Press, 1992. Out of print.

—. *A Train to the City* (The Micki and Daniel Series). Toronto: Annick Press, 1993. Out of print.

—. *The Wedding* (The Micki and Daniel Series). Toronto: Annick Press, 1993. Out of print.

—. *A Light in Space.* Toronto: Annick Press, 1994 Paper 1-55037-975-5; Cloth 1-55037-368-4.

—. *Yancy & Bear.* Toronto: Annick Press, 1996 Paper 1-55037-502-4, Cloth 155037-503-2.

—. *It's Raining, Yancy & Bear.* Toronto: Annick Press, 1998 Paper 1-55037-528-8; Cloth 1-55037-529-6.

Thompson, Richard. *The Last Story, The First Story* (Annick Young Novels Series). Toronto: Annick Press, 1988 Paper 0-55037-024-3; Cloth 1-55037-025-1.

—. *Zoe & the Mysterious X.* Toronto: Annick Press, 1990. Out of print.

Westell, Kerry. *Amanda's Book.* Toronto: Annick Press, 1991. Out of print.

From *It's Raining, Yancy & Bear*

Roger Paré
AUTHOR/ILLUSTRATOR

Born
November 25, 1929, Ville-Marie, Quebec

Where I live now
Montreal, Quebec

Career
Illustrator

Family
Three grown-up children

The room where he creates
Studio in his house

Spare time
One of Roger's favorite "sports" is to walk in Montreal searching for new faces and new expressions. He also enjoys cross-country and downhill skiing, birdwatching and fishing.

When he was growing up
Roger received formal education only until the end of Grade 10 in the Quebec community of Ville-Marie. His teachers encouraged him to paint and draw. As a result of developing his talents as an artist at an early age, he enjoyed a 25-year career with Radio Canada as a graphic artist for children's television programs.

His first book
His career as a children's book illustrator began in 1979 with *Une Fenêtre dans ma Tête*. Since that time he has built an enviable reputation in both French and English Canada publishing worlds.

Where his ideas come from
Roger spends a good deal of time thinking about the kind of children's books he wants to produce. He checks libraries and bookstores, noting what is not available. "For me, books begin through surveying existing children's books, then asking mothers, teachers, and publishers about the real needs of children. This is very important. I also try to observe personally what books kids prefer. My intention is to have fun making a book, so that the kid will also have fun looking at it."

How he works
"I have a small studio in my home where I write and draw. I do a lot of thinking while sitting in a rocking chair. I've kept to a strong discipline which helps me stay at my drawing table a minimum of six to eight hours a day, seven days a week until a project is completed. It takes me as much as a year to finish a book." Roger has now retired from Radio Canada and works full-time at his children's books.

Illustrating for children
It is evident that, even though his illustrations emphasize humour, Roger is very serious about what he wants to accomplish with his children's books. He has a great deal of respect for children's capacity to appreciate good art in a picture book. "What I want for children's books are illustrations that will have the quality of a painting. I think that children are sensitive and can feel what an artist can tell with images. When an illustration is so explicit, there needs to be little writing — the image must reach the reader above all."

Roger Paré

Bibliography

Inglehart, Anne. *Radio Dog*. New York: Elsevier Dutton, 1979. Illustrations by Roger Paré. Out of print.

Paré, Roger. *A, B, C... Read with Me*. Montreal: la courte échelle, 1985. Illustrations by the author. Out of print.

—. *123...Count with Me*. Trans. by David Homel. Toronto: Annick Press, 1986. Out of print.✦

—. *The Annick ABC*. Trans. by David Homel. Toronto: Annick Press, 1987 Annikin Paper 1-55037-059-X. Illustrations by the author.✦

—. *A Friend Like You*. Trans. by David Homel. Toronto: Annick Press, 1988 Paper 0-920303-05-6; Annikin Paper 0-920303-80-3. Illustrations by the author.✦

continued...

—. *L'Alphabet: A Child's Introduction to the Letters and Sounds of French.* Lincolnwood, IL: NTC Publishing, 1990 Cloth 0-8442-1395-0. Illustrations by the author.

—. *Un elephant.* Montreal: la courte échelle, 1993 1-89021-199-1. Illustrations by the author.

—. *Un chat.* Montreal: la courte échelle, 1993 1-89021-198-3. Illustrations by the author.

—. *Plaisirs de vacances.*Montreal: la courte échelle, 1995 2-89021-253-X. Illustrations by the author.

—. *Les contraires.* Montreal: la courte échelle, 1996 2-89021-272-6. Illustrations by the author.

—. *Les couleurs.* Montreal: la courte échelle, 1997 2-890021-304-8. Illustrations by the author.

Paré, Roger, and Bertrand Gauthier. *Summer Days.* Trans. by David Homel. Toronto: Annick Press, 1989 Paper 1-55037-044-8; Cloth 1-55037-043-X. Illustrations by Roger Paré.♣

—. *Circus Days.* Trans. by David Homel. Toronto: Annick Press, 1990 Paper 1-55037-020-0; Cloth 1-55037-021-9. Illustrations by Roger Paré.♣

—. *Play Time.* Trans. by David Homel. Toronto: Annick Press, 1990 Paper 1-55037-086-3; Cloth 1-55037-087-1. Illustrations by Roger Paré.♣

—. *Winter Games.* Trans. by David Homel. Toronto: Annick Press, 1991 Paper 1-55037-184-3; Cloth 1-55037-187-8. Illustrations by Roger Paré.♣

—. *Animal Capers.* Trans. by David Homel. Toronto: Annick Press, 1992 Paper 1-55037-244-0; Cloth 1-55037-243-2. Illustrations by Roger Paré.♣

Awards
1979 Canada Council Children's Literature Prize for *Une Fenêtre dans ma Tête*

1985 Canada Council Children's Literature Prize for *L'Alphabet (ABC)*

From *Winter Games*

Dušan Petričić
ILLUSTRATOR

Where I live now
Toronto, Ontario

My favourite books when I was young
Winnie the Pooh, Alice in Wonderland, The Boys from Pavel's Street

My favourite book now
The Giving Tree by Shel Silverstein

Career
Professor of illustration and book design at the Faculty of Applied Arts, Belgrade, Yugoslavia and at Sheridan College, Oakville, Ontario; freelance editorial cartoonist, *The Toronto Star*; freelance illustrator for *The New York Times, Scientific American, The Wall Street Journal, Canadian Geographic*

Family
Married, four children

The room where I create
"Small room on the second floor, with a working desk surrounded by walls. Wide windows with a view onto the street. Shelves with books, and an incredible mess everywhere."

Spare time
"No spare time, I am working continuously."

When I was growing up
"I enjoyed very much lying on the floor of my room, reading books and eating (at the same time) sugar and lemon."

My first book (and how it happened)
"I got 17 funny poems about dragons and monsters from my friend, an already famous children's poet in my country, Yugoslavia. I created a variety of funny monsters doing nasty, bad and forbidden things and designed a picture book. After that, we started to search for a publisher. Finally, it appeared to become extremely successful, and a favourite book for generations of kids in Yugoslavia."

Where my ideas come from
"From my childhood, from my children."

Who and what influenced me
"Authors and illustrators like A.A. Milne, Dušan Radovic, Norman Rockwell, Maurice Sendak, and above all, one old encyclopedia with thousands of black and white drawings."

How I work
"I illustrate every picture book the same way a director directs a movie — making my own screenplay and my own rhythm based on the author's text. My books all flow as a movie."

Something nobody knew about me (until now)
"As a boy, I had a dilemma whether to be a fireman or a priest when grown up!"

My favourite book that I've created
"*Bone Button Borscht* by Aubrey Davis, published by Kids Can Press."

Tips for young creators
"Creating illustrations for kids is not just a profession. It is a kind of play itself. The more you enjoy the game, the better result you get."

Dušan Petričić

Bibliography

Davis, Aubrey. *Bone Button Borscht.* Toronto: Kids Can Press, 1995 Paper 1-55074-326-0; Cloth 1-55074-224-8. Illustrations by Dušan Petričić.

—. *The Enormous Potato.* Toronto: Kids Can Press, 1997 Paper 1-86388-979-5; Cloth 1-55074-386-4. Illustrations by Dušan Petričić.

Funston, Sylvia. *Scary Science.* Toronto: Owl Books, 1996 Paper 1-895688-53-1; Cloth 1-895688-52-3. Illustrations by Dušan Petričić.

continued...

Gryski, Camilla. *Let's Play: Traditional Games of Childhood.* Toronto: Kids Can Press, 1995 Cloth 1-55074-256-6. Illustrations by Dušan Petričić.

Shalom, Vivienne and Dušan Petričić. *The Color of Things.* New York: Rizzoli, 1995 Cloth 0-8478-1866-7. Illustrations by Vivienne Shalom and Dušan Petričić

Dušan has also had over 20 books published in Yugoslavia.

Awards
Dušan has won nine Yugoslav and international awards from cities including Belgrade, Bratislava, Ljubljana, Leipzig and Moscow.

From *The Enormous Potato*

Stéphane Poulin
AUTHOR/ILLUSTRATOR

Born
December 6, 1961, Montreal, Quebec

School
College Ahuntsic, Montreal, Quebec

Where I live now
Montreal, Quebec

My favourite book when I was young
"*Babar the Elephant, Becassine, Tintin*, and the medical encyclopedia."

Career
Illustrator

Family
Two children, Gabriel and Camille

When I was growing up
"I am from a family of nine kids. My father was very talented in every kind of artistic expression but he didn't take it too seriously. He practised art as a sideline but encouraged us to draw and to create things for our own pleasure.

"I really enjoyed reading books but television fascinated me the most. Television was my first open window on the world."

Who and what influenced me
"When I decided to be an illustrator, I had no idea of the kinds of things an illustrator could do. Then I met Lise Monette, who was as passionate about drawing as I was. We started to draw together, and we are still sharing the same eraser."

Because of Lise, Stephane enrolled at College Ahuntsic. "It was exciting and fascinating to be with all those students who cared about art as I did. In the college's library there were many books about famous artists. I learned to love and understand their paintings. Lise was studying education and taught me about child development. I read most of her children's books. They captivated me, and that's when I decided to draw for children."

My first book (and how it happened)
"When I was 19, I received a Special Mention in the Communication Jeunesse Children's Illustration Contest. The next year I won the First Prize as best illustrator. Tundra Books asked me to do my first children's book. The concept of the book was an incredible challenge. It took me six months to complete it. The book, *A Beautiful City ABC*, received critical acclaim. I was 22.

"The hardest part was to come. Tundra asked me for a second book which had to be better than the *ABC*. I was scared. But I received the Canada Council Children's Literature Prize for Illustration for 1986 for *Have You Seen Josephine?* (Tundra) and *Album de famille* (Michel Quintin). For the first time, the Canada Council couldn't decide between two nominated books, so they gave the prize to both."

Where my ideas come from
"I was and I am still extremely curious about everything. I am visual, but I am not passive. I don't only look... I have a lot to say, and I wish I could have more time to say it all. I am always thinking of new paintings, new books. I can work a long time on a picture and I want it perfect but my mind is already on the next picture."

How I work
"In the past I worked with many kinds of mediums. I finally picked oil painting because when Tundra asked me for the *ABC*, Lise and I were expecting our first baby. I worked at home and I wanted to take care of the baby too, so I needed a medium which would allow me to stop at any time: oil takes a long time to dry.

"An artist must find the medium that suits his vision and his sensibility. I work only with the primary colours (blue, red, yellow), ochre and white. I use only these colours because it is easier to preserve their original brilliance. A red is more bright when you darken it with blue instead of using black. You can feel the blue inside the red while black just stays black."

Creating a children's book

"Drawing for children is something very special, a privilege. Knowing that somebody, somewhere is reading your book and may like it... It feels like this: when you are six years old and you show your mother a picture you are proud of. What a feeling you get when she decides to put it on the fridge where everybody can see it."

Stéphane Poulin

Bibliography

All books illustrated by Stéphane Poulin

Beaudin, Louise. *Animals in Winter* (Mr. Click Series). Trans. Alan Brown. Waterloo, QC: Quintin Publishers, 1992 Paper 2-920438-94-8; Cloth 2-920438-93-X.✤

Jo, Mary and Peter Collier. *The King's Giraffe*. New York: Simon and Schuster, 1996 0-689-80679-5.

Lamarche, Hélène. *Leonardo For Children Young And Old*. Trans. Judith Terry. Montreal: Montreal Museum of Fine Arts, 1987. Out of print.✤

Lenain, Thierry. *Petit Zizi*. Laval: Les 400 coups, 1997 Paper 2-921620-16-2.

Major, Henriette. *The Christmas Elves*. Trans. by Alan Brown. Toronto: McClelland and Stewart, 1988 Cloth 0-7710-5473-4.✤

Marcotte, Danielle. *Poil de serpent dent d'araignée*. Laval: Les 400 coups, 1996 2-921620-06-5.

Peant, Stanley. *Un petit garçon qui avait peur de tout et de rien*. Montreal: la courte échelle, 1998 2-89021-320-X.

Poulin, Stéphane. *Ah! Belle cité/ A Beautiful City ABC*. Montreal: Tundra Books, 1985. Out of print.

From *Petit Zizi*

—. *Have You Seen Josephine?* Montreal: Tundra Books, 1986 Cloth 0-88776-180-1.✤

—. *Can You Catch Josephine?* Montreal: Tundra Books, 1987 Paper 0-88776-214-X.✤

—. *Could You Stop Josephine?* Montreal: Tundra Books, 1988 Paper 0-88776-216-6; Cloth 0-88776-216-6.✤

—. *Benjamin and the Pillow Saga*. Toronto: Annick Press, 1989 Paper 1-55037-068-5; Cloth 1-55037-069-3.✤

—. *My Mother's Loves: Stories and Lies from My Childhood*. Toronto: Annick Press, 1990 Paper 1-55037-148-7; Cloth 1-55037-149-5.✤

—. *Travels for Two: Stories and Lies from My Childhood*. Toronto: Annick Press, 1991 Paper 1-55037-204-1; Cloth 1-55037-205-X.✤

—. *Family Album* (Mr. Click Series). Translated by Alan Brown. Waterloo, QC: Quintin Publishers, 1991 Paper 2-920438-92-1; Cloth 2-920438-91-3.✤

Quintin, Michel. *Endangered Animals* (Mr. Click Series). Translated by Alan Brown. Waterloo, QC: Quintin Publishers, 1992. Out of print.

—. *Dinosaurs* (Mr. Click Series). Translated by Alan Brown. Waterloo, QC: Quintin Publishers, 1992. Out of print.

Stinson, Kathy. *Teddy Rabbit*. Toronto: Annick Press, 1988. (English title out of print.)✤

Zipes, Jack. *The Outspoken Princess and the Gentle Knight*. New York: Bantam, 1994. Out of print.

Awards

1986 Canada Council Children's Literature Prize for *Album de Famille* and *Have You Seen Josephine?*

1988 Elizabeth Mrazik-Cleaver Canadian Picture Book Award for *Can You Catch Josephine?*

1988 Boston Globe Award of Excellence for *Can You Catch Josephine?*

1989 Vicky Metcalf Award for a body of work

1989 Governor General's Literary Award for *Benjamin and the Pillow Saga*

1992 Mr. Christie's Book Award for *Travels for Two*

1997 Mr. Christie's Book Award for *Poil de serpent dent d'araignée*

1997 Governor General's Award for *Poil de serpent dent d'araignée*

1998 Prix Jeunesse du salon du livre de Trois Rivière for *Petit Zizi*

Selected articles about Stéphane Poulin

Peel, Claudia. "French Author-Illustrator Shares Memories in Books." *Cornwall Ontario Daily* 22 Apr. 1988.

Pierre Pratt
AUTHOR/ILLUSTRATOR

Born
February 8, 1962, Montreal, Quebec

School
Graphic Arts at College Ahuntsic, Montreal, Quebec

Where I live now
Montreal, Quebec

My favourite book when I was young
"*Le Lotus Bleu* in the series *Tintin* by Hergé."

My favourite book now
The Incredible Painting of Felix Clousseau by Jon Agee

Career
Illustrator

Family
"I love cats but I'm really allergic to them."

The room where I create
"I work in a room facing a quiet street."

Spare time
"I play music, mostly the accordion. My repertoire includes jazz and central European music."

When I was growing up
"I began to draw very early. My mother recalls that, at age five, at the opening of the subway in Montreal, I saw a young girl crying because her ice cream cone had slipped out of her hands. I must have been touched by that, because when we got home, I drew her situation. When my father took me to hockey games, I would go home and draw the players. As a teenager, I wrote and illustrated my own comic strip."

My first book (and how it happened)
"...was done in 1985. It's not really a book, it's a long image that's folded up like an accordion. It was commissioned by Philippe Béha (an illustrator) and published in Quebec by Ovale under the title *Le Frigo*.

Follow That Hat! was the first picture book that Pierre both wrote and illustrated. "After *Uncle Henry's Dinner Guests* I wanted to do a book about transportation. Once a friend and I were in a car, when a hat went sailing by. I said, 'Follow that hat!' and he said, 'There's your story!'"

Where my ideas come from
"Mostly from what I observe around me, the people with whom I live, my friends and experiences. I have lots of ideas, but sometimes it's difficult to get them out. Once I start working though, the ideas usually begin to flow."

Who and what influenced me
"First, it's clear that Hergé influenced me. Then there are illustrators like Ian Pollock and Lionel Koechlin and painters like Jean Dubuffet and Georges Rouault."

How I work
"That depends on what kind of book I'm doing and what feelings I should render. I use different techniques: sometimes acrylics, sometimes inks or watercolours. I like mixed media very much."

My favourite book that I've created
"Usually my preferred one is the latest, in fact, *Marcel et André*, published by Gallimard in Paris is my preferred. I also really like *The Magic Boot, Follow That Hat* and the very last one, *La vie exemplaire de Martha et Paul*, a book that I wrote and illustrated, soon to be published in Paris by Seuil Jeunesse."

Tips for young creators
"Do what you want, impose your personality on your work. But also think of the people to whom you want to communicate."

Pierre Pratt

Bibliography

Duchesne, Christiane. *A Drawing for Tara.* Hull: CIDA, 1989. Illustrations by Pierre Pratt. Out of print.♣

Duchesne, Christiane. *Benjamin's Travels.* Hull: CIDA, 1990. Illustrations by Pierre Pratt. Out of print.♣

Evelyn, A. *Herman Henry's Dog.* Lexington: D.C. Heath & Co., 1995. Illustrations by Pierre Pratt.

Froissart, Bénédicte. *Uncle Henry's Dinner Guests.* Toronto: Annick Press, 1990 Paper 1055037-140-1; Cloth 1-55037-141-X. Illustrations by Pierre Pratt.

Pratt, Pierre. *Le frigo.* Montreal: Editions Ovale, 1985. Illustrations by the author. Out of print.

—. *Follow That Hat!* Trans. David Homel. Toronto: Annick Press, 1992 Paper 1-55037-259-9; Cloth 1-55037-261-0. Illustrations by the author.♣

—. *Marcel et André.* Gallimard/Le sourire qui mord, 1994. Illustrations by the author.

—. *Hippo Beach.* Toronto: Annick Press, 1997 Cloth 1-55037-419-2. Illustrations by the author.

Sage, James. *Sassy Gracie.* London: Macmillan Children's Books, 1998 Paper 0-333-684281; Cloth 0-333-68427-3. Illustrations by Pierre Pratt.

Simard, Rémy. *My Dog is an Elephant.* Trans. David Homel. Toronto: Annick Press, 1994 Paper 1-55037-976-3; Cloth 1-55037-977-1. Illustrations by Pierre Pratt.♣

—. *The Magic Boot.* Trans. David Homel. Toronto: Annick Press, 1995 Paper 1-55037-410-9; Cloth 1-55037-411-7. Illustrations by Pierre Pratt.♣

—. *Mister Once-Upon-a-Time.* Toronto: Annick Press 1998. Illustrations by Pierre Pratt.

Vandal, A. *Le rêve de Maggie.* Montreal: Editions Ovale, 1988. Illustrations by Pierre Pratt. Out of print.

Awards

1990 Governor General's Literary Award for *Uncle Henry's Dinner Guests*

1991 Mr. Christie's Book Award for *Uncle Henry's Dinner Guests*

1992 UNICEF Award (Bologna) for *Benjamin's Travels*

1993 Golden Apple Award (Bratislava) for *Follow That Hat!*

1994 Governor General's Literary Award for *My Dog is an Elephant*

1994 Mr. Christie's Book Award for *My Dog is an Elephant*

1994 TOTEM (Paris) best French picture book for children for *Marcel et André*

From *Sassy Gracie*

Barbara Reid
AUTHOR/ILLUSTRATOR

Born
November 16, 1957, Toronto, Ontario

School
Lawrence Park Collegiate Institute and Ontario College of Art, both in Toronto, Ontario

Where I live now
Toronto, Ontario

My favourite book when I was young
"I really loved the Narnia books by C.S. Lewis."

My favourite book now
"I love Robertson Davies, and other people's picture books I wish I'd done."

Career
Freelance illustrator

Family
Husband Ian Crysler; daughters Zoë and Tara, and a fox terrier named Ruby

The room where I create
"My studio is the top room of the house."

Spare time
"Read and garden, but I never really have spare time!"

When I was growing up
"When I was a kid I loved to read and draw. I copied favourite characters from books or made up my own if I didn't like the illustrations. I didn't realize that that was a good way to learn to be an illustrator!

"My favourite place to read was in a tree at my summer cottage. At least once every summer I would secretly stay awake all night — reading a book from cover to cover."

My first book (and how it happened)
"Scholastic gave me the job of illustrating *Mustard* by Betty Waterton. It was a low-budget, two-colour paperback. Although it was fun to do, when I saw the printed piece I realized I had a lot more to learn!

"My first real book was *The New Baby Calf*. Scholastic decided to give my Plasticine artwork a chance. By that time I had learned more and I was thrilled to work on a full-colour, hardcover book, especially in Plasticine."

Where my ideas come from
"First, I read the manuscript until I get right inside the story. Then I surround myself with reference material, from cuttings, picture files, books and magazines to fabrics and music. I plan the book out and then I start drawing and making notes. I keep filling my head with information and emotions until an idea comes. It's kind of magic — all you can do is set the stage and hope the idea makes an entrance."

Who and what influenced me
"In high school I got a book about the illustrator N.C. Wyeth for Christmas. I practically memorized it.

"I was also influenced by my high school art teacher who prodded me towards the Ontario College of Art. Arthur Rackham's art, illustrators who draw people, animals and characters, mood and emotion influence me as well. Ernest Shepard, Edward Ardizzone, Pauline Baines and Toulouse Lautrec are illustrators/ artists I love."

How I work
"After I've received a manuscript and spent a few weeks thinking about the story and collecting research, I plan the pictures out with pencil and paper. These drawings guide me when I start to put down the Plasticine.

"To start a picture, I spread a thin layer of Plasticine with my thumbs onto a piece of illustration board or stiff cardboard.

This provides a sticky surface to add on smaller details and textures. I make shapes with my fingers and add them on, building up layers from the background. Round pancake shapes can be pebbles on a beach or somebody's fat cheeks. A long snake shape can make hair, a kite string or smoke rising from a chimney.

"I use a knife to cut shapes like fence posts and doors; a comb to press a grassy or furry texture into the Plasticine; a sharp pencil to poke whisker lines or nostrils or nail holes with. I think up textures I want and I look around the house for tools to help me.

"Each page takes two to five days to make. A complicated picture like the birthday cake scene in *The Party* took six days to create.

"When all the pictures are finished, they are photographed; it is the photo of the Plasticine art that you see in my picture books. My husband Ian Crysler has photographed all of my books, and helped create lots of great effects."

My favourite book that I've created

"Each book is a different creation — parts of them I'm proud of, parts of them I wish I could change, parts of them I like because of something that was happening when I was working on them. Once they are done, though, like grown up children, they are on their own — not mine any more."

From *The Party*

Tips for young creators

"Read, write, draw. Most importantly — amuse yourself. I think spending time alone, being 'bored,' can lead to a lot of creativity. When your brain isn't being babysat by television or organized activities, there is freedom to just let your ideas play."

Barbara Reid
Bibliography

Allinson, Beverly. *Effie*. Richmond Hill: Scholastic Canada, 1990 Paper 0-590-74031. Illustrations by Barbara Reid.♣

Blakeslee, Mary. *It's Tough to be a Kid*. Richmond Hill: Scholastic Canada, 1983. Illustrations by Barbara Reid. Out of print.

Bogart, Jo Ellen. *Gifts*. Richmond Hill: Scholastic Canada, 1994 Cloth 0-590-24177-X. 1996 Paper 0-590-24935-5. Illustrations by Barbara Reid.

Chase, Edith Newlin. *The New Baby Calf*. Richmond Hill: Scholastic Canada, 1984 Cloth 0-590-71456-2; Big Book 0-590-71404-X. 1990 Paper 0-590-73678-7. Illustrations by Barbara Reid.♣

continued...

Downie, Mary Alice. *Jenny Greenteeth*. Toronto: Kids Can Press, 1984. Illustrations by Barbara Reid. Out of print.

Gold, Carol. *Have Fun With Magnifying*. Toronto: Kids Can Press, 1987. Illustrations by Barbara Reid. Out of print.

Irvine, Joan. *How to Make Pop-Ups*. Toronto: Kids Can Press, 1987 Paper 0-921103-36-0. Illustrations by Barbara Reid.

Linton, Marilyn. *Just Desserts and Other Treats for Kids to Make*. Toronto: Kids Can Press, 1986. Rev. ed. 1998 Paper 0-921103-02-6. Illustrations by Barbara Reid.

Oppenheim, Joanne. *Have You Seen Birds?* Richmond Hill: Scholastic Canada, 1986 Paper 0-590-71577-1; Cloth 0-590-71596-8; Big Book 0-590-71576-3. Illustrations by Barbara Reid.✤

Reid, Barbara, comp. *Sing a Song of Mother Goose*. Richmond Hill: Scholastic Canada, 1987. 1991 Paper 0-590-73838-0; Cloth 0-590-71781-2; Big Book 0-590-71380-9. Illustrations by the author.✤

—. *Playing With Plasticine*. Toronto: Kids Can Press, 1988 Paper 0-921103-41-7. Illustrations by the author.✤

—. *The Zoe Series*. Toronto: HarperCollins Canada, 1991. Illustrations by the author.
  Zoe's Rainy Day 0-00-223764-4
  Zoe's Windy Day 0-00-223763-6
  Zoe's Sunny Day 0-00-223759-8
  Zoe's Snowy Day 0-00-223758-X

—. *Two By Two*. Richmond Hill: Scholastic Canada, 1992 Cloth 0-590-73656-6. 1994 Paper 0-590-74407-0. Illustrations by the author.✤

—. *The Party*. Richmond Hill: Scholastic, 1997 Cloth 0-591-12385-8. Illustrations by the author.✤

—. *Fun with Modelling Clay*. Toronto: Kids Can Press, 1998 Paper 1-55074-510-7. Illustrations by the author.

—. *First Look Board Books* (Nature Series). Toronto: HarperCollins Canada, 1998.
  Caterpillar to Butterfly 0-00-224007-6
  Acorn to Oak Tree 0-00-224006-8
  Tadpole to Frog 0-00-224005-X
  Seed to Flower 0-00-224004-1

Waterton, Betty. *Mustard*. Richmond Hill: Scholastic Canada, 1983. Illustrations by Barbara Reid. Out of print.

Awards
1986 IODE Book Award - Toronto Chapter for *Have You Seen Birds?*

1986 Canada Council Children's Literature Prize for *Have You Seen Birds?*

1987 Elizabeth Mrazik-Cleaver Canadian Picture Book Award for *Have You Seen Birds?*

1988 UNICEF – Ezra Jack Keats Award of Excellence in Children's Book Illustration for *New Baby Calf, Sing a Song of Mother Goose*, and *Have You Seen Birds?*

1987 Ruth Schwartz Children's Book Award for *Have You Seen Birds?*

1992 Mr. Christie's Book Award for *Zoe* (Series)

1993 Elizabeth Mrazik-Cleaver Canadian Picture Book Award for *Two By Two*

1995 Amelia Frances Howard-Gibbon Illustrator's Award for *Gifts*

1997 Governor General's Literary Award for *The Party*

1997 Amelia Frances Howard-Gibbon Illustrator's Award for *The Party*

Selected articles about Barbara Reid
Goldsmith, Annette. "The Art of the Children's Book Illustrator." *Quill & Quire* Oct. 1985: 11-12.

McDougall, Carol. "Barbara Reid." *Presenting Canscaip*. Ed. Barbara Greenwood. Markham: Pembroke Press, 1990: 155-159.

Gertridge, Alison. *Meet Canadian Authors and Illustrators: 50 Creators of Children's Books*. Richmond Hill: Scholastic Canada, 1994.

Bill Slavin
ILLUSTRATOR

Born
February 12, 1959, Belleville, Ontario

School
Sheridan College, Oakville, Ontario

Where I live now
"An old farmhouse on the edge of the village of Millbrook, Ontario."

My favourite book when I was young
"Anything by Thornton W. Burgess."

My favourite book now:
Tuesday by D. Wiesner

Career
Illustrator

Family
Wife, Esperança Melo

The room where I create
"A large sunny room in the upstairs of our house."

Spare time
"Travel, gardening, reading, rummaging around medieval ruins."

When I was growing up
"I was the second youngest in a family of eight. I have been drawing since I can remember, and have wanted to illustrate books for just about as long. My first commercial success was an anti-smoking-in-bed poster I did in Grade 3, which won first prize and paid me $25. In Grade 3 I also produced my first illustrated book, called *Zok the Caveman*. This was such a success that I promptly created a sequel, *The Adventures of Black Cloud, Son of Zok*.

"I continued to write and illustrate books as well as draw profusely. I graduated to pen and ink at a fairly early age. Fortunately, my mother was a tolerant person and put up with the many bottles of ink spilt on the living room carpet."

My first book (and how it happened)
"I worked for many years as an art director/illustrator/layout artist for a small publishing house in the Ottawa Valley. When I moved to Toronto, I took my portfolio around trying to get a job illustrating kid's books. Finally, Kids Can Press offered me *Too Many Chickens*. Since then I have illustrated a number of children's books. It is work I love, and I consider myself very fortunate to be working in this industry."

How I work
"I work primarily in watercolour and inks, although my first children's book, *Too Many Chickens*, was in pastel.

I tend to work quickly and impetuously at my art, but am trying to learn to slow down. Until now I have had very little contact with the authors whose books I am illustrating, and it works well, allowing each party to have free rein on their creative vision. However, I am thinking that it would be interesting to try a book where I worked more closely with the author."

Where my ideas come from
"I work mainly from my imagination. Dreams and that point before you fall asleep or wake up are my most creative times."

Who and what influenced me
"My influences are all over the place. My parents encouraged me, and my older brothers and sisters drew as well. Early heroes were Uderzo (illustrator on *Asterix*) and early *Mad* comic illustrators."

Something nobody knew about me (until now)
"I'm bald on top."

My favourite book that I've created
The Stone Lion

Tips for young creators
"If you want to illustrate, draw all the time. Don't watch too much television — it turns your brain to porridge — and never forget how to see. If you think you know what something looks like, you will stop seeing it for what it actually is.

"Never set limitations on your dreams and don't become frustrated when things don't work out. Improving is a lifetime process. If you never forget your dream, you will get there. Every action you take will directly or indirectly lead you there."

Bill Slavin

Bibliography

All books illustrated by Bill Slavin

Bourgeois, Paulette. *Too Many Chickens.* Toronto: Kids Can Press, 1990 Paper 1-55074-067-9. ♣

—. *The Sun.* Toronto: Kids Can Press, 1995 Cloth 1-55074-158-6. 1996 Paper 1-55074-330-9.

—. *The Moon.* Toronto: Kids Can Press, 1995 Cloth 1-55074-157-8. 1996 Paper 1-55074-332-5.

Brooks, Ben. *Lemonade Parade.* Toronto: Kids Can Press, 1991. ♣

Cockerill, A.W. *Emma on Albert Street.* Cobourg: Black Cat Press, 1997

Drake, Jane and Ann Love. *A Kid's Guide to the Millennium.* Toronto: Kids Can Press, 1998. Paper 1-55074-436-4; Cloth 1-55074-556-5. ♣

Engel, Howard. *A Child's Christmas in Scarborough.* Toronto: Key Porter, 1997.

Granfield, Linda. *Extra! Extra! The Who, What, Where, When and Why of Newspapers.* Toronto: Kids Can Press, 1993 Paper 1-55074-122-5. ♣

—. *1987, the Year I Was Born.* Toronto: Kids Can Press, 1994 Paper 1-55074-144-6.

—. *1988, the Year I Was Born.* Toronto: Kids Can Press, 1995 1-55074-192-6.

—. *1984, the Year I Was Born.* Toronto: Kids Can Press, 1996 1-55074-309-0.

Hancock, Pat. *1985, the Year I Was Born.* Toronto: Kids Can Press, 1996 1-55074-308-2.

King, Bob. *Sitting on the Farm.* Toronto: Kids Can Press, 1991 Paper 1-55074-149-7. ♣

Lewis, Amanda, and Tim Wynne-Jones. *Rosie Backstage.* Toronto: Kids Can Press, 1994 Paper 1-55074-148-9; Cloth 1-55074-148-9. ♣

McFarlane, Brian. *Hockey! The Book for Kids.* Toronto: Kids Can Press, 1990. Rpt. as *Hockey for Kids: Heroes, Stats, Tips and Facts* 1994 Paper 1-55074-215-9. ♣

MacLeod, Elizabeth. *The Phone Book.* Toronto: Kids Can Press, 1995 Paper 1-55074-220-5.

—. *Get Started: Stamp Collecting.* Toronto: Kids Can Press, 1996 Paper 1-55074-313-9; Cloth 1-55074-279-5. Illustrations also by Esperança Melo.

Nicolson, Cynthia Pratt. *Earthdance: How Volcanoes, Earthquakes, Tidal Waves and Geysers Shake Our Restless Planet.* Toronto: Kids Can Press, 1994 Paper 1-55074-155-1.

—. *The Earth.* Toronto: Kids Can Press, 1996 Cloth 1-55074-314-7. 1997 Paper 1-55074-327-9.

—. *The Planets.* Toronto: Kids Can Press, 1998 Cloth 1-55074-512-3.

Ross, Catherine Sheldrick. *Circles: Shapes in Math, Science and Nature.* Toronto: Kids Can Press, 1992 Paper 1-55074-064-4. ♣

—. *Triangles: Shapes in Math, Science and Nature.* Toronto: Kids Can Press, 1994 Paper 1-55074-194-2.

—. *Squares: Shapes in Math, Science and Nature.* Toronto: Kids Can Press, 1996 Paper 1-55074-273-6.

Slavin, Bill. *The Cat Came Back.* Toronto: Kids Can Press, 1992. 1994 Paper 1-55074-183-7. ♣

—. *The Stone Lion.* Red Deer AB: Northern Lights Books for Children-Red Deer College Press, 1996 Cloth 0-88995-154-3.

Staunton, Ted. *Morgan Makes Magic.* Halifax: Formac Publishing, 1997 Paper 0-88780-390-3; Cloth 0-88780-391-1.

Wynne-Jones, Tim, adapt. *The Hunchback of Notre Dame.* By Victor Hugo. Toronto: Key Porter, 1996. 1997 Paper 1-55013-872-3.

Zimelman, Nathan. *How the Second Grade Got $8,205.50 to Visit the Statue of Liberty.* Mortin Grove, IL: Albert Whitman, 1992 Cloth 0-8075-3431-5.

Awards

1997 Storytelling World Awards Honour title for *The Stone Lion*

From
The Stone Lion

Martin Springett
ILLUSTRATOR

Born
October 18, 1947, London, England

School
Hastings School of Art, England

Where I live now
Toronto, Ontario

My favourite books when I was young
Dan Dare, Pilot of the Future, by Frank Hampson; *Lord of the Rings* by J.R.R. Tolkien

My favourite books now
Lord of the Rings by J.R.R. Tolkien; *Winter's Tale* by Mark Helprin; *Tigana*, by Guy Gavriel Kay

Career
"As an immigrant to Canada (1965) I had many different jobs, from working in a hospital to landscape gardening. I also played guitar and sang in many bands. I was a songwriter for a recording studio in Vancouver. When I moved to Toronto I worked in every field where illustration is required: magazines, newspapers, educational publishing, advertising, record and CD covers. I have also designed and illustrated many young adult book covers. In 1988 I was asked to illustrate my first children's book, *Mei Ming and the Dragon's Daughter.* The most recent job I have had is creating concept illustrations for a television series based on Ann Macafree's *Dragon Riders of Pern* books."

Family
Wife, Hilary; daughters, Rebecca and Miriam; and Buddy the mad Cocker Spaniel

The room where I create
"I have a basement studio. We live on the top floor of a house owned by my wife's aunt, and after many years of working in the room next to the kitchen, Aunt Kathleen very kindly allowed me the use of a large basement room. I have two drawing tables, an extensive library of art books of all kinds, and a table with all my inks, paints, brushes, pencils, laid out in a messy array. I also have an air compressor for my air brush. At the other end of my studio I have all my music gear, guitars and recording equipment."

Spare time
"I love to play my guitar, read books, listen to music, go to movies and hang out with my family."

When I was growing up
"The first books I 'illustrated' were in fact incredibly dull math books that I had in Grade 5. I would fill these dreary textbooks with drawings of spaceships and vast battle scenes. At the end of school term my teacher discovered that I had at least six of these books with my doodles, and I had to erase them all. Things had improved by the time I went to art school, although I spent most of my time there learning to play the guitar. You can see that I was doing the right things at the wrong time, but I always had lots of fun. A sense of humour is essential in the life of an artist; that's one of the most important things I learned when I was growing up."

My first book (and how it happened)
"*Mei Ming and the Dragon's Daughter*, written by Lydia Bailey, was the first children's book I illustrated. I had been illustrating and designing many covers for adult novels, and one of these, *The Darkest Road*, was a favourite book of an editor at Scholastic. She liked the cover so much that I was asked to come in with my portfolio, and after looking at my work, she offered me the job of illustrating *Mei Ming*. I had always had a great love of Chinese art and design, so creating the pictures for this story was like receiving a gift."

Where my ideas come from

"Inspiration and ideas come from life I have lived, my interests, the places I have visited, my friends and family. The everyday, as well as the amazing, can ignite ideas. I have always loved the challenge of creating an image that wasn't there before. I love drawing kids, but to illustrate kids' books one has to be able to draw many things. I am always learning about the world and art, and this leads to inspiration."

Who and what influenced me

"While growing up I was always looking at art of all kinds, whether it was fine art or illustrations, and I still do exactly that. I have a large sheet of paper which I cover in tiny drawings, and from one of these scribbles will come the finished illustration. The next day I take the sketch I like and enlarge it to the size I wish to work at. The following day I return to my thumbnails and work on the next part of the story until all the ideas for the illustrations have been worked out. These are shown to the editor and art director at the publishers, who then give the go-ahead for the final stage.

"It's at this point that I have to decide which technique to use, acrylic paint, coloured pencil, pen and ink, watercolour or air brush."

My favourite book that I've created

"Usually my favourite book is the last one I illustrated; in this case it's *Too Many Suns*, by Julie Lawson."

Tips for young creators

"When you are looking for ideas for a picture, remember there are no such things as mistakes. If you draw something you don't like, think of it as a stepping stone to the next idea. Keep 'playing' with ideas."

Martin Springett

Bibliography

Anderson, John. *Witch What and the Wye of Tyme*. Toronto: Napoleon, 1992 Cloth 0-929141-15-6. Illustrations by Martin Springett.

Bailey, Lydia. *Mei Ming and the Dragon's Daughter*. Toronto: Scholastic, 1990 Cloth 0-590-73369-9. 1992 Paper 0-590-73370-2. Illustrations by Martin Springett.

Lawson, Julie. *Too Many Suns*. Toronto: Stoddart Kids, 1996 Cloth 0-7737-2897-X. Illustrations by Martin Springett.

Thompson, Richard. *Who*. Victoria: Orca Publishers, 1993 Cloth 0-920501-98-2. Illustrations by Martin Springett.

Yochida, Yoshika. *The Wise Old Woman*. New York: Margaret K. McElderry Books, 1994 Cloth 0-689-50582-5. 1997 Paper 1-56334-747-4. Illustrations by Martin Springett.

Articles about Martin Springett

"Essence of What's Going On... Frieda Wishinsky Speaks with Martin Springett." *Books in Canada* Nov. 1996.

From *Too Many Suns*

Daniel Sylvestre
AUTHOR/ILLUSTRATOR

Born
Montreal, November 29, 1952

School
CEGEP in Montreal

My favourite book when I was young
Tom Sawyer by Mark Twain

My favourite book now
Noeuds et dénouement by Annie Proulx

Career
"Illustrator for the past 25 years (children's books, book illustrations, logos, etc.). Animation films for two years at the National Film Board."

Family
"Three brothers; two children: Alma, 21 years old and Antoine, 3 years old."

The room where I create
"Over the years, I have had many studios. I also worked on kitchen tables and in hotels. Now I have a studio in the basement and another one in an engraving and lithography studio. I like the space I can have working on big tables."

Spare time
"I have played the guitar since I was 13 years old and I'm not too bad. I regularly read, I like newspapers and I do sculpture."

When I was growing up
"In the spring, I loved making barricades of snow to control the water running along the sidewalk. In the summer, I would spend hours constructing dams in the streams. I humbly confess that, at the seaside, my sand castles were noticed. I have rediscovered these pleasures with my children. I did it with Alma who is grown up now and I will do it with Antoine too: still making castles and constructions. I use the children as an excuse and then my youthful pleasure is always with me."

My first book (and how it happened)
"Bertrand Gauthier, Zunik's author, got in touch with me for my first book. He had seen one of my illustrations in a magazine and the 'Montreal look' hooked him. So we did our first book *Un jour d'été à fleurdepeau*, in 1978. Then we started the Zunik's series, of which there are now 10 titles."

Where my ideas come from
"They come from my family life and the people and objects that surround me. I love Montreal. I was born there and I have always been curious about urban life: buildings, alleys, bridges, trains and 'greasy spoons.' I'm also very interested in art history. My parents had a lot of French and English magazines at home (*l'Express, le Nouvel Observateur, Life, Look, The New Yorker*) and I was attracted by their illustrations. Sempé affected me and still affects me now with his sensibility and his intelligence. I like American illustrations because their humour and their lack of taste is irresistible."

How I work
"I do a lot of sketches. I draw a storyboard of the story and finally I very freely draw all of the book. This last part is very lively and full of hidden treasures.

"Then I do some refining and I present the sketches to the publisher to receive the go-ahead. Then I do the final illustrations while trying to preserve as much lightness in the sketches as possible. For me this is the biggest part of the job, and disappointments can happen."

Something nobody knew about me (until now)
"Almost 20 years ago, I wanted to get fit and to find a sport or an activity. So, at the same time, I took up tap dancing and boxing but I finally chose bicycling. I bicycled from Montreal to Halifax (all right, so I returned by train)."

My favourite book that I've created

"It is impossible to say. Rather, I would say that I like the characters I've created: Zunik, Not Dog, Murphy the Rat."

Tips for young creators

"Relax, it's a game and enjoy yourself. Work is an art; it is your art and you should be like an explorer moving forward in a wild forest."

Daniel Sylvestre

Select bibliography

Duggan, Paul. *Murphy the Rat: Tales of Tough City*. Red Deer: Red Deer College Press, 1992 Cloth 0-88995-084-9. Illustrations by Daniel Sylvestre.

Farmer, Patti. *Amanda Adams Loves Herbie Hickle*. Toronto: Scholastic, 1998 Paper 0-590-12444-7; Cloth 0-590-12445-5. Illustrations by Daniel Sylvestre.

Gauthier, Bertrand. *Un jour d' été a fleurdepeau*. Montreal: la courte échelle, 1978. Illustrations by the author. Out of print.

—. *The Yuneek* Series. Trans. David Homel. Montreal: la courte échelle. Illustrations by Daniel Sylvestre.

> *I'm Yuneek*. 1984.✤
> *The Championship*. 1986.✤
> *The Winner*. 1987.✤
> *The Present*. 1987.✤
> *The Wawabongbong*. 1989.✤
> *Camping Out*. 1989.✤
> *Le spectacle*. 1991.
> *Le dragon*. 1991.
> *Le rendez-vous*. 1994.
> *Le grand magicien*. 1998.

Sylvestre, Daniel. *À chat perché*. St. Lambert: Héritage, 1997 2-7625-8704-2. Illustrations by the author.

Awards

1984 Alvine-Bélisle Award for Best Children's Book for *Je suis Zunik (I'm Yuneek)*

1992 Award of Excellence from l'Association des consommateurs du Quebec for *Le dragon*

From *Le grand magicien*

C.J. (Carrie) Taylor
AUTHOR/ILLUSTRATOR

Born
August 31, 1952, Montreal, Quebec

Life
Self-taught

Where she lives now
Chateauguay, Quebec

Lifestyle
Artist

Family
Husband, Norman Keene; three children, Matthew, Kristy and Joseph. Two grandsons, Andrew (six years old) and Morise (eight months old)

Spare time
"Since January 1992, I have been the host of a weekly radio program called 'Earthsongs' on CKRK FM, Mohawk Radio in Kahnawake, Quebec. Books are reviewed, songs by and about natives are played, stories are told, and ecological concerns are aired."

When she was growing up
"I started painting when I was 16 years old with an old set of oil paints that belonged to my mother. I sold my first painting for five dollars. My talent comes from my mother. My subject matter comes from my father. My father's mother was a Mohawk, who lost her status when her first husband died and she remarried a non-native. She was a sad woman, and her sadness intrigued me."

Discovering her native roots when she was six years old, Carrie has been fascinated with legends ever since. "We lived in the country in the middle of nowhere and I was always by myself. It gave me a chance to think things through to find out who I was."

Her first book (and how it happened)
May Cutler, president of Tundra Books admired Carrie's work and asked if she wanted to write and illustrate native legends for children. Tundra launched her first book, *How Two-Feather was saved from loneliness*, which is based on an Abenaki tale of a lonely man who becomes enchanted with a mystical woman. "The book takes in three origins — how corn, communal living and fire came into the world," Carrie says.

Where her ideas come from
Carrie's interest in native legends peaked when she began to investigate her own native heritage. "I've been on a lifelong search to find my heritage and personality. My art and books are an extension of that."

How she works
The legends Carrie chooses to illustrate are the ones she sees most vividly in her imagination. "In all my books I'm looking for the qualities of a hero and whether the legend is a good story with good morals for children."

Research is also an important part of Carrie's work. "When I'm researching a story I have to make sure that the environment is authentic, that the style of dress the natives wear is authentic and the type of spirituality I'm portraying is authentic. This is important because I want to dispel the stereotypes about natives." Carrie works in acrylic, pencil, watercolour and oils.

C. J. Taylor

Bibliography
Taylor, C. J. *How Two-Feather was saved from loneliness: An Abenaki Legend*. Montreal: Tundra Books, 1990 Cloth 0-88776-254-9. 1992 Paper 0-88776-282-4. Illustrations by the author.✲

—. *The Ghost and Lone Warrior: An Arapaho Legend*. Montreal: Tundra Books, 1991 Cloth 0-88776-263-8. 1993 Paper 0-88776-308-1. Illustrations by the author.✲

—. *Little Water and the gift of the animals: A Seneca Legend*. Montreal:

Tundra Books, 1992 Cloth 0-88776-285-9. 1997 Paper 0-88776-400-2. Illustrations by the author. ✢

—. *How we saw the world: Nine Native stories of the way things began.* Montreal: Tundra Books, 1993 Cloth 0-88776-302-2. 1996 Paper 0-88776-373-1. Illustrations by the author.

—. *The secret of the white buffalo: An Oglala Sioux Legend.* Montreal: Tundra Books, 1993 Cloth 0-88776-321-9. 1997 Paper 0-88776-399-5. Illustrations by the author. ✢

—. *Bones in the basket: Native stories of the origin of people.* Montreal: Tundra Books, 1994 Cloth 0-88776-327-8. Illustrations by the author.♣

—. *Monster from the swamp: Native legends about demons, monsters and other creatures.* Toronto: Tundra Books, 1995 Cloth 0-88776-361-8. Illustrations by the author.

—. *Messenger of Spring.* Toronto: Tundra Books, 1997 Cloth 0-88776-361-8. Illustrations by the author.

Selected articles about C. J. Taylor

Clemence, Verne. "Books Express Native Spirituality and Identity." *The Star Phoenix* [Saskatoon] 21 Mar. 1992.

Tousley, Nancy. "Native Author Brings Legends to Life." *Calgary Herald* 24 Mar. 1992 A10-11.

Van Luven, Lynne. "Network Needed for Communication among Natives, Metis Author Says." *The Edmonton Journal* 23 Mar. 1992.

Varcoe, Chris. "Art and Words Capture Traditional Indian Legends." *The Leader-Post* [Regina] 4 Apr. 1992.

From *Bones in the basket*

Jan Thornhill
AUTHOR/ILLUSTRATOR

Born
1955, Sudbury, Ontario

School
Elementary and high school in Richmond Hill and Thornhill, Ontario; Ontario College of Art, Toronto, Ontario

Where I live now
"In the woods near Havelock, Ontario in a house my husband and I built."

My favourite book when I was young
The Bad Child's Book of Beasts by Hilaire Belloc

My favourite book now
Precious Bane by Mary Webb

Career
"Illustrator and writer, although I once spent six months sewing beads and sequins on Dolly Parton's dresses."

Family
"Husband, Fred Gottschalk. We have a new dog called Betty Boots, and an ancient cat, Morag."

The room where I create
"I have a little studio where I write, and I do all my illustrations on the dining room table."

Spare time
"Gardening, seed-saving, mushroom-hunting, swimming, travelling, reading, making a mess."

When I was growing up
"I've made pictures since I could hold a crayon, partly because my mother, an artist, always encouraged me. My family went on regular weekend walks in the country which gave me an early and long-lasting appreciation of nature, particularly because my father is a walking encyclopedia of the sciences. By the time I was 10, I'd collected so many birds' nests and animal skulls, fossils and shells, feathers and leaves, that I turned our basement into a museum and charged five cents to get in. My mother was the only one who paid."

My first book (and how it happened)
"*The Wildlife ABC* was the result of three things: I was bored with drawing hands, money and unattractive businessmen for newspapers and magazines; I'd become involved in environmental issues; and I thought if I made a kids' book, I'd make wheelbarrows full of money (ha).

"I came up with the concept of an ABC using Canadian wildlife because I couldn't find anything similar in the library. I did four sample illustrations, wrote four sample 'nature notes', wrote the rhyming text, researched Canadian publishers at the library, and then sat on the

whole thing for two years. My husband finally forced me to send it to a publisher. I chose Greey de Pencier, now Owl Books, because of their nature and science interest. They called me immediately and accepted my proposal. Much later I found out how rarely things happen this way in children's book publishing."

Where my ideas come from
"Ideas come from different places. The tree book developed after I'd spent a few weeks making maple syrup in the open woods, staring for hours at the leafless trees. After noticing all the scars and broken limbs and woodpeckers looking for nesting holes, it occurred to me that each tree had a separate and unique story to tell. The book evolved from that point.

"I often come up with what seems like a simple concept, and then the project gets more complicated as I progress. The idea of linking retold animal folk tales in *Crow and Fox* seemed simple, but ended up being an almost endless task of searching for, listing, categorizing, and juggling two-animal tales until my head was spinning."

Who and what influenced me
"The wonders of the natural world. My parents and a couple

of extraordinary teachers in school. Artists from all cultures, both ancient and modern. My husband, Fred, who with one cutting remark, made me rethink my illustration style and loosen up so that I could do something that was all my own. That was in 1982 and I've been happy ever since."

How I work

"The illustrations in my first three books were all done on scratchboard — white card covered with a thin, smooth layer of white clay. I would paint with gouache (an opaque watercolour paint), then shade with coloured pencils, then outline with black ink. After that I would use a variety of sharp tools to scratch away paint so that the white base showed through. This was a particularly effective technique for highlights and fur. My hand hurts too much these days to use the scratching tools, so now I just paint, beginning with black outlines. It's almost like paint-by-number, but is a bit more complicated, and I'm the only one who knows the numbers.

"Because I often use a lot of detail that can be repetitious and tedious, I'd go out of my mind if I didn't have the company of radio or television. In the morning I listen to CBC Radio, and in the afternoons I work in front of the television listening to — this is embarrassing — three different soaps."

Something nobody knew about me (until now)

"Whenever I start a final illustration, after the rough pencil drawing is done, I'm always

From *Crow and Fox and Other Animal Legends*

afraid that it's going to be awful when it's finished. I feel that way until almost the minute that it's done, which is sometimes two or three weeks later. It's a scary process, but I think it keeps me from being bored while I work."

Tips for young creators

"If you want to write, you have to read. So read, read, and read some more. If you like drawing, draw. Draw anything. Draw your hand in different positions. Look at other people's drawings and paintings and try to figure out what they did to create different effects. Don't be impatient. I spend up to three weeks working on one illustration, sometimes 14 hours a day. Don't give up. I've been drawing almost every day for more that 35 years and I'm still not always sure of myself or happy with what I've done, but that doesn't stop me from trying."

Jan Thornhill

Bibliography

Crease, Skid. *In the Great Meadow*. Willowdale: Annick Press, 1994 Paper 1-55037-998-4; Cloth 1-55037-999-2. Illustrations by Jan Thornhill.

Thornhill, Jan. *The Wildlife ABC: A Nature Alphabet*. Toronto: Owl Books, 1988 Cloth 0-920775-29-2. 1994 Paper 1-895688-13-2. Illustrations by the author.

—. *The Wildlife 123: A Nature Counting Book*. Toronto: Owl Books, 1989 Cloth 0-920775-39-X. 1994 Paper 1-895688-14-0. Illustrations by the author.

—. *A Tree in the Forest*. Toronto: Owl Books, 1991 Paper 1-895688-18-3; Cloth 0-920775-64-0. Illustrations by the author.

—. *Crow and Fox and Other Animal Legends*. Toronto: Owl Books, 1993 Cloth 1-895688-11-6. Illustrations by the author.

—. *Wild in the City*. Toronto: Owl Books, 1995 Cloth 1-895688-33-7. Illustrations by the author.

—. *Before and After: A Book of Nature Timescapes*. Toronto: Owl Books, 1997 Cloth 1-895688-61-2. Illustrations by the author.

Awards

1990 UNICEF – Ezra Jack Keats International Award for Excellence in Children's Book Illustration for *The Wildlife 123*

1992 Information Book Award for *A Tree in the Forest*

Selected articles about Jan Thornhill

Siamon, Sharon. "Introducing Jan Thornhill." *CANSCAIP News* 19.3 (1997): 1-4.

Mark Thurman
AUTHOR/ILLUSTRATOR

Born
September 27, 1948, Toronto, Ontario

School
Toronto Island School, Lord Dufferin School, Central Technical School, all in Toronto

Where I live now
"Half the year in Toronto, half the year near Owen Sound, Ontario."

My favourite books when I was young
"Comic books: *Mad Magazine, Sick, Green Lantern, Superman, Spiderman, Batman.*"

My favourite books now
Alice in Wonderland, Amusing Ourselves to Death, Brave New World

Career
Illustrator, author, teacher, artist, designer, painter

Family
Partner, Marianne Dworkin; white German Shepherd, Sherwood

The room where I create
"My second-floor studio where I've worked for 25 years. I also work in cafés in downtown Toronto."

Spare time
"Read, play tennis, go to movies, draw and paint, think, play guitar."

When I was growing up
"I loved to draw from before I can remember. I drew cartoons for my friends and was known as 'the artist'. From the time I was eight until I was 15, my family went away every summer to a log cabin in northern Ontario. There was no electricity, no running water and no indoor toilet, just an outhouse. We hiked, swam, watched animals, made forts, created mischief, learned about nature, played cards, told scary stories and didn't watch television or listen to the radio."

My first book (and how it happened)
"I made up a story for my nieces about an elephant with a worse cold than theirs. I decided to turn it into a picture book. As a mental exercise, I planned and designed the illustrations in my head as I took the streetcar to work every morning. It seemed easier than trying to sketch on a packed streetcar. (It also proved to be a valuable lesson in visualizing.) Six years later I went to a publisher about a completely different job and took a few original paintings from *The Elephant's*

Cold. I showed them, she liked them, and that was it."

Who and what influenced me
"My parents for their love and for looking at an endless stream of drawings. My large and loving family and my teachers who encouraged and supported me. Meeting the Masters in art school: Michelangelo, da Vinci, Rembrandt, Carravaggio, Vermeer, Goya, Van Gogh, Degas: and, later, meeting the masters of illustration: Wyeth, Parrish, Rackham, Heinrich Kley, C.D. Gibson, Mucha and Beardsley."

How I work
"I work in two ways depending on whether it is someone else's story or my own. If I'm hired, I read the story many times until I get a feeling for the text and images come fast and furious. I do small pencil sketches to capture the images, but the real work begins when I start to move things around and play with the characters, action and backgrounds. After meetings with the art director and editor, I work on more detailed sketches and once they're approved, I start the final artwork. This whole process can take a year.

"When I work on my own, I usually have a flash! Ideas come to me whole, the story with all the images, like an edited-down movie. Or, sometimes, ideas will work their way to the surface of my imagination very, very slowly. I 'catch' those ideas by writing and doodling in my sketchbook. Slowly, the characters, problems and settings take form. Sometimes I draw the whole story first, sometimes I write it first. After developing the characters and trying numerous techniques for the illustrations, I show my story to publishers. That's the difficult part."

My favourite book that I've created

"*One, Two, Many*. A close second is *Some Sumo*. The 154 issues of 'The Mighty Mites' comic for *Owl Magazine* that Emily Hearn and I created stands as a favourite project, all 16 years worth."

Tips for young creators

"Draw and write everyday. Carry a notebook, and sketch and jot down all your ideas. Copy styles of writing that you like. Copy the art of the Masters. This will teach you style, form and improve your technique."

Mark Thurman

Bibliography

Alexander, Wilma. *What to Do About Babe*. Toronto: ITP Nelson, 1997. Illustrations by Mark Thurman. Out of print.

Bodger, Joan. *Belinda's Ball*. Toronto: Stoddart/Oxford University Press Canada, 1981. Illustrations by Mark Thurman. Out of print.

Choyce, Lesley. *Go for it Carrie*. Halifax: Formac, 1997 Paper 0-88780-392-X; Cloth 0-88780-393-8. Illustrations by Mark Thurman.

Dunn, Sonja. *Primary Rhymerry*. Markham: Pembroke Publishers, 1993 Paper 1-55138-005-6. Illustrations by Mark Thurman.

—. *Gimme a Break, Rattlesnake!: Schoolyard Chants and Other Nonsense*. Toronto: Stoddart, 1994 Paper 0-7737-5696-5. Illustrations by Mark Thurman.

Granfield, Linda. *Postcards Talk*. Markham: Pembroke Publishers, 1998 Paper 1-55138-033-1. Illustrations by Mark Thurman.

Haffner, Margaret. *Fearless Jake*. Toronto: Scholastic, 1995 Cloth 0-590-124308-X. Illustrations by Mark Thurman.

Hearn, Emily. *Good Morning Franny, Good Night Franny*. Toronto: Women's Press, 1984. Illustrations by Mark Thurman. Out of print.

—. *Race You Franny!* Toronto: Women's Press, 1986. Illustrations by Mark Thurman. Out of print.

—. *Franny and the Music Girl*. Toronto: Second Story Press, 1989 Paper 0-929005-03-1. Illustrations by Mark Thurman.

Hearn, Emily. *Draw & Write Your Own Picture Book*. Markham: Pembroke Publishers, 1990 Paper 0-921217-46-3. Illustrations by Mark Thurman.✦

Hearn, Emily, and Mark Thurman. *Illustration Ideas for Creating Picture Books*. Markham: Pembroke Publishers, 1990 Cloth 0-921217-48-X. Illustrations by Mark Thurman.

—. *Helping Kids Draw & Write Picture Books*. Markham: Pembroke Publishers, 1990 Paper 0-921217-47-1. Illustrations by Mark Thurman.

Mabin, Geraldine, and Lynn Seligman. *Cookie Magic*. Toronto: Stoddart/Oxford University Press, 1994 Paper 0-19-540994-9. Illustrations by Mark Thurman.

Roberts, Ken. *Pop Bottles*. Toronto: Groundwood, 1987 Paper 0-88899-059-6. Toronto: ITP Nelson, 1998 Paper 0-17-607444-9. Illustrations by Mark Thurman.

continued...

From *One, Two, Many*

Swede, George. *I Want to Lasso Time*. Toronto: Simon & Pierre, 1991 Paper 0-88924-234-8. Introduction by Emily Hearn. Illustrations by Mark Thurman.

Thurman, Mark. *The Elephant's Cold* (Douglas the Elephant Series). Richmond Hill: Marrello, 1979. Rev. ed. 1989. Illustrations by the author. Out of print.

—. *The Elephant's New Bicycle* (Douglas the Elephant Series). Richmond Hill: Marrello, 1980. Rev. ed. 1989. Illustrations by the author. Out of print.

—. *The Birthday Party* (Douglas the Elephant Series). Rev. ed. Richmond Hill: Marrello, 1981. Illustrations by the author. Out of print.

—. *The Lie That Grew And Grew* (Douglas the Elephant Series). Richmond Hill: Marrello, 1981. Rev. ed. 1989. Illustrations by the author. Out of print.

—. *Two Pals on an Adventure* (Douglas the Elephant Series). Richmond Hill: Marrello, 1982. Rev. ed. 1989. Illustrations by the author. Out of print.

—. *City Scrapes* (Two Pals on an Adventure Series). Richmond Hill: Marrello, 1983. Rev. ed. 1989. Illustrations by the author. Out of print.

—. *You Bug Me* (Two Pals on an Adventure Series). Richmond Hill: Marrello, 1985. Rev. ed. 1989. Illustrations by the author. Out of print.

—. *Old Friends, New Friends*. Richmond Hill: Marrello, 1985. Illustrations by the author. Out of print.

—. *Two Stupid Dummies*. Richmond Hill: Marrello, 1989. Illustrations by the author. Out of print.

—. *Cabbagetown Gang*. Richmond Hill: Marrello, 1989. Illustrations by the author. Out of print.

—. *Who Needs Me?* Richmond Hill: Marrello, 1989. Illustrations by the author. Out of print.

—. *Some Sumo* (Two Pals on an Adventure Series). Richmond Hill: Marrello, 1989. Illustrations by the author. Out of print.

—. *How to Plan Your Drawings*. Markham: Pembroke Publishers, 1992 Paper 0-921217-84-6. Illustrations by the author.

—. *Fun-tastic Collages*. Markham: Pembroke Publishers, 1992 Paper 0-921217-83-8. Illustrations by the author.

—. *One, Two, Many*. Toronto: Penguin Books Canada, 1993. 1996 Cloth 0-670-84537-X. Illustrations by the author.

Thurman, Mark, and Emily Hearn. *Mighty Mites in Dinosaurland*. Toronto: Owl Books, 1981. Illustrations by Mark Thurman. Out of print.

—. *Illustration Ideas for Creating Picture Books*. Markham: Pembroke Publishers, 1990 Cloth 0-921217-48-X. Illustrations by Mark Thurman.

Waldron, Kathleen Cook. *Ivan and the All Stars*. Toronto: Boardwalk, 1995 Paper 1-895681-08-1. Illustrations by Mark Thurman.

Selected articles about Mark Thurman

Hearn, Emily "Introducing: Mark Thurman." *CANSCAIP News* 5.1 (Dec. 1982): 1-2.

"Mark Thurman." *Quill & Quire* (Oct. 1985).

"The Write Stuff: Mark Thurman." *Classroom* (Oct.-Nov. 1988): 29.

Gilles Tibo
AUTHOR/ILLUSTRATOR

Born
July 18, 1951, Nicolet, Quebec

School
Self-taught

Where I live now
Montreal, Quebec

My favourite book when I was growing up
Tintin by Hergé.

Career
Illustrator

Family
Two children, Simon and Marlene

The room where I create
"In my studio."

Spare time
"I play tennis and percussion music. I'm a conga player."

When I was growing up
"When I was little I lived in Longueuil, a small town facing Montreal on the south side of the St. Lawrence River. Our house had bookshelves in every room, full of novels, essays and dictionaries. Most were very serious and didn't have many illustrations or pictures.

"What I loved were comic-strips, especially those that were printed in the supplement to the Montreal newspaper, *La Presse*. I remember the smell of the printer's ink, the pleasure of turning the pages and, of course, the excitement of following the adventures of my favourite heroes.

"I began by copying everything I saw printed in newspapers and magazines. From a very young age I knew that I wanted to be an illustrator. Every day I did a drawing that I dated and numbered. My parents had no other choice but to encourage me. They enrolled me in painting and drawing classes in the basement of our church."

My first book (and how it happened)
"I self-published my first book *L'Oeil Voyeur* in 1970. It was drawn in black and white and was 40 pages long. I participated in every stage of production and learned all about printing and publishing a book. It was an extraordinary experience to watch the book come together, stage by stage. I sold it myself, bookstore to bookstore. For the next couple of years, I created several books, until, in 1976, I met Bertrand Gauthier of la courte échelle. Together, we produced my first book for young people, *Le prince sourire and le lys bleu.*"

How I work
"There are two moments that I love the best. The first is that magic moment when ideas are born and one feels that one has created something quite extraordinary (this isn't always the case). The next thing I love the best is when I put down the colour and plunge into the light of the picture. That's when the characters come to life.

"There is a lot that goes into creating a picture: research, rough drawings, cutting out masks to protect the part of the picture I don't want to get ink on, making the outlines with the airbrush and the details with the pencil crayons. Theoretically, I work five days a week from 9:00 to 5:00, just like a bureaucrat, but it is very rare to draw for a whole day. Usually, there are meetings with editors, authors, and designers; there are new projects to expand; and the latest books in production to oversee. There are shows to mount, book signings to go to, and visits with children in schools. Sometimes I'm obliged to hide behind my answering machine to draw in peace."

Tibo's technique
"I work with an airbrush. It's a little gun that shoots ink out through a tiny hole like a pen. I use an ink called Ecoline, which is transparent and very smooth. With the airbrush, I control the intensity and depth of colour and create well-defined forms.

The airbrush allows me to play with the light of an image and to really define the atmosphere. For me, light is the most important part of my illustration. It's what first hits the reader. After I've finished with the airbrush, I draw in the details of the illustration with coloured pencils. One image takes about a week of work."

Research

"I do a lot of research especially when I'm going to draw animals in a realistic style. I consult encyclopedias and reference books. The most research I've done was for *The Wonderful History of Birth*. The author gave me at least 30 books devoted to the subject. Because we couldn't make a single error, we were also supervised by an obstetrician. I think that each drawing was redone more than once."

Where my ideas come from

"When I'm thinking of my next book, usually I have a vague idea of what it will be about. Sometimes it's on a subject that interests me, other times it's the principal character that imposes himself on me.

"Whenever I have an idea, I make a note of it. Afterwards, I put down all the ideas that could come from the original idea. Presently, I have ten books in the 'idea' stage. Some have lots of ideas, others only have one or two. In a few years, some of these projects will become books and others will fall by the wayside."

Tips for young creators

"There's only one piece of advice that I can give to young authors and illustrators: work, work, and work some more. Illustrating has a long apprenticeship. You have to take formal courses to learn techniques and above all, you

must develop a personal style. Your style comes from your originality and is what makes you different from everyone else. Don't be afraid to have many experiences and to try several mediums. You always have to risk making mistakes in order to find your way."

Gilles Tibo

Select Bibliography

All books illustrated by Gilles Tibo

Filion, Pierre. *Pikolo's Night Voyage*. Toronto: Annick Press, 1994 Paper 1-55-37-364-1; Cloth 1-55037-365-X.

Guillet, Jean-Pierre. *The Magic Powder* (Ecological Tales Series). Trans. Sheila Fischman. Waterloo: Quintin Publishing, 1992 Cloth 2-920438-72-7. 1993 Paper 2-920438-73-5. ♣

—*Castle Chaos* (Ecological Tales Series). Trans. Frances Morgan. Waterloo: Quintin Publishing, 1993 Paper 2-89435-023-6; Cloth 2-89435-022-8. ♣

Munsch, Robert. *Giant or Waiting for the Thursday Boat*. Toronto: Annick Press, 1989.

From *Simon at the Circus*

Tibo, Gilles. *Simon and the Snowflakes*. Montreal: Tundra Books, 1988 Paper 0-88776-274-3; Cloth 0-88776-218-21991. ♣

—*Simon and the Wind*. Montreal: Tundra Books, 1989 Cloth 0-88776-234-4. 1991 Paper 0-88776-276-X.♣

—. *Simon Welcomes Spring*. Montreal: Tundra Books, 1990 Cloth 0-88776-247-6. 1993 Paper 0-88776-278-6. ♣

— *Simon in Summer*. Montreal: Tundra Books, 1991 Cloth 0-88776-261-1; Paper 0-88776-2808.♣

—*Simon and His Boxes*. Montreal: Tundra Books, 1992 Paper 0-88776-345-6; Cloth 0-88776-287-5. ♣

—*Simon in the Moonlight*. Montreal: Tundra Books, 1993 Paper 0-88776-347-2; Cloth 0-88776-3162. ♣

—. *Simon Finds a Feather*. Montreal: Tundra Books, 1994 Cloth 0-88776-340-5. 1997 Paper 0-88776-402-9. ♣

—*Simon Makes Music* Montreal: Tundra Books, 1995 Cloth 0-88776-359-6. 1997 Paper 0-88776-398-7. ♣

—*Simon Finds a Treasure*. Montreal: Tundra Books, 1996 Cloth 0-88776-376-6. ♣

—*Simon at the Circus*. Toronto: Tundra Books, 1997 Paper 0-88776-416-9; Cloth 0-88776-4142. .♣

Tibo, Gilles, and Pierre Filion. *Paper Nights*. Toronto: Annick Press, 1992 Paper 1-55037-224-6; Cloth 1-55037-225-4. ♣

Tibo, Gilles, and Francois Vaillancourt. *Mr. Patapoum's First Trip*. Toronto: Annick Press, 1993 Paper 1-55037-294-7; Cloth 1-55037-293-9. Illustrations by the authors.

Awards

1992 Governor General's Literary Award for *Simon and His Boxes*

1996 Governor General's Literary Award for *Noémie, le secret de Madame Lumbago*

Frances Claire Tyrrell
ILLUSTRATOR

Born
Kirkland Lake, Ontario

School
Elementary School and High School in Montreal, Sheridan College (secretarial!) and three years at the University of Western Ontario

Where I live now
Oakville, Ontario

My favourite books when I was young
The *Narnia* books, by C.S. Lewis

My favourite book now
Till We Have Faces, by C.S. Lewis

Career
"Once a secretary who doodled a lot, now an artist/illustrator and mother."

Family
"Our son, Neil, and Sweet William the dog."

The room where I create
"A small, nice, pink and white room, not tidy, but packed tight with books old and new, shelves old and new, portfolios, papers, art supplies, models (including shells and the castle from *Kate's Castle*), music and book tapes, a Victorian washstand and my big work table (not to mention the dog!)."

Spare time
"When a book is in progress, with deadlines, there is little spare time. I steal time from sleep in order to read or sew. But *between* books I paint on the walls of my house, go to Scottish country dancing or Cape Breton step dancing, canoe, dig a new flower bed, and spend even more time than usual making mud pies or chalk drawings with my son."

When I was growing up
"I have been drawing since I could hold a pencil, and have never really stopped. My brother and I used to draw together on our blackboard, or on long sheets of brown wrapping paper. We would crayon large 'maps' of imaginary neighbourhoods and events."

My first book (and how it happened)
"My mother first prompted me to paint a 'Huron Carol' Christmas card, which was printed and well-enough received to lead to three more. The series of four was picked up by Carlton cards and sold well. One of my cards was given to Lester and Orpen Dennys, and the book was underway. From 1989 to 1990 was a very exciting time — I learned about how a book is made, and yet was given so much artistic freedom."

How I work and where my ideas come from
"Typically, the ideas for a picture, or a series of pictures, arrive in my imagination complete, like a gift dropped into my lap. Usually this happens while doing something apparently unrelated to work — walking the dog or doing the dishes or gardening. I write down the ideas first, and do the drawing later. Those first notes and sketches are like keys to a much bigger file. The detailed drawings take a day or two each, and each painting takes a week or two — or three! I do love the painting part — lovely colours and details becoming richer under my brush, then the final dot of light in the eye that makes the picture wink back at me."

Who and what influenced me
"The earliest influences in my life, apart from my parents, came from books, especially the second-hand books my mother collected. I remember in particular a certain older book of nursery rhymes, and a beautiful copy of *Idylls of the King*."

My favourite book that I've created
"*The Huron Carol* was a joy to work on, inspiring and rewarding, having history, humanity and an eye to heaven."

139

Tips for young creators

"My pictures, up until I was about 12, show more enthusiasm than ability! Keep drawing, for the joy of it, and dream your dreams."

Frances Tyrrell

Bibliography

Brebeuf, Jean de. *The Huron Carol*. Toronto: Key Porter, 1990 0-88619-280-3. Illustrations by Frances Tyrrell.

Forrester, Maureen comp. *Joy to the World*. Toronto: Stoddart Kids, 1992 1-895555-19-1. Illustrations by Frances Tyrrell.

Lawson, Julie. *Kate's Castle*. Toronto: Stoddart Kids, 1992 0-540842-X. Illustrations by Frances Tyrrell.

Pickthall, Marjorie. *The Worker in Sandalwood*. Toronto: Stoddart Kids, 1991 1-985555-10-8. Illustrations by Frances Tyrrell.

Tyrrell, Avril. *The Christmas Clown*. Oakville: Treasure Seeker Studio, 1993 Paper 0-9697421-0-X. Illustrations by Frances Tyrrell.

Tyrrell, Frances. *Woodland Christmas*. Toronto: Scholastic, 1995 Cloth 0-0590-24430-2. 1997 Paper 0-590-12390-4. Illustrations by the author.

From *Woodland Christmas*

Vlasta van Kampen
AUTHOR/ILLUSTRATOR

Born
August 22, 1943, Belleville, Ontario

School
Ontario College of Art and Design, Toronto, Ontario

Where I live now
Toronto, Ontario

My favourite book when I was young
Pumpkinhead

Career
Illustrator

Family
Two children, Saskia and Dimitri; cat

The room where I create
"When the children moved out I finally got 'a room of my own.' I painted it bright yellow, filled it with all of my favourite things and called it my happy room where I create."

Spare time
"Read, listen to music, cook and prepare new recipes, entertain friends at the family cabin in the country."

When I was growing up
"I lived out in the country. My brother and I had a wonderful big tabby cat. One winter day he disappeared. We were very sad and for several weeks we searched everywhere for him, calling him and asking all the neighbours if they'd seen him. Finally one day we found him frozen at the edge of the pond. Together we lugged him back home (he was extremely heavy for two small children). We asked our mother to please thaw him out because he must be very cold. Very calmly our mother put him by the fire and told us that she would see what she could do. We were ushered off to bed with some hot chocolate and hugs and kisses. Needless to say, in the morning, the cat was gone and my mother, in her wisdom, told us that he had disappeared in the night. To this day we still believe he just melted away."

As a child, Vlasta was always drawing. "I drew for school exhibitions and took part in an art program in high school. There, I designed posters, set designs for school productions and decorations for school dances." But there was very little recognition of art in high schools then. "You did it, and you did it quietly. Only the students who excelled in academics and sports got awards. But the night of the graduation ball and banquet, something special happened. One teacher stood up and said that while he wouldn't mention any names, some very talented kids had been responsible for all the wonderful decorations in the room. His recognition of our work was wonderful and made me feel so good!"

My first book (and how it happened)
"*ABC, 123 The Canadian Alphabet and Counting Book* started out as a concept for a colouring book for Hurtig Publishers. Mel Hurtig became interested in seeing it as a picture book with strong Canadian overtones in all of the illustrations and the text. Since 1982 was an important year in Canadian history (the patriation of the Constitution), we decided to have a birthday party for Canada. The book went on to win the Canada Council Prize.

More art
Parks Canada commissioned paintings of eight natural habitats for a permanent exhibit in Kouchibouguac National Park, N.B. Commercial work includes: CD covers for CBC Enterprises; ads for Pondocillin (Leo Laboratories), a children's medication, using nine different animals; two sets of children's posters for Posters International; and puzzles for The Great American Puzzle Factory. In addition, the National Library of Canada purchased entire body of artwork, research, and related back-up work for Vlasta's *Rockanimals*.

Where my ideas come from

"A walk in the park, listening to music, sharing ideas and thoughts with my family, seeing an interesting shape or object." Ideas for new books also come from observing other children's books to see what has or hasn't been done already."

Who and what influenced me

"The illustrator Arthur Rackham and everything in nature."

How I work

"Watercolours and mixed media. I do lots of research of subject matter before starting to sketch."

My favourite books that I've created

Beetle Bedlam, The Last Straw

Tips for young creators

"Be observant of the world around you. Research your topic before beginning. Read what others have written. Look at what others have illustrated. Draw from their strengths and weaknesses."

Vlasta van Kampen

Bibliography

All books illustrated by Vlasta van Kampen

Corrigan, Kathy. *Emily Umily.* Toronto: Annick Press, 1984. Out of print.

Gugler, Laurel Dee. *Muddle Cuddle.* Toronto: Annick Press, 1997 Paper 1-55037-434-6; Cloth 1-55037-435-4.

—. *Monkey Tales.* Toronto: Annick Press, 1998 Paper 1-55037-530-X; Cloth 1-55037-531-8.

Harris, Dorothy Joan. *Four Seasons for Toby.* Richmond Hill: Scholastic Canada, 1987 Paper 0-590-71676-X; Cloth 0-590-71677-8. ✤

—. *Racing Stripes for William.* Toronto: Three Trees Press, 1987. Out of print.

Johnson, Arthur. *King of Cats.* Toronto: Stoddart, 1992 Cloth 0-7737-2589-X.

Manning, Linda. *Dinosaur Days.* Toronto: Stoddart, 1993 Cloth 0-7737-2699-3.

—. *Animal Hours.* Don Mills: Stoddart/Oxford University Press, 1990 Paper 0-19-540844-6.

Pearson, Debora. *Cookie Critters* (Activity Book Package). Toronto: Somerville House, 1997 1-895897-97-1.

Quinlan, Patricia. *My Dad Takes Care Of Me.* Toronto: Annick Press, 1987 Paper 0-920303-76-5; Cloth 0-920303-79-X.

Shapiro, Arnold. *God Loves You* (A Pop-Up Book). Nashville TN: Nelson, 1996 0-7852-7419-7.

Thury, Fredrick H. *The Last Straw.* Toronto: Key Porter Books, 1997 Cloth 1-55263-022-6.

van Kampen, Vlasta. *ABC, 123: The Canadian Alphabet and Counting Book.* Edmonton: Hurtig Publishers, 1982. Out of print.

—. *Beetle Bedlam.* Toronto: Key Porter Books, 1997 Cloth 1-55013-777-8.

—. *Birds and Beasts/Sea and Sky* (Puzzles). Great American Puzzle Factory, 1998 1-56646-380-7/1-56646-379-3.

van Kampen, Vlasta and Irene Eugen. *Orchestranimals.* Richmond Hill: Scholastic Canada, 1989 Cloth 0-590-73161-0, Big Book 0-590-73163-7. 1991 Paper 0-590-73162-9.

—. *Rockanimals.* Richmond Hill: Scholastic Canada, 1991 Cloth 0-590-73660-4. 1993 Paper 0-590-73661-2 Out of print.

Whitaker, Muriel, ed. *Great Canadian Animal Stories.* Edmonton: Hurtig Publishers, 1978. 1995 Cloth 0-7710-8818-3.

— ed. *Great Canadian Adventure Stories.* Edmonton: Hurtig Publishers, 1979. Out of print.

— ed. *Stories from the Canadian North.* Edmonton: Hurtig Publishers, 1980. Out of print.

— ed. *The Princess, the Hockey Player, Magic and Ghosts.* Edmonton: Hurtig, 1981. Out of print.

Wilger, Jennifer Root. *Abraham* (A Bible Big Book). Loveland CO: Group Publishing, 1995 1-55945-437-7.

Awards

1982 Canada Council Children's Literature Prize for *ABC, 123: The Canadian Alphabet and Counting Book*

From *Beetle Bedlam*

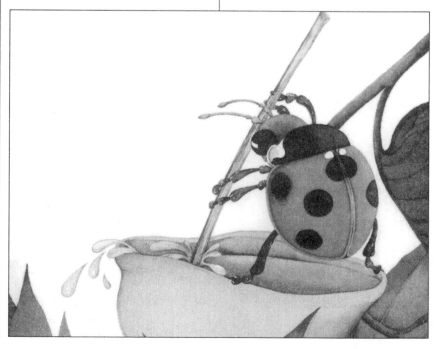

Andrea Wayne von Königslöw
AUTHOR/ILLUSTRATOR

Born
1958, Toronto, Ontario

School
Marymount School, Cuernavaca, Mexico; Thornton School for the Arts, Toronto, Ontario; Queen's University, Kingston, Ontario

Where I live now
Toronto, Ontario

My favourite books when I was young
"Dr. Seuss books, Nancy Drew and all fairy tales."

My favourite book now
"Authors I enjoy are John Irving, Barbara Gowdy, Margaret Atwood, Timothy Findley and a lot of Canadian children's writers. I still love a good picture book."

Career
Writer and illustrator of children's books

Family
Husband, Rainer von Königslöw; three children, Alexis, Tai and Keir; three cats, Nishy, Whoopi and Grizzabela

The room where I create
"I have a studio in my house where I write and illustrate. It overlooks my garden. I work there almost every day. When my kids come in, I give them paints and they paint at the table beside me."

Spare time
"I exercise, cook and garden. I love plays and movies. I love to spend time with my husband and children most. There is so much to do in Toronto."

When I was growing up
"I was born in Toronto, but when I was eight years old, we moved to Mexico. While we lived there, I learned to speak Spanish and eat raw chili peppers.

"When we returned to Canada, I spent summers at the family cottage on Mary Lake in Ontario's Muskoka area. I stayed in the water so long that my mother was sure I had gills. I loved playing with my friends, and going for long walks and I always drew and painted. I loved painting Muskoka landscapes and animals. I was always a storyteller and told a lot of fibs."

My first book (and how it happened)
"I wrote my first children's book when I was still in university. I sent it to Annick Press. They liked my concepts but it took years to get a good book together. Annick was very patient and they were wonderful to me. I think I'm very lucky. Now I write and illustrate for many publishers."

Where my ideas come from
"I get my ideas from anyone and anything. Sometimes I am just out driving in my car and an idea for a story comes to me. Sometimes I get a story together and sometimes I just write down the idea for a time when a story happens. A story idea may sit in my brain for years until I can write it. Sometimes the stories are good, and sometimes they are not great. My children are also a great source of inspiration."

Who and what influenced me
"I think that Dr. Seuss was my greatest inspiration. I loved his humour. I am writing more poems now because of him. Robert Munsch, Maurice Sendak, Mercer Mayer, Judith Viorst and Stephen Kellogg are also influences. I always loved Michael Martchenko's art; even his pencil lines have action and a life of their own. I love the art of Mireille Levert, and Stéphane Poulin, and would love to paint like them. I also love Barbara Reid's work."

How I work
"I write anytime I can. I always have a few stories on the computer that I work on. Sometimes I will think of a new story in the middle of the night and I have to start it right then. Painting is

more difficult. I need a few hours of uninterrupted time all together. If I mix up just the right colour and the phone rings... the paint dries. I try not to answer but with three children there are always distractions."

Something nobody knew about me (until now)

"It is very hard for me to think of something that no one knows about me. I am a very open person. I tell people almost anything that's on my mind. I love to talk and I especially like to talk about myself."

My favourite book that I've created

"It is so hard to say which of my books is my favourite. I think that my favourite is always the one that I am working on now. If I start a new book, it becomes my favourite."

Tips for young creators

"Keep creating and don't let anyone tell you to stop. If something interesting happens to you, write about it. It may make a good story. Take lots of art classes, especially life drawing. Save all your art and stories and reread them every few years. Keep your imagination open."

Andrea Wayne von Königslöw

Bibliography

Dunn, Sonja. *Rapunzel's Rap.* Goderich: Moonstone Press, 1992 Paper 0-92025-939-1. Illustrations by Andrea Wayne von Königslöw.

Wayne von Königslöw, Andrea. *Toilet Tales* (Annick Toddler Series). Toronto: Annick Press, 1985 Paper 0-92030313-7; Cloth 0-920303-14-5. 1987 Annikin Paper 0-920303-81-1. Illustrations by the author.

—. *A Tail Between Two Cities.* Toronto: Annick Press, 1987. Illustrations by the author. Out of print.

—. *Peas, Please!* Windsor: Black Moss Press, 1987 Paper 0-88753-191-1. Illustrations by the author.

—. *Catching Problems.* Toronto: Annick Press, 1990. Illustrations by the author.

—. *That's My Baby?* (Annick Toddler Series). Toronto: Annick Press, 1986. Rev. ed. 1990 Paper 0-92303-57-9. Illustrations by the author.

—. *Frogs.* Toronto: HarperCollins, 1993 Cloth 0-00-223895-0. 1996 Paper 0-00-648057-8. Illustrations by Michael Martchenko.

—. *Would You Love Me?* Toronto: Annick Press, 1997 Paper 1-55037-430-3; Cloth 1-55037-431-1. Illustrations by the author.

Wayne-von Königslöw, Andrea and Linda Granfield. *The Make-Your-Own-Button Book.* Toronto: Somerville House, 1993 Paper (with button kit) 0-921051-89-1. Illustrations by Andrea Wayne von Königslöw.

From *Bing and Chutney*

My favourite book that I've created

When a student asks Ian this question, he asks them if they have any brothers and sisters and if they say yes, he answers, "And if I asked your parents which of their children they loved most, what do you think they would say?"

"They love us all equally," says the child.

"Exactly" says Ian. "I love all of my books to the same degree, but in different ways and for different reasons. Each book I created has taught me something new about writing and illustrating in the same way that you and each of your brothers and sisters teach your parents something new about raising kids every day."

Tips for young creators

"Be courageous and never give up, even when your own doubts and fears seem to overwhelm your confidence."

Ian Wallace

Bibliography

All books illustrated by Ian Wallace

Andrews, Jan. *The Very Last First Time.* Toronto: Groundwood Books, 1985 Cloth 0-88899-043-X.

Davidge, Bud. *The Mummer's Song.* Toronto: Groundwood Books, 1993 Cloth 0-88899-178-9.

Jam, Teddy. *The Year of Fire.* Toronto: Groundwood Books, 1992 Cloth 0-88899-154-1.

Lottridge, Celia Barker. *The Name of the Tree.* Toronto: Groundwood Books, 1989 Cloth 0-88899-097-9.

Wallace, Ian. *Julie News.* Toronto: Kids Can Press, 1974. Out of print.

—. *The Christmas Tree House.* Toronto: Kids Can Press, 1976. Out of print.

—. *Chin Chiang and the Dragon's Dance.* Toronto: Groundwood

From *Sarah and the People of Sand River*

Books, 1984 Cloth 0-88899-020-0. 1992 Paper 0-88899-167-3.

—. *Morgan the Magnificent.* Toronto: Groundwood Books, 1987 Cloth 0-88899-056-1. 1992 Paper 0-88899-166-5.

—. *Mr. Kneebone's New Digs.* Toronto: Groundwood Books, 1991 Cloth 0-88899-143-6.

—. *The Sparrow's Song.* Toronto: Groundwood Books, 1986. 1994 Paper 0-88899-204-1.

—. *Hansel and Gretel.* (Canadian Fairy Tales Series). Toronto: Groundwood Books, 1994 Cloth 0-88899-212-2.

—. *A Winter's Tale.* Toronto: Groundwood Books, 1997 Cloth 0-88899-286-6.

Wallace, Ian and Angela Wood. *The Sandwich.* Toronto: Kids Can Press, 1975. Rev. ed. 1985 Paper 0-919964-02-8. Illustrations by the authors.

Wynne-Jones, Tim. *Architect of the Moon.* Toronto: Groundwood Books, 1988. 1991 Paper 0-88899-150-9.

Valgardson, W.D. *Sarah and the People of Sand River.* Toronto: Groundwood Books, 1996 Cloth 0-88899-255-6.

Awards

1984 Amelia Frances Howard-Gibbon Illustrator's Award for *Chin Chiang and the Dragon's Dance*

1984 IODE Book Award – Toronto Chapter for *Chin Chiang and the Dragon's Dance*

1986 White Raven Selection of the International Youth Library, Munich for *The Very Last First Time*

1990 Elizabeth Mrazik-Cleaver Canadian Picture Book Award for *The Name of the Tree*

1990 Mr. Christie's Book Award for Illustration for *The Name of the Tree*

1998 IODE Book Award-Toronto Chapter for *A Winter's Tale*

Selected articles about Ian Wallace

Margo Beggs, "What's in the Picture? Exploring the art of Ian Wallace." *Children's Book News* (Spring 1998): 15-17.

Booth, David, ed. *Writers on Writing.* Don Mills: General Publishing, 1989.

The New Advocate Spring 1998.

Ross, Val. "Toronto Illustrator Gives Grimm Tale a Canadian Twist." *The Globe and Mail* [Toronto] 24 Dec. 1994: C16.

Wallace, Ian. "When Fort Nelson's Kids Won Ian Wallace". *Quill & Quire* Feb. 1985: 8.

Ian Wallace
AUTHOR/ILLUSTRATOR

Born
March 31, 1950, Niagara Falls, Ontario

Where I live now
"In a lovely three-storey Edwardian house in Toronto."

My favourite book when I was young
The Wind in the Willows

My favourite book now
Where the Wild Things Are

Career
Illustrator and author

Family
"My family is quite small, just my wife and me. No goldfish or budgies or chickens."

The room where I create
"A room in the back of my house overlooking the yard. It is much quieter there than in the front of the house."

Spare time
"I 'hang out' with my wife."

When I was growing up
"I never imagined that someday I would be writing and illustrating books of my own. In fact, I never made the connection that books were created by people who made that work their profession. At one point, I remember thinking that the librarian who loaned me the books had created them all. Miss Albrandt was a very busy lady in her off hours!"

My first book (and how it happened)
"My first full-colour, hardcover, jacketed book, was inspired one cold February day during the Chinese New Year celebrations when I saw my first Dragon's Dance. I was so excited by what I saw, I knew I had to tell a story encompassing this impressive tradition. I didn't realize six years would pass until the book was published."

Where my ideas come from
"The books that I have written and/or illustrated have been inspired by an incident that has captured my imagination, delighted me visually, and caused my ears to perk up. It always amazes me that these tiny fragments can take my creative energies down paths that I have never trod, into cultures that I have only witnessed from afar, and under the skins of characters I would be proud to call 'friend'."

Who and what influenced me
"Good stories have always interested and excited me. At the end of a good story the reader comes away knowing that the characters have been changed by the experience and will never be the same. In some small measure, I hope that I will never be the same either and will be richer for having let those characters into my life."

How I work
"Each book has its own gestation period. Some are gifts and develop quickly, while others are nothing short of hard labour." Regardless, Ian works closely with his editor on each manuscript, writing and rewriting until he has achieved what he feels is the perfect story.

Once the story has been approved, he begins working on small pencil sketches, again in consultation with his editor. When the sketches are approved, he starts on more detailed pencil roughs and proceeds to finished pencil drawings. He uses the medium, the design, the colour and the perspectives that most capture the spirit and the inner voice of the story. He works five or six days a week, at least six hours a day, to a maximum of 14 hours a day, when he is working to a tight deadline.

Something nobody knew about me (until now)
"I am a Coke-a-holic. I love Coca Cola Classic. Diet Coke and ordinary Coke don't interest me in the least. I can tell the difference between Pepsi and Coke, even though other people cannot."

Janet Wilson
ILLUSTRATOR

Born
November 20, 1952, Toronto, Ontario

School
Ontario College of Art, Toronto.

Where I live now
Eden Mills, Ontario

My favourite book when I was young
"*Greyfriars Bobby.*"

My favourite book now
"The last book I couldn't put down was the biography of Andrew Wyeth, *A Secret Life.*"

Career
Illustrator and aspiring author

Family
"Husband and business partner Chris. Two grown sons: Cory, and Graeme. We share our house with nieces Shannon and Heather who go to high school in Guelph, an obstreperous chihuahua, Chimi, and a flirtatious springer spaniel, Lulu."

The room where I create
"We converted a garage into my studio, put in big windows so that there is good northern light and stuffed it with books and art supplies. One window overlooks the river where I can watch the village kids skate in the winter and catch crayfish in the summer. Through the other window I watch the villagers meander over the bridge."

Spare time
"At least once a week I go life drawing. I also enjoy landscape painting excursions."

When I was growing up
"My hands were always busy. I was a knitting fool and never went anywhere without my wool and needles. Drawing was a secret pastime and I was very shy about showing anyone my sketches."

My first book (and how it happened)
"My first picture book was *Daniel's Dog.* I had been illustrating textbooks and was gaining a reputation for drawing realistic-looking children, especially of racially diverse groups. Because *Daniel's Dog* was based on an African folk tale, the publisher was looking for an artist who could draw a child of African descent."

Where my ideas come from
"When I read through a manuscript I give much consideration to the first images that come into my thoughts. I have learned to trust my intuition. Then I do an enormous amount of research. Ideally I like to visit the area where the story is set. My paintings for *In Flanders Fields* and *Sarah May and the New Red Dress* would not have had the same visual impact had I not visited France and Pender Island. If it's just not possible to be there, I watch videos, visit museums and libraries to learn about the time and the place. I have my own picture file too. After my research is done, I then go back to my original ideas and rethink them."

Who and what influenced me
"I am inspired greatly by artists I admire, especially the book illustrators from the 'Golden Age of Illustration.' The Wyeths, especially N.C., are great favourites. Presently I'm taken with Winslow Homer's watercolours."

How I work
"My process for making a picture book is probably typical. It may differ when painting the pictures because I work on all of them at the same time. My attention span for working on one picture is about two hours. Then I switch to a different canvas and I get excited about that one. If I've been away from a picture for a few days, I see it with a fresh eye and notice problems that I wasn't aware of before.

"I spend a goodly amount of time reposing on my studio couch looking at the painting on my easel. It may look as if I'm goofing off, but actually I'm figuring out what to do to make it better. This is my most productive and valuable time. My favourite medium is oil paints although I am learning to enjoy watercolours. And I'm devoted to the HB pencil and its trusty sidekick, the electric pencil sharpener.

"As for getting models, now that I live in a tiny hamlet, I am turning into a modern day Norman Rockwell, and eventually I think everyone in Eden Mills will end up in one of my picture books."

Something nobody knew about me (until now)

"People assume that artists have wonderful imaginations. I do not. Perhaps that's why I am fascinated by reality. I work very hard at trying to be more observant. I'm constantly taking pictures with the camera in my head to store for a future purpose. You might also be surprised at how often I put down my brush and use my fingers to push the paint around. Just like kindergarten!"

My favourite book that I've created

"This is like asking a parent which child they like best. I am very pleased with how the *Selina* books came out. But my favourite is always the next one because of the fun and challenge of creating new images."

Janet Wilson

Bibliography

Alexander, Carol. *Rachel Carson, Writer and Scientist*. Ohio: Modern Curriculum Press, 1995 Cloth 0-8136-5732-6; Paper 0-8136-5738-5. Illustrations by Janet Wilson.

Bayless, Maureen. *Howard's House is Haunted!* Richmond Hill: Scholastic Canada, 1993 Paper 0-590-74559-X. Illustrations by Janet Wilson.

Beattie, Owen and John Geiger. *Buried in Ice*. Toronto: Madison Press, 1992 Illustrations by Janet Wilson. Out of print.

Bogart, Jo Ellen. *Daniel's Dog*. Richmond Hill: Scholastic Canada, 1990 Cloth 0-590-73344-3; Paper 0-590-73205-6. Illustrations by Janet Wilson.

Carney, Margaret. *At Grandpa's Sugarbush*. Toronto: Kids Can Press, 1997 Cloth 1-55074-341-4. Illustrations by Janet Wilson.

Duffey, Betsy. *The Math Whiz*. New York: Viking Children's Books, 1990 Paper 0-14-038647-5. Illustrations by Janet Wilson.

—. *The Gadget War*. New York: Viking Children's Books, 1991 Paper 0-670-84152-8. Illustrations by Janet Wilson.

—. *How To Be Cool In The Third Grade*. New York: Viking Children's Books, 1993 Paper 0-670-84798-4. Illustrations by Janet Wilson.

Farmer, Patti. *What's He Doing Now?* Richmond Hill: Scholastic Canada, 1996 Paper 0-590-24542-2. Illustrations by Janet Wilson.

continued...

From *Lucy Maud and the Cavendish Cat*

The Storymakers: Illustrating Children's Books

Gaetz, Dayle. *Heather Come Back* (Series 2000). Toronto: Maxwell Macmillan, 1993 Paper 0-02-954207-3. Illustrations by Janet Wilson. Photographs by Peter Paterson.

Godfrey, Martyn. *Break Out* (Series Canada). Toronto: Maxwell Macmillan, 1988 Paper 0-02-953543-3. Illustrations by Janet Wilson.

Gordon, Katherine and Joshua Willoughby (eds.) *The Eramosa Anthology.* 1996 Paper 0-9681055-0-5. Illustrations by Janet Wilson.

Granfield, Linda. *In Flanders Fields: the story of the poem by John McCrae.* Toronto: Stoddart Publishing, 1996 Cloth 0-7737-2991-7; Paper 0-7737-5925-5. Illustrations by Janet Wilson.

—. *Amazing Grace: the Story of the Hymn.* Toronto: Tundra Books, 1997 Cloth 0-88776-389-8. Illustrations by Janet Wilson.

Green, Susan and Sharon Siamon. *Danny's Dollars.* Toronto: Gage, 1986. Illustrations by Janet Wilson. Out of print.

Hehner, Barbara. *Let's Find Out About Cats.* Toronto: Random House, 1990. Illustrations by Janet Wilson. Out of print.

—. *Let's Find Out About Dogs.* Toronto: Random House, 1991. Illustrations by Janet Wilson. Out of print.

Heneghan, James. *The Trail of the Chocolate Thief.* Richmond Hill: Scholastic Canada, 1993 Paper 0-590-74514-X. Illustrations by Janet Wilson.

Kropp, Paul. *We Both Have Scars* (Series 2000). Toronto: Maxwell Macmillan, 1990 Paper 0-02-953984-6. Illustrations by Janet Wilson.

Little, Jean. *Jess Was the Brave One.* Toronto: Penguin Books Canada, 1991. Illustrations by Janet Wilson. Out of print.

—. *Revenge of the Small Small.* Toronto: Penguin Books, 1992 Cloth 0-670-84471-3; Paper 0-14-05555-63-3. Illustrations by Janet Wilson.

Lohans, Alison. *Secret of the Lunchbox Criminal.* Richmond Hill: Scholastic Canada, 1990. Illustrations by Janet Wilson. Out of print.

—. *Germy Johnson's Secret Plan.* Richmond Hill: Scholastic Canada, 1992. Illustrations by Janet Wilson. Out of print.

Manuel, Lynn. *Lucy Maud and the Cavendish Cat.* Toronto: Tundra Books, 1997 Cloth 0-88776-397-9. Illustrations by Janet Wilson.

Martin, Elaine. *Baby Games: the Joyful Guide to Child's Play from Birth to Three Years.* Toronto: Stoddart Publishing, 1994 (Rev. ed.) Paper 0-7737-5637-X. Illustrations by Janet Wilson.

—. *Kid's Games: How to Have Great Times with Your 3 to 6 year Old.* Toronto: Random House, 1989 Paper 0-394-22103-6. Illustrations by Janet Wilson.

McNicoll, Sylvia. *Jump Start* (Series Canada). Toronto: Maxwell Macmillan, 1989 Paper 0-02-953928-5. Illustrations by Janet Wilson.

McVaugh, Jenifer. *Hello, Hello* (Series 2000). Toronto: Maxwell Macmillan, 1991 Paper 0-02-954081-X. Illustrations by Janet Wilson.

Quinlan, Patricia. *Tiger Flowers.* Toronto: Stoddart Publishing, 1993 Cloth 1-895555-58-2. Illustrations by Janet Wilson.

Scribner, Virginia. *Gopher Draws Conclusions.* New York: Viking USA, 1994. Illustrations by Janet Wilson. Out of print.

—. *Gopher Takes Heart.* New York: Viking USA, 1995 Paper 0-14-036311-4. Illustrations by Janet Wilson.

Siamon, Sharon. *The Laughing Cake.* Toronto: Gage, 1987. Illustrations by Janet Wilson. Out of print.

Skelton, Mora. *The Baritone Cat.* Toronto: Stoddart Publishing, 1994 Cloth 1-895555-52-3. Illustrations by Janet Wilson.

Smucker, Barbara. *Selina and the Bear Paw Quilt.* Toronto: Stoddart Publishing, 1996 Paper 0-7737-5837-2; Cloth 0-7737-2992-5. Illustrations by Janet Wilson.

Wilson, Janet. comp. *The Worm Song (and Other Tasty Tunes).* Richmond Hill: Scholastic Canada, 1993 Paper 0-590-74095-4. Illustrations by Cory Wilson.

Zach, Cheryl. *Benny and the Crazy Contest.* New York: Bradbury Press, 1991. Illustrations by Janet Wilson. Out of print.

—. *Benny and the No-Good Teacher.* New York: Bradbury Press, 1992. Illustrations by Janet Wilson. Out of print

Ludmilla Zeman
AUTHOR/ILLUSTRATOR

Born
Czech Republic, April 23, 1947

School
Czech College of Art in Uh. Hradiste

Where I live now
Montreal, Quebec

My favourite books when I was young
"Since I was very young, I have loved all fairy tales and legends. Some of my favourites were: *Arabian Nights*, Hans Christian Andersen's fairy tales, *The Iliad*, *The Odyssey*, *Beowulf*, *Ivanhoe*, *Treasure Island*, *Robinson Crusoe*, *Tom Sawyer* and *Huckleberry Finn*."

Career
Filmmaker, writer and illustrator

Family
My husband, Eugene Spaleny, and two daughters Linda and Malvina

The room where I create
"I work on my pictures in a small room in my house. This small studio has a large table with many wooden boxes filled with pencils, paint brushes and other tools that I use for my pictures. I also have a large window and a wall-sized bookshelf that is filled with my favourite books and magazines. I have many pictures and paintings on my walls. Some are from my previous books and others are from my films."

Spare time
"I like to see movies in the theatre and read books. In the summer, I play tennis with my friends and in the winter I ski with my family."

When I was growing up
"I grew up in a filmmaker's family, five minutes away from a major studio where my father, Karel Zeman, a renowned film director, worked. My father made films mostly for children and I spent all my free time by his side. I admired the way he could sketch, plan the storyboards and direct his crew. The film studio was like a real kingdom for me. I was usually helping to make puppets, painting backgrounds for different films and most importantly, I was sitting in the projection room watching movies. Today when I work, I still think of everything that I learned in the studio and from my father."

My first book (and how it happened)
"My husband and I had finished working on our film *Lord of the Sky*, and in order to start the next film, we needed to raise some money. It was nearly impossible, and in desperation I took a few screenplays and sketches to Tundra Books in Montreal. The publisher, May Cutler, liked my pictures and storyboards very much and gave me the opportunity, support and freedom to make the *Gilgamesh* trilogy."

Where my ideas come from
"My ideas come from the many books that I read during my childhood. They gave me a lot of knowledge and understanding about life."

Who and what influenced me
"My greatest influences and inspiration come from my father, Karel Zeman, as well as illustrators such as Arthur Rackham, Maurice Sendak, Ralph Steadman and Ronald Searle."

How I work
"For each project, whether it is a film or a picture book, I first search for an original way to visualize the story, making it attractive and fresh. When creating a picture book, I start with sketches and build the storyboard similarly as for animated film. My skills gained from film making are helpful in making the illustrations full of movement, space and action. I want

children to feel that they are walking through the incredible world that I create in my pictures and become part of history. When I feel that the preliminary drawings are telling the story well, I start to look for an appropriate style of design. I work long hours on the picture book for eight to nine months."

My favourite book that I've created

"*Gilgamesh the King*. It is still my favourite book because it was the first one that I created in Canada. It is also one of the most unique and incredible epics ever written. It is the oldest story of mankind, unravelling the beginning of human civilization. When I started to retell the *Epic of Gilgamesh* I fell in love with this beautiful, old poem and during my research I realized how important the wisdom and examples of human experience are for children's intellectual and cultural development.

"Creating the *Gilgamesh* trilogy was quite a difficult task since not many visual references related to this story exist. I spent over two years researching and collecting information concerning artifacts from Mesopotamia that exist in museums around the world. To take a jewel of human history, and revive it in a new form which has never been done before, was a big challenge and a great source of inspiration."

Ludmilla Zeman

Bibliography

Zeman, Ludmilla. adapt. *Gilgamesh the King*. Montreal: Tundra Books, 1992 Cloth 0-88776-283-2. Illustrations by the author.

—. adapt. *The Revenge of Ishtar*. Montreal: Tundra Books, 1994 Cloth 0-88776-315-4. Illustrations by the author.

—. adapt. *The Last Quest of Gilgamesh*. Montreal: Tundra Books, 1994 Cloth 0-88776-328-6. Illustrations by the author.

—. *The First Red Maple Leaf*. Montreal: Tundra Books, 1997 Cloth 0-88776-372-3. Illustrations by the author.

Awards

1995 Governor General's Literary Award for *The Last Quest of Gilgamesh*

Selected articles about Ludmilla Zeman

"Between the Lines, Stories Live." *Canadian Children's Literature* 73 (1994).

From *The First Red Maple Leaf*

Ange Zhang
ILLUSTRATOR

Born
March 19, 1951, Beijing, China

School
China Central Academy of Drama; Banff Centre of the Arts

Where I live now
Toronto, Ontario

My favourite book when I was young.
War and Peace by Leo Tolstoy

My favourite books now
"I like Ralph Steadman and Michael Sowa's illustrations."

Career
Children's book illustrator; theatre set designer

Family
Wife, Pingna Sheng; son, Eric Zhang

The room where I create
"…is a small sunroom facing north. It has a messy drawing table where there is always some unfinished work. There is also a computer table, bookshelves and a tool cabinet."

Spare time
"I like to listen to classical music, watch movies, go to the theatre, and play badminton."

When I was growing up
"I did not get a chance to go to the high school. Instead, I was working as a farmer in a small village in the northwest of China. One day, my friend showed me some colourful tubes. He said 'These are oil paints, let's use them and be artists.' We went to the lakeside, and, after half an hour, my friend gave up. But my first oil painting experience opened a new world for me. I knew I wanted to be an artist."

My first book (and how it happened)
"When I was working at the Stratford Festival design department, I often went to the Stratford Art Gallery for life drawing classes. I met an artist named Ken, who organized the drawing classes, and his drawings were very impressive to me. Later, I was told that he was also a well-known children's book illustrator. After seeing my art, Ken [a.k.a. Eric Beddows] kindly suggested that I should show my portfolio to Groundwood Books. I did, and six months later, I received the manuscript for *Thor*, my first book."

Where my ideas come from
"When I design a set for the theatre, I try very hard to find a concept, a key image. But for children's book illustration, the ideas come in a more natural way. I search for my character. I may not be familiar with children who live at Lake Winnipeg or Nova Scotia, but I can feel them; I try to draw something I know underneath the characters. Feelings are universal and cross-cultural, so even though I haven't lived the lives of the book characters, I can understand their feelings."

Who and what influenced me
"My family and I have been through some tough times during the Cultural Revolution in China. Most Chinese people in their 60s and 70s share this dark history. Also, like every new immigrant, we worked very hard to build a new home in this peaceful land. Those experiences will influence my creations in subtle ways.

"The two artist's work I admire most are Ming Cho Lee, an American-Chinese set designer, and Wu-Qi Chao, a French oil painter."

How I work

"I always like to surround myself with a great amount of research to start with. Then I create my characters; sometimes I draw them from my imagination, sometimes they are based on real people. For instance, the boy Thor was directly drawn from my son's classmate. I try to draw a character from different angles that might be useful when I progress to the more detailed drawing.

"In the rough drawings I like to show the basic composition, characters, and style. If necessary, I paint a coloured sample to show my technique. This way, the art director and the publisher will have a clear idea about the finished illustration. I prefer to work with opaque colours such as gouache or coloured pencil."

Something nobody knew about me (until now)

"I am basically a shy person, plus, English is not my mother tongue. So when I go to meet people like publishers, art directors or theatre directors, I always try to make my portfolio speak louder."

My favourite book that I've created

"*The Fishing Summer* is my latest book. I tried some new colour combinations, and I enjoyed what I did."

Tips for young creators

"If you want to know somebody better when you draw them, you can start your sketches from different angles — front, side, top, bottom, and even the back."

Ange Zhang

Bibliography

Jam, Teddy. *The Fishing Summer*. Toronto: Groundwood, 1997 Cloth 0-88899-285-8. Illustrations by Ange Zhang.

Valgardson, W.D. *Thor*. Toronto: Groundwood, 1994 Cloth 0-88899-209-2. Illustrations by Ange Zhang.

Wieler, Diana. *To the Mountains by Morning*. Toronto: Groundwood, 1995 Cloth 0-88899-227-0. Illustrations by Ange Zhang.

Awards

1995 Mr. Christie's Book Award for *Thor*

Selected articles about Ange Zhang

Citron, Paula. "Beijing Designer Bridges Cultural Gap at Blyth." *The Toronto Star* 6 Aug. 1992.

Winsor, Christopher. "Drawing with Light." *The Globe and Mail* [Toronto] 5 Oct. 1996.

From *The Fishing Summer*

Song Nan Zhang
AUTHOR/ILLUSTRATOR

Born
June 22, 1942, Shanghai, China

School
Central Institute of Fine Arts, Beijing, China

Where I live now
Montreal, Quebec

My favourite books when I was young
The children's stories of Hans Christian Anderson

My favourite book now
Paintings in the Musée d'Orsay

Career
Artist (oil painter); children's book illustrator

Family
Wife, Sheng Li Wang; sons Hao Yu Zhang and Hao Yong Zhang

The room where I create
"I usually work at home, at my dining room/studio. I like the two big north windows there; they let in plenty of natural light, just perfect for oil painting."

When I was growing up
"I was fond of drawing cartoons. I often copied down good cartoon drawings from newspapers on bigger pieces of paper and posted them on walls near school. Later on, I volunteered as the fine arts editor for the wall bulletins of the Shanghai Youth Centre. When I started my academic studies of art, I spent most of my time studying Chinese-style painting. I changed my mind later on, after seeing a retrospective Russian oil exhibit in Beijing. I knew from then on that oil would be my painting medium."

My first book (and how it happened)
"My first book is titled *A Little Tiger in the Chinese Night*. It is an illustrated autobiography of my 50 years in China. May Cutler, the former president of Tundra Books, was the one who first encouraged me to do an illustrated children's book of my own story. I was humbled and surprised at first. I consider the story of myself rather ordinary; I wondered if children of the Americas would be interested in it. After a lot of sweat and hard work, the book was published in 1993. *A Little Tiger*, my first book ever, won a Mr. Christie's Book Award in 1993."

Where my ideas come from
"I think book ideas come from life. Pay attention to the things that happen around us every day. When you go on a trip, observe things that are interesting and take notes. Of course, when you finally decide to write a book, observation alone is not enough. On subjects that you are not so sure about, research will always help."

Who and what influenced me
"I made up my mind when I was 15 that I wanted to become an artist, an oil painter. During the past four decades or so, many artists and many paintings have influenced me. A Chinese saying (on how to achieve success) perhaps best describes my experience: "journey 10 thousand miles, and read 10 thousand books." One has to keep learning new things every step of the way. In my case, I can probably add 'study 10 thousand paintings.'"

How I work
"Before I start to illustrate a book, I always try to familiarize myself with the subject as much as possible. I then compile an image file on the subject. During research, I constantly take note of new ideas and draw small sketches. These small sketches will then one day be the bases of the final illustrations."

Something nobody knew about me (until now)
"My books, so far, are all published in English. But only people close to me know that I

speak very little English. When I write a book, I write in Chinese first. My son then translates them into English. Last year (1997), when Canada's annual Governor General's Literary Awards organization committee sent me a boxful of books and asked me to become a selection committee member, I had to return the books."

My favourite book that I've created

The Children of China.

Tips for young creators

"Success is achieved with determination, creativity, and above all — hard work."

Song Nan Zhang

Bibliography

Granfield, Linda. *The Legend of the Panda.* Toronto: Tundra Books, 1998 Cloth 0-88776-421-5. Illustrations by Song Nan Zhang.

Zhang, Song Nan. *A Little Tiger in the Chinese Night.* Toronto: Tundra Books, 1993 Cloth 0-88776-320-0. 1995 Paper 0-88776-356-1. Illustrations by the author.

—. *Five Heavenly Emperors: Chinese Myths of Creation.* Toronto: Tundra Books, 1994 Cloth 0-88776-338-3. Illustrations by the author.

—. *The Children of China: A Painter's Journey.* Toronto: Tundra Books, 1995 Paper 0-88776-448-7; Cloth 0-88776-363-4. Illustrations by the author.

—. *Cowboy on the Steppes.* Toronto: McClelland and Stewart, 1997 Cloth 0-88776-410-X. Illustrations by the author.

The Ballad of Mulan. Union City, CA: Pan Asian Publications, 1998 Cloth 1-57227-054-3. Illustrations by Song Nan Zhang.

Awards

1993 Mr. Christie's Book Award for *A Little Tiger in the Chinese Night*

Selected articles about Song Nan Zhang

"Day Care, Canada, and two views of the Far East." *The Globe and Mail* 13 Sept. 1997

From *The Children of China*

Werner Zimmermann

AUTHOR/ILLUSTRATOR

Born

"November 20, 1951, Wörgl, Austria. They exported me on the first available cattle boat to Canada a year later. I had my first birthday on that boat. Boy was I excited!"

School

"Most of my time served was at Fruitland Public School in, where else, Fruitland, Ontario. It's now a banquet hall, and there isn't a fruit tree in sight. From there I went to Saltfleet and Orchard Park Secondary. Naturally, the school was parked right over an orchard, thus the name, and sadly not one tree got out from under it. My final escape was to the University of Guelph, which I liked a lot, learned the most and forgot to graduate from."

Where I live now

"Gwelf, Ontario. Some people spell it wrong: Guelph, but it doesn't sound that way. I've never heard anybody say the 'p'!"

My favourite book when I was young

"Didn't. I hated books and hated reading."

My favourite book now

The Little Prince by Antoine de Saint-Exupéry.

Career

"When I grow up..."

Family

"Two sons, and one super, amazing, one-of-a-kind dog, Mupps."

The room where I create

"The front room of the old house we've restored. But work is underway on an addition so I can have a new studio. It will have French doors looking onto my small garden and lily pool. I need to look onto a garden, no matter how small, to keep my sanity in a city. I have another larger studio in the centre of town, but I seem to spend less and less time there."

Spare time

"I race with my son in his sailboat. He's crazy and we spend a lot of time sideways or upside down!" Werner also enjoys kayaking.

When I was growing up

"What!! It ended? Actually, I couldn't wait for it to end. Summers were horribly long and boring. The first summer I loved was when I was 16 years old and worked on a dairy farm. I worked till I dropped: milking cows, cleaning pigs, driving tractors, baling hay... all of it to glorious sunrises over the Grand River which flowed just behind the barn, or fluffy clouds above a majestic oak tree that someone with foresight let grow in the middle of a wheat field. There was time to lie on your back and watch the clouds float by, fence rows to follow, curves in streams to discover, even the sight of cows emerging out of early morning fog on their way to the barn. For me, it was my first summer of magic."

Who and what influenced me

"Most of my real influences came out of my time in the Arctic. It wasn't that I started to draw like the Inuit, but they taught me to see and feel at the same time. It may sound crazy, but you need to see with your senses and feel with your eyes. Other than that, I've learned the most from older people. I have a lot of friends in their 70s and 80s and they are treasure troves of advice and balance."

How I work

"I should call this work? I suppose, because it takes far more discipline than I've got, and sometimes, it's very hard. I admit, I never learned about planning and dedication and seeing it through, or even working with others. Word of advice: forget everything else you learned in school, but don't forget to take on projects, no matter how small (though do yourself a favour and keep things small), and learn to plan them out and learn to get them done, finished, completed, no matter what! I'm still not very good at that."

Something nobody knew about me (until now)

"I'm shy."

My favourite book that I've created

"Yikes! Put me on the spot why don't you. Every book has something special, and something I die about every time I see it. But, all things considered, it's got to be *Henny Penny*. Doing it was crazy, but the characters are so much like me and people I know, that I get the greatest chuckle out of it. But, as I said before,

there are parts I wish I hadn't done the way I did."

Tips for young creators

"Don't be shy. Ask others for advice but don't impose. There are ways to learn from everyone if you're willing to keep yourself open. The worst thing is an attitude, 'Man, I got talent, ain't nobody gonna tell me nothin'. Yes, you've got to believe in yourself, protect your time and energy, but realize there's always something to be learned, even if you've heard it before.

"Final advice: start simple, work simple and keep it simple. With time, your work will naturally gain more complexity, but in simple things there is power, strength and elegance."

Werner Zimmermann

Bibliography

All books illustrated by H. Werner Zimmermann

Baker, Kent. *Finster Frets*. Toronto: Stoddart, 1994 Cloth 0-19-541055-6.

DeVries, John. *In My Back Yard*. Richmond Hill: Scholastic Canada, 1992 Cloth 0-590-73307-9; Paper 0-590-73681-7; Big Book 0-590-74064-4.

Lawson, Julie. *Whatever You Do, Don't Go Near that Canoe!* Richmond Hill: Scholastic Canada, 1996 Cloth 0-590-24429-9.

Richards, Nancy Wilcox. *Farmer Joe Babysits*. Richmond Hill: Scholastic Canada, 1997 Cloth 0-590-24977-0.

—. *Farmer Joe Goes to the City*. Richmond Hill: Scholastic Canada, 1990 Cloth 0-590-73362-1; Paper 0-590-73361-3.

—. *Farmer Joe's Hot Day*. Richmond Hill: Scholastic Canada, 1987 Cloth 0-590-71717-0; Paper 0-590-74280-9; Big Book 0-590-71714-6.

Wishinsky, Frieda. *Each One Special*. Victoria: Orca Book Publishers, 1998 Cloth 1-55143-122-X.

Zimmermann, H. Werner. *Henny Penny*. Richmond Hill: Scholastic Canada, 1989 Cloth 0-590-73159-9; Paper 0-590-71929-7; Big Book 0-590-71755-3.

—. *Alphonse Knows... Twelve Months Make a Year*. Toronto: Stoddart, 1990 Cloth 0-19-540798-9.

—. *Alphonse Knows... Zero is Not Enough*. Toronto: Stoddart, 1990 Cloth 0-19-540797-0.

—. *Alphonse Knows... a Circle is Not a Valentine*. Toronto: Stoddart, 1992 Paper 0-19-540928-0.

—. *Alphonse Knows... the Colour of Spring*. Toronto: Stoddart, 1992 Paper 0-19-540927-2.

Selected articles about Werner Zimmermann

Maruszeczka, Greg. "The Electronic Artist in Residence: Being There." *CM* 21.4 (Sept. 1993): 117-120.

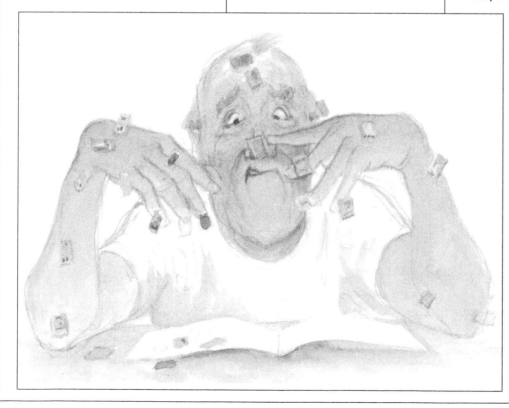

From *Each One Special*

A Word About Us

A national, non-profit organization founded in 1976, The Canadian Children's Book Centre promotes and encourages the reading, writing and illustrating of Canadian children's books.

We are here for anyone who cares about the books that children read. We assist parents, teachers, librarians and students as well as writers, illustrators, publishers and booksellers.

The Canadian Children's Book Centre organizes Canadian Children's Book Week, the single most important celebration of books and reading in this country. Every November, thousands of children and adults meet authors and illustrators in schools, libraries, bookstores and community centres throughout this week-long, national festival.

The Centre also has a reference library of Canadian children's books, as well as extensive information on Canadian children's authors, illustrators and the book trade, both in print and on our web site. Our collection is accessible to the public in five different sites across the country — at our national office in Toronto and in Halifax, Winnipeg, Edmonton and Vancouver.

If an illustrator you are researching is not included in this book, please contact The Canadian Children's Book Centre.
We have information on more than 300 authors and illustrators on file and each year these resources expand.

You, too, can become a member of The Canadian Children's Book Centre. As a member, you'll receive *Our Choice,* our guide to the best of Canadian children's books and media; as well as our magazine, Children's Book News, which will keep you up-to-date on what's happening in the Canadian children's book world.

For further information on becoming a member, ordering our publications, or learning more about the Centre's work, please contact us at:

The Canadian Children's Book Centre
35 Spadina Road, Toronto, Ontario M5R 2S9
Tel: (416)975-0010 Fax: (416) 975-1839
E-mail: ccbc@sympatico.ca
www3.sympatico.ca/ccbc